The Moment of Rupture

INTELLECTUAL HISTORY
OF THE MODERN AGE

Series Editors
Angus Burgin
Peter E. Gordon
Joel Isaac
Karuna Mantena
Samuel Moyn
Jennifer Ratner-Rosenhagen
Camille Robcis
Sophia Rosenfeld

The Moment of Rupture

Historical Consciousness
in Interwar German Thought

Humberto Beck

PENN

UNIVERSITY OF PENNSYLVANIA PRESS

PHILADELPHIA

Published by
University of Pennsylvania Press
Philadelphia, Pennsylvania 19104-4112
www.upenn.edu/pennpress

Printed in the United States of America on acid-free paper
1 3 5 7 9 10 8 6 4 2

Library of Congress Cataloging-in-Publication Data
Library of Congress Cataloging-in-Publication Data

Names: Beck, Humberto, author.
Title: The moment of rupture: historical consciousness in interwar German thought /
    Humberto Beck.
Other titles: Intellectual history of the modern age.
Description: 1st edition. | Philadelphia: University of Pennsylvania Press, [2019] | Series:
    Intellectual history of the modern age | Includes bibliographical references and index.
Identifiers: LCCN 2019007399| ISBN 9780812251593 (hardcover: alk. paper) | ISBN 0812251598
    (hardcover: alk. paper)
Subjects: LCSH: Germany—History—20th century—Philosophy. | Time perception—
    Germany—Philosophy—History—20th century. | Time perception in literature. |
    Jünger, Ernst, 1895–1998—Criticism and interpretation. | Benjamin, Walter, 1892–1940—
    Criticism and interpretation. | Bloch, Ernst, 1885-1977.
Classification: LCC DD97.B43 2019 | DDC 901—dc23
LC record available at https://lccn.loc.gov/2019007399

CONTENTS

INTRODUCTION

This book explores the rise in significance of instantaneous time—the sudden temporality of *the instant* (*Augenblick*)—in several currents of German thought during the first decades of the twentieth century. Between 1914 and 1940, in response to the experiences of abrupt discontinuity and social and political rupture, a new form of historical time consciousness was born in Germany, which articulated itself around the notion of *instantaneity*. Three German writers in particular—Ernst Jünger, Ernst Bloch, and Walter Benjamin—fused the consciousness of war, crisis, catastrophe, and revolution with the literary and philosophical formulation of *the instantaneous* as a category of thought. Their work employed instantaneity as a conceptual framework for the description and interpretation of the experiences of rupture and discontinuity, both personal and collective. Together, they produced a constellation of concepts and figures of sudden temporality that contributed to the formation of a distinct instantaneist "regime of historicity"[1]—a mode of experiencing time based on the notion of a discontinuous present.

The creation of this new formula for the perception of temporality drew considerably from a modern tradition of reflection on the concept of the instant as a philosophical and aesthetic category, a tradition that spanned the poetry of Johann Wolfgang von Goethe, the historical self-understanding of the French Revolution, the aesthetics of early Romanticism, the philosophies of Søren Kierkegaard and Friedrich Nietzsche, Charles Baudelaire's theory of *modernité*, and the artistic and literary practices of the historical avant-gardes. Given the existence of this previous tradition of reflection on instantaneity, what was created in Germany during this period was not a qualitatively new idea of the instant—a philosophical concept that goes back as far as Plato—but, rather, the transformation of *suddenness* and *abrupt discontinuity* into the foundations of a new organization of the experience of time. Jünger, Bloch, and Benjamin turned to the figure of instantaneity in order to intellectually represent an era marked by shocks in individual perception and other historical and political crises. Through their works, the instant became a defining figure of the era's historical consciousness.

Germany, 1914–1940: Experiences of Historical Discontinuity and Crisis

Between the years 1914 and 1940—that is, between the outbreaks of the First World War and the Second—Germany experienced an almost uninterrupted series of violent ruptures. The feeling of euphoric expectation that preceded the First World War was followed by the traumatic experiences of the troops on the battlefield and the devastation of a calamitous military defeat. At the conclusion of the war in 1918, the proclamation of the new Weimar Republic marked the beginning of a period of extreme social and political turmoil after which would come, in turn, the rapid establishment, in 1933, of a brutal dictatorship and the eruption of a new world war a few years later. Before these political upheavals, German society had already undergone shock-like experiences and perceptions brought about by new technologies and urbanization. Berlin, capital of both the Reich and the Republic, typified the new mass industrial metropolis. The entire European continent shared the experience of historical rupture brought about by war, revolution, accelerated modernization, and crisis, but in Germany the rupture was the most extreme. From 1914 to 1940, the nation endured a turbulent progression of events. War, military defeat, imperial collapse and change of regime, failed revolution, economic breakdown, general strikes, unsuccessful putsches, rule by emergency powers, the increase of political radicalism and violence, and the rise of a totalitarian dictatorship—these were just some of the events that crowded these tumultuous years. Their accumulation generated an intense sensation of *discontinuity*, both historical and perceptual. The recurrence of the feeling of discontinuity throughout the interwar years contributed to the formation of a sense of perplexity that became the characteristic feature of the experience of time during this unstable era.

Taking into consideration this historical context, *The Moment of Rupture* asks a question about the relationship between ideas and events in modern European intellectual history: What role did the concept of *instantaneous temporality* play in German thought between 1914 and 1940?[2] My proposition is that instantaneity represents a crucial concept for the development of the historical and time consciousness of the period. The notion of the instant was understood as the isolated *now* of abrupt discontinuity. Its importance arises from a certain correspondence between the instant's conceptual features—above all, its connection with suddenness and rupture—and the nature of the interwar years as unstable and marked by recurrent radical change. Given the defining qualities of this period in German history, it is possible to speak of an "elective affinity"[3] between the experiences of crisis and rupture and the instant as a conceptual device. The grounds for this affinity reside in the instant's ability, as a notion, to posit certain questions that would remain obscure under a conventional understanding of temporality as continuous duration. With its close connection to suddenness, the instant cultivates a sensibility attuned to the exceptional and the unexpected. This sensibility became fundamental to historical and time consciousness in Germany during the first decades of the twentieth century.

Oswald Spengler, one of the most representative authors of the era, seems to have made an argument similar to mine in *The Decline of the West* when he wrote: "In the Classical world years played no role, in the Indian world decades scarcely mattered; but here [in Germany in 1918] the hour, the minute, even the second is of importance. Neither a Greek nor an Indian could have had any idea of the tragic tension of a historic crisis like that of August 1914, when even moments seemed of overwhelming significance."[4] Following this line of interpretation, I analyze historically and conceptually the variations on the theme of instantaneous temporality that were articulated during this period of German history. The history of these variations is significant for understanding fundamental aspects of twentieth-century intellectual history, such as the role of historicism and antihistoricism in modern visions of temporality, and transformations in the notion of individual and collective experience.

Previous approaches to this topic include Karl Heinz Bohrer's conceptualization of suddenness as a motif in European modernist literature; Anson Rabinbach's examination of the critical reactions of German intellectuals to the experience of catastrophe after the end of the two world wars; and Michael Löwy's study of the relations between Jewish messianism and libertarian socialism in Central European thought.[5] Stephen Kern's panoramic analysis of the "culture of time and space" in Europe at the turn of the century and Modris Eksteins' characterization of Germany's perspective on the First World War as a central moment in the emergence of modern consciousness have also addressed the interaction between representations of time and historical events.[6] *The Moment of Rupture* intends to contribute to this area of inquiry by constituting an intellectual history of the operation of the motif of instantaneous time in the work of three authors in whose writings instantaneity functions as a crucial notion for the conceptual mediation of the experiences of war, revolution, and crisis.

The Intellectual Representation of Suddenness

The affinity between the concept of the instant and the experiences of historical discontinuity found its most consummate expression in the works of Ernst Jünger, Ernst Bloch, and Walter Benjamin, each of whom addressed the question of historical and perceptual discontinuity from the point of view of instantaneous temporality. In the writings of this constellation of authors, the instant presented itself as a formidable instrument for the intellectual representation of a time of crisis. In spite of their cultural and political differences, these authors shared a fundamental dilemma: how to *name* the novel experiences of rupture in historical consciousness and individual perception as well as the particular social consequences of these forms of rupture. They resorted to the language of instantaneity to capture the unprecedented and sometimes contradictory quality of these new forms of experience, which seemed to break with the conventional expectation of time as a linear progression and to present crisis, catastrophe, and danger as new bases of perception.

The differences in these authors' political persuasions are considerable. Jünger was involved with nationalist and militaristic circles, whereas Bloch and Benjamin distinctively combined revolutionary Marxism and Jewish messianism. But their belonging to opposite political fields does not obviate their commonalities. Rather, it is a telling symptom of the existence of a deeper frame of mind in this period of German history and a general outline for the perception of temporality that cut across the ideological spectrum. Central to this outline was a vision of instantaneity as a unifying category for collective and individual experience under the cultural and political conditions of the early twentieth century.

A series of significant characteristics connected these authors' understanding of the instant. Most fundamentally, they shared an interpretation of instantaneous time as a temporal modality based on suddenness. They also adopted the instant as a notion that was simultaneously political and aesthetic, and they articulated this notion as a category that was, at the same time, a vehicle of historical consciousness and a mode of subjective perception. As a result of these convergences, Jünger, Bloch, and Benjamin created an influential collection of images of instantaneity, in which the main features of their era's conception of temporality came together. With instantaneity as the basis of discontinuous interpretations of temporality, these images especially negated—or transfigured—the perception of historical time as *progress*, and thus expressed a powerful antiteleological tendency. The notion of the instant posits disruptive and singular events as a sort of historical ex nihilo creation—either through violence, decision, or revolution—in opposition to the notion of a historical reason gradually accomplishing itself along the lines of a predetermined goal or telos. This was true even when these authors looked into the past to develop their respective notions of instantaneity, as the return of past elements can itself be a form of sudden interruption. As a consequence, each of these authors disavowed linearity and continuity and postulated a caesura in time as the premise for a new conception of history.

These images of instantaneity also contributed to the fashioning of a new conception of experience.[7] In such formulations as Jünger's "danger," Bloch's "darkness of the lived moment" or Benjamin's "shock," the conventional contrast between "ordinary" and "extraordinary" experience dissolves and sudden perception becomes identified with actual sensations that the the individual subject faces. Each of these conceptions points to a form of exceptional experience that, as a consequence of the cultural and political conditions of twentieth-century modernity, became part of the common structure of temporal consciousness and of a new standard of perception. Furthermore, novel forms of mediation between the subjective and historical dimensions of the experience of time furthered the dissolution of these boundaries. In these authors' writings, notions derived from individual perception helped to articulate the sense of a collective historical experience, and, at the same time, their concepts of historical and political crisis conditioned the subjective experience of temporality. This process is made clear in Jünger's, Bloch's, and Benjamin's engagement with the avant-garde aesthetics of sudden juxtaposition and their distinct temporalities—Jünger's "terror," Bloch's "noncontemporaneity," and Benjamin's "now-time." In each, the formal principle of montage becomes a paradigm of historical consciousness and sensory perception.

The constellation formed by Jünger, Bloch, and Benjamin takes central stage in this book because of these convergences in their treatment of instantaneity. But in this period of German intellectual history, there were other important authors who also developed reflections on diverse facets of instantaneous temporality: Edmund Husserl, Karl Jaspers, Martin Heidegger, and Carl Schmitt, among others. I did not include them centrally in my inquiry because fundamental aspects of the instantaneity *chronotope* (a term I discuss below) were not present in their works—such as the correlation between the historical and subjective dimensions of time, or the integration of the principles of avant-garde aesthetics into a vision of temporality. But, even though these writers are not my main object of study, I do analyze their ideas when they touch upon the development of my central argument.

The Origins of the Instant: A Brief History

The concept of the instant, and its ramifications in the intellectual history of Germany during the years of the Great War, the Weimar Republic, and the rise of National Socialism, are central to *The Moment of Rupture*, but what, exactly, is an "instant"? An instant is the shortest span in which time can be divided and experienced. The instant is, then, a moment without time, that infinitely short moment in which there is no interval or duration, no before or after, but only an *atemporal present*. Because of its timelessness, the instant is associated with *eternity*, and therefore alludes to the paradoxical experience of the *eternal* in the *ephemeral*. The instant is that interruption that happens in the "blink of an eye": it evokes fractures in permanence and negates the idea of time as an "empty continuum" in which the now is merely an abstract boundary between the past and the future.[8] The vision of the now that derives from the instant is, rather, reminiscent of *kairos* (καιρός), the ancient Greek word that denotes the "timely" occurrence of an event,[9] as opposed to the uniform, quantitative time of *chronos* (Χρόνος). Kairos designates the happening of the unrepeatable and exceptional, as well as the unique time for auspicious action, especially in a moment of crisis.

The concept of the instant is, in this sense, analogous to the notion of the *event*: that unexpected disruption of the flow of time that seems to emerge out of nowhere—an episode of singularity that opens up the horizon of thinking and action by introducing a previously inconceivable possibility.[10] Because it distills experience into a fleeting, transitory moment, the instant has been prominently associated with suddenness, a concept that poses two fundamental themes: the discontinuity of time and the occurrence of the radically new.[11] In the realm of human subjectivity, the instant has been considered the privileged space for the expression of the spirit's inner life, the form and limits of sensory perception, and the mental and moral ground of freedom and resolution.[12] As Rüdiger Safranski has pointed out, the instant "means a different experience of time and the experience of a different time. It promises sudden turns and transformations, perhaps even arrival and redemption, but at any rate it enforces decision."[13]

In the Western tradition, the concept of the instant originated in Plato's speculations about change as a sudden, unexplainable alteration in the qualities of being, and, later, in Saint Paul's doctrine of *parousia*—the second coming of Christ at the end of time—as an abrupt and radical transformation of the cosmos. In the *Parmenides*, Plato defines the instant as the moment when the change from one quality to another—for example, from stillness to movement—takes place. Since an object cannot exist simultaneously in two different states, Plato conjectures that there must be a moment outside of time during which the transformed object is in neither state and when the transition actually occurs. This moment, which Plato calls an *atopos*—a *non*-place but also a non-*time*—is the instant.[14] In his *Physics*, Aristotle departs from Plato's discontinuous vision of temporality and posits instead an account of time as an uninterrupted flow.[15] His alternative to Plato's instant is the now, whose function is analogous to that of a point on a line: to connect and, likewise, to signal the end of a duration or "length" in temporality.[16] By virtue of being, just like the point, simultaneously a *link* and a *limit*, the now establishes both the *continuity* of time and its *division* into past and future. Nevertheless, insofar as it was indivisible, as the point in space, Aristotle's now is a purely conceptual reality that did not correspond directly with anything perceptible. In the end, Aristotle's continuous account of time, and not Plato's emphasis on interruption, became the more influential in the history of philosophy, and, as a consequence, it became the foundation for most of the later treatments of temporality. This situation remained unaltered until the arrival of the modern thinkers of the instant, such as Søren Kierkegaard and Friedrich Nietzsche.

Saint Paul's vision of final redemption is the other significant source of the concept of the instant. In the Epistles, Paul outlines his eschatological thinking, a central tenet of which is the belief that the end of the world will happen suddenly, in the propitious moment, or "favorable time," of an instant.[17] In the First Epistle to the Corinthians, he famously describes the moment of the *parousia* as an instantaneous event: "in a moment, in the twinkling of an eye, at the last trumpet. For the trumpet will sound, and the dead will be raised imperishable, and we shall be changed."[18] In the early Christian worldview shaped by Paul's eschatology, Christ's return was expected to happen in the "twinkling of an eye." As a result of this expectation, *any* instant could in effect become the ultimate one, the potential scenario for the consummation of time. This ever-present latency of the end did nothing but intensify the awareness of the present moment. Paul's identification of the instant with the "twinkling of an eye" would become a fundamental concept in modern philosophical thought. Following Luther's translation of Paul, Kierkegaard and Heidegger referred to the instant with terms that recalled the original Pauline image—the Danish *øjeblik* and the German *Augenblick* (both of which mean "in the blink of an eye").

After Plato and Saint Paul, the next defining chapter in the history of the instant would arrive in the fourth century with the writings of Saint Augustine, who introduced—most notably in his *Confessions*—an enduring association between instantaneity and subjectivity. Like Aristotle, Augustine regards the moment of the immediate present as indivisible, but, in contrast to the abstractions of Aristotelian thought, the theologian rejects the perception of the now as an impersonal limit and instead centers his understanding on the concrete, subjective experience of temporality. Augustine thus became the first thinker to focus his analysis on the personal aspect of time. He defined time as a "distension" of the soul, which measures the effects that fleeting things have on it. Because of its immediate nature, Augustine considers the instant the only genuine reality of time, in opposition to the past (that has already been) and the future (that has not yet been), as well as to other measures of temporality, such as the year, the month, the day or even the hour, all of which, if studied carefully, are revealed to be illusory.[19] Nevertheless, he also realizes that the instant, since it has no duration, does not, strictly speaking, exist either. Augustine draws out the paradox of instantaneous temporality: the only point of contact with time is the present but the present moment is not in time. His proposed resolution to the paradox is to relocate it in the realm of subjective experience. It does not matter, he argues, if time's only reality, the instant, lacks a true outward expanse, because the measuring of time is not an external reality but an activity that takes place in an altogether different dimension—that is, in the soul.

The reflections on the instant in Plato, Paul, and Augustine established the foundations of the notion of instantaneity in the Western tradition. Some of the basic tenets of this conception would reappear in medieval philosophy and theology—as in the scholastic idea of *nunc stans* (or "eternal present") as an attribute of God, or in the ecstatic visions of Meister Eckhart and other Christian mystics. Other isolated aspects of the doctrines can be found in early modern thinkers, such as the implied decisionism of Blaise Pascal's famous "wager" or René Descartes' principle of the re-creation of the world at every instant. But what ultimately predominated in Western thought, at least until Immanuel Kant and Georg Wilhelm Friedrich Hegel, was rather a continuous and Aristotelian idea of time as uninterrupted flow. As Chapters 1 and 2 will show, toward the end of the eighteenth and the beginning of the nineteenth centuries, a series of influential discourses on the instant broke with the dominance of temporal Aristotelianism and reintroduced instantaneity as a key concept in philosophy, aesthetics, and politics. The aesthetic ideas of Goethe and the early German Romantics, the French revolutionary spirit, and the philosophies of Kierkegaard and Nietzsche brought instantaneity to the center of European intellectual history. In the early twentieth century, European thinkers took up this tradition of reflection on the instant in order to explore the "essential discontinuity of Time"[20] in the cultural and political context of their era. The triad of Jünger, Bloch, and Benjamin embodied a powerful incarnation of this tradition's revival by transforming some of the features of the concept into the premises of a general vision of time consciousness.

The Rhetoric of Instantaneity

Given the philosophical history of the concept, and following Karl Heinz Bohrer's analysis of suddenness as an aesthetic category,[21] I here use *instantaneity* to refer to an abrupt discontinuity that resists integration into a regular and coherent flow. Instantaneity is a form of temporality dissociated from stability, permanence, or accumulation. I treat instantaneity as a *trope*, which means that the term implies a certain fixed identity denoted in its conceptual structure. A trope is a rhetorical expression that introduces a change in ordinary meaning—from the Greek for a movement or turn—by establishing a new relationship between two words or terms.[22] The relationship that the trope of instantaneity has typically established is the unforeseen juxtaposition between two contrasting or unconnected elements, which triggers the aesthetic effect of suddenness. As the foundational examples of Plato, Paul, and

Augustine, or the more modern incarnations in Kierkegaard or Nietzsche, attest, instantaneity has traditionally alluded to the abrupt association of two apparently contradictory components: the ideas of time and eternity.

Although treating instantaneity as a trope permits its identification through time, it does not exclude its examination as a properly *historical* object of study. The figure of instantaneity can also be comprehended, in this sense, as a *motif*,[23] that is, as a pattern of thought that continually recurs and is reappropriated in diverse historical contexts. The history of the instant resides, above all, in the tracing of these uses and "strategic deployments"[24] in specific intellectual traditions, historical conjunctures, conceptual universes, and political moments. This history also entails, then, the tracking of the concept's "ramifications" and "historical inscriptions"[25] in concrete social and political settings, which mediate between the events and their intellectual representation. Since the first formulations of the instant in antiquity up to the years of the Weimar Republic, for example, there have been essential changes in the intellectual, cultural, and political implications of its use. The diverse intersections between the idea and concrete historical processes have resulted in the coinage of novel connotations in response to new circumstances. As a consequence, in each iteration of the instantaneity motif, both the conceptual pattern of sudden juxtaposition and the images of the temporal and the eternal have been variously interpreted, reinvented, adapted, or extrapolated.

The treatment of instantaneity as a motif can account for the seeming paradox of using a notion belonging to such an old tradition to describe a modern historical era. The paradox dissipates if one takes into account the distinction between the different dimensions in the usages of instantaneity. Although there is certainly a continuity in the *structure* of the idea, there is also a manifest *dis*continuity in the theoretical reach of each dimension. These deployments have ranged from the utilization of the instant as a *concept* in certain philosophical and theological doctrines—as in the writings of Plato and Saint Paul—to its role as a defining notion in more systematic aesthetic and political *discourses*, such as the French revolutionary consciousness and German Romanticism. One must distinguish, in turn—and this is the main thesis of *The Moment of Rupture*—between those more circumscribed or local uses of instantaneity as a discourse or concept and what took place in Germany during the interwar years: the formation of a distinct *regime of historicity* that adopted the figure of the instant as a wide-ranging formula for the configuration of that epoch's forms of temporal experience. The modern discourses predicated on instantaneity anticipated this new regime of historicity, while never attaining the chronotope's quality of a full-fledged, systematic representation of an entire historical period. The birth of such representation would happen only in the 1914–1940 period in Germany. Then, in the writings of a handful of emblematic authors, the motif of instantaneity presented itself as the most appropriate conceptual and rhetorical device for capturing a historical consciousness and subjective perception of a time defined by intense discontinuity and the ensuing experience of an immediate and fragmentary present seemingly dislocated from anything in the past. Accordingly, even though the rhetoric of instantaneity has appeared in different historical periods, it was only in the early decades of the twentieth century in Germany that the "historical inscription" of the instant became a crucial element of the "common intellectual horizon" of an entire era.[26]

The Instantaneist Chronotope

This book analyzes the deployment of the instantaneity motif in the cultural and political context of early twentieth-century Germany. I demonstrate that in these years—the years of the First World War and its aftermath, of the Russian Revolution and its reverberations, and of extreme economic and political crises throughout Europe—instantaneous temporality became the fundamental idea of a new and distinctive chronotope and regime of historicity. I use the term *chronotope*[27] in Hans Ulrich Gumbrecht's adapted sense, meaning a general conception of the experience of temporality.[28] I also argue that instantaneity constitutes a distinct *regime of historicity*, the French historian François Hartog's phrase meant to designate "a way of expressing and organizing experiences of time—that is, ways of articulating the past, the present, and the future—and investing them with sense."[29] For Hartog, a regime of historicity is a tool for "highlighting modes of relation to time" and "exploring forms of temporal experience."[30] Although the notions of regime of historicity and chronotope originated in different intellectual genealogies, throughout this book I will use them interchangeably in their more general sense as a conceptual framework for the organization and interpretation of the experience of temporality.

To historical agents, a regime of historicity represents their relationship to historical temporality—that is, their way of being in time. To the historian, it represents an instrument for the comparison of historical consciousness at different historical moments. For Hartog, the regime of historicity concept is, primarily, an "artificial construct" created by the historian, the chief value of which is its "heuristic potential."[31] Following Hartog, I use the concept both as a paradigm of historiographical interpretation and as a general category for the perception of temporality as historical subjects themselves represent it. In my application of the concept to the interwar years in Germany, I will emphasize it as a "mode of experience"[32] that comprehends figures of collective historical consciousness as well as the subjective and individual dimension of time perception—and the correspondences, ramifications, and different forms of articulation between the two.

The formation of the instantaneist regime of historicity, or *instantaneism*, was the result of a theoretical and historical juncture that took place in Germany during the first decades of the twentieth century, when the forms of historical consciousness that had been shaped by the experiences of war, crisis, and revolution fused with a modern tradition of reflection on instantaneity as a category of perception. As a result of this merging of philosophical and aesthetic evolutions with intellectual and historical occurrences, a corpus of thinking formed, which provided a substantial series of concrete embodiments of the instant as a category for the experience of the historical and the political. The writings of Jünger, Bloch, and Benjamin constitute the most influential expression of this instantaneist body of work. Their writings offer a set of categories, images, and figures of sudden temporality that expressed the particular experience of time that characterized the interwar years in Germany. By means of this new language, they attempted to give "order"[33] to the new forms of temporal experience (sweeping interruptions, sudden breaks, radical turmoil and crises) as well as to the sensations, feelings, and moods derived from those experiences (surprise, alarm, astonishment, perplexity, disorientation). The result was the thematization of instantaneity as a trope or figure of thought, and the associated formation of instantaneism as a novel formula of historical and time consciousness.

With instantaneism, the rhetoric of the instant was adapted to a historical setting characterized by the multiplication of episodes of political and perceptual discontinuity. In this new form, the nature of both historical consciousness and everyday subjective experience was conveyed by the figure of *fragmentation*. Under the influence of the avant-garde's aesthetics of juxtaposition and its manifestation in the practice of visual and literary montage, the instantaneist works of Jünger, Bloch, and Benjamin emphasized the affinities between fragmentation and crisis. In moments of critical rupture, gaps in the continuity of consciousness are created, resulting in the production of fragments of historical experience or subjective perception. Jünger, Bloch, and Benjamin also emphasized, in turn, the affinities between fragmentation and suddenness. Given its rhetorical structure, the concept of the instant has always presupposed the encounter—the simultaneous presence—between the two contrasting realities of the temporal and the eternal and the subsequent aesthetic effect of suddenness. But in the twentieth-century version of instantaneity, the aesthetic effect of this simultaneity was usually attributed to the encounter of two incoherent or disconnected fragments. In the instantaneist regime of historicity, the relationship between the temporal and the eternal was reinterpreted in terms of the juxtaposition of *fragments* of experience.

As a regime of historicity, instantaneism represents a unique form of time consciousness. In order to understand its singularity, let me point out how it differs from other regimes, most notably *historicism*, the archetypally modern chronotope. Historicism is based on the notions of historical continuity and progress, and it prevailed in Europe from the Enlightenment to the end of the twentieth century. The main feature of the historicist regime is its belief in the future as a primordial dimension of time capable of illuminating both the present and the past. Historicism turns the future into the supreme source of meaning by means of the enunciation of a telos—such as the idea of progress—that situates historical events within a gradual and comprehensive logic of development. In this regime, the past loses any value as a point of reference, and the present is reduced to an ephemeral moment of transition,[34] justified only by the role it may play in a process of expansion into an indefinitely open future.

Instantaneity need also be distinguished from the time consciousness of *presentism*, the predominant chronotope after the crisis of historicism in the last decades of the twentieth century. In presentism, Hartog and Gumbrecht argue, the present replaces the future as a point of reference and the focus of historical attention. The present moment is no longer a space of transition or anticipation: it now occupies the whole space of temporal experience. In the presentist regime, the present can manifest itself as the time of flows, mobility, and acceleration; but precisely because these movements lack any direction, it also presents itself as the temporality of inactivity, paralysis, and stagnation. The future fades away because it has been stripped of any promises or certainties. The future no longer represents an open horizon of possibilities, but becomes instead a place of confluence for menaces to come, such as the demographic explosion or global warming.[35] Moreover, the past is no

longer "past" because it has flooded the present with the augmented capacities for the digital storage of information and the new "culture of memory." As
a result, the new present of presentism is not actually ephemeral, as if it were
a swift point of transition, but rather "slow" and "broad."[36]

In contrast to presentism and historicism, the present in instantaneism
entails neither a mere moment in the path toward progress nor a sense of
expanded stagnation; it represents, rather, the irruption of an "event breaking
into history, an event that transcends and is heterogeneous to it."[37] The present understood as irruption has distinct implications for the experience of
temporality. For example, while in historicism the meaning of crises is always
integrated within a larger rationality and every rupture is construed as a step
within a process toward a goal, in instantaneism the experiences of discontinuity and break constitute forms of an *atemporal* historical consciousness,
which are significant in themselves. In contrast to the historicist understanding of crisis as a moment in which the meaning and purpose of the unalterable
teleology behind all events is exposed, instantaneism sees crises as authentic
instants—that is, interruptions or suspensions of the teleological. Moreover,
while presentism presents passivity and rest as the opposite of historicism's
typical forward movement, instantaneism offers a different opposition: the
instant, which is distinct from both the prospective, goal-oriented activism
of historicism and the stasis of presentism. Despite its transient quality, the
instant is not like other passing moments (e.g., the moments of progress,
repetition, or acceleration) but utterly singular. The time of instantaneism is
neither the pure ephemerality of transition nor the immobility of a "broad
present," but rather the *actuality of the now*, the time when history is completed, not in a process, but in its very interruption. While in the historicist
regime an all-encompassing historical sense devours the possible significance
of individual moments, and while in the presentist chronotope this sense has
vanished altogether, in instantaneism forms of historical meaning are still
attainable, but only abruptly, accomplished in the instant itself.

The Narrative of This Work

The first part of this book describes the formation of the modern tradition of thinking about instantaneity by tracing two of its most important
trajectories. The first is the reflection on instantaneous temporality that
begins with the poetry of Goethe and the French Revolution's historical

self-understanding as an absolute historical beginning. The early German Romantics, in turn, continued this reflection in their deployment of suddenness and nearness as literary and intellectual tropes. Later, instantaneism would be philosophically consolidated in the thought of Kierkegaard and Nietzsche. The second trajectory is the lineage of aesthetic reflection that began with Baudelaire's use of the concept of modernity (*modernité*) as a formula to appraise the new field of perception that mass urban city life had brought about and continued with the historical avant-gardes of the early twentieth century. Each of these trajectories created constellations of ideas that contributed to the formulation of a fundamental vocabulary for talking about instantaneous experiences in modernity. Chapters 1 and 2 sketch the antecedents of the instantaneist chronotope by tracing the history of the rhetorical deployments of the instantaneity motif in modern intellectual history. These deployments extend from the appearance of suddenness as a category of aesthetic perception (with Romanticism), to the appearance of suddenness as a category of political change (with the French Revolution's self-interpretation), and, in Chapter 2, to the formation of an "aesthetics of juxtaposition" in the avant-garde practice of montage.

The lineages identified in each of these two chapters—from Goethe to Nietzsche in Chapter 1, and from Baudelaire to Breton in Chapter 2—respond to different but equally crucial problems that instantaneity raises in various contexts. Chapter 1, with its discussion of Goethe, the German Romantics, and the French revolutionary consciousness, introduces the distinction between subjective and the collective perceptions of temporality, and discusses the interaction between the two. Additionally, in analyzing the philosophies of Kierkegaard and Nietzsche, it presents the possibility of an *ahistorical* form of time consciousness. Chapter 2, with its attention to the avant-garde and the poetry of Baudelaire, introduces the aesthetic perceptions of ephemerality and discontinuity in the setting of urban modernity, as well as the subsequent blurring of the distinction between "everyday" and "limit" experience and the search for new forms of experience adapted to this setting.

Chapter 1 thus explores a series of landmarks in the intellectual history of instantaneous temporality. It argues that the two sources for the modern conceptualization of the instant are the literary work of Goethe and the French Revolution's historical self-understanding. Goethe's *Faust* contains one of the most influential articulations of the instant: Faust's wager, which is sealed by the familiar verse: "If I ever say to the moment 'Linger on, you are so beautiful' . . . Then I will gladly perish." Voicing an everlasting frustration with the present, Goethe's influential formulation helped to define the instant as a category of subjective experience in modernity. Similarly, by devising a new calendar and the organization of revolutionary festivals, the French Revolution articulated a form of historical consciousness that helped establish the concept's historical and political dimension. The French revolutionaries interpreted their own political action as the enactment of a radical new beginning in history—the event of an instantaneous, ex nihilo foundation of a new era with no links with the past. Chapter 1 also examines the varied contributions of early German Romantic authors, such as Friedrich Schleiermacher, Friedrich Schlegel, and Friedrich Hölderlin, to a treatment of instantaneity that emphasizes one fundamental theme: the discovery of suddenness as a temporal modality. Finally, the chapter examines the consolidation of the instant as a philosophical category in the works of Kierkegaard and Nietzsche, the two authors who framed the terms of the debate on instantaneous temporality for the twentieth century. Kierkegaard understood instantaneity as one part of a new kind of radical freedom, in which existential decisions, even though they take place in time, determine the individual's eternal fate in damnation or redemption. The instant, that point of encounter between time and eternity, represents the moment when these decisions are made. For his part, Nietzsche argued for the value of instantaneous *ahistoricity* (the condition of existing only in the present) against the perils of *historical sickness* (the impossibility of forgetting the past). Nietzsche also grounded the instant's existential decisiveness in the eternal return such that the instant is the name for the affirmation of everlasting being—everything that is, has been, or will be—in the cycles of recurrence: a "saying yes" to all of existence.

Chapter 2 studies how the avant-garde artistic and literary movements of the early twentieth century articulated the notion of sudden temporal rupture and the role this articulation played in the transformation of the modern perception of time in aesthetics and beyond. Both in their historical self-understanding and in their aesthetic practice, the avant-gardes—futurism, Dadaism, and, above all, surrealism—represent a significant elaboration and redeployment of the perceptual categories of instantaneity. The avant-gardes conceived of themselves as ground-breaking movements into "newness," and this self-understanding manifested itself in an artistic sensibility and a set of creative techniques that were prominently based on the figure of suddenness. Photomontage, collage, simultaneist poetry, and automatic writing were some of the techniques of their "aesthetics of juxtaposition," one of whose most significant consequences was the affirmation of a new understanding of the instantaneous present as the site of sudden, shock-like apparitions. As a result, the avant-garde practice of montage presented itself as the privileged form of aesthetic mediation for the intensified and fragmented nature of human perception in the setting of urban modernity. Chapter 2 identifies the poetry of Baudelaire as the original source of some of the central themes and formal features of the avant-garde stance, as well as of the awareness of "modernity" as the experience of historical time in the ephemeral character of instantaneity. Surrealism later supplied some of the most innovative thematizations of the new character of experience in urban city life. In works such as André Breton's *Nadja* or Louis Aragon's *Paris Peasant*, the occurrence of chance encounters and sudden associations introduce a vision of beauty based on discontinuity and interruption, present a form of perception in which the distinction between "everyday" and "limit" experiences is obscured, and embrace ephemerality as a "divinity" within a new "mythology of the modern."

Chapters 3, 4, and 5 present detailed analyses of the formation of the instantaneist chronotope in the intellectual production of Jünger, Bloch, and Benjamin, respectively. These authors turned to the conceptual features of instantaneity to elaborate a discourse on time consciousness, both collective and individual, historical and subjective. They sought to make sense of contemporary historical events marked by the sudden rupture of long-established expectations, practices, and institutions. They outlined a form of time consciousness in which the conceptual features of instantaneity were expanded into a general framework for making sense of the experiences of historical and individual temporality in their historical period.

Chapter 3 examines Ernst Jünger's recourse to instantaneous temporality as a conceptual method for the description and interpretation of the experience of historical and cultural crisis entailed by the First World War and the unstable years of the Weimar Republic. An officer in the German Army during the war and a renowned chronicler of life on the battlefront, Jünger was also a prolific author of a wide variety of works, from personal diaries to social criticism. In Jünger's writings from the Weimar era, instantaneity provides the intellectual framework for the analysis of the sudden ruptures in both historical consciousness and subjective perception that characterized that turbulent time. For Jünger, the war had implied a profound civilizational change: the establishing, as a universal principle of organization, of "total mobilization"—that is, the all-encompassing and incessant utilization of the sum of a society's resources for war purposes. Total mobilization was a directive that also invaded the space of civilian life, erasing the distinctions between war and peace, and creating the conditions for a world of permanent crisis. In contradiction to the bourgeois version of progress, the result of this process of modernization was not a situation of more but less security: a world where danger prevailed as the constant possibility of abrupt shock or death in accident, war, or revolution. The everyday pervasiveness of perils and threats effectuated a deep transformation of the human psyche, which had to assimilate suddenness as a mode of subjective perception. To Jünger, the technology of photography offered both a faithful reflection of this transformation and a device that dealt with the omnipresence of danger in modern society. Under the influence of the avant-garde, and particularly, the surrealist aesthetics of suddenness, Jünger also developed in his more literary pieces the category of "terror." For Jünger, terror was an aesthetic modality for capturing the intensified risk that sociopolitical instability and industrial technology brought about. Because they present the personal experience of crisis as the subjective counterpart to the period's historical ruptures, Jünger's writings from the period exemplify the affinity between instantaneous temporality and crisis in a particularly compelling fashion.

Chapter 4 explores the different manifestations of the instantaneity concept in German philosopher Ernst Bloch's thought. Developed in midst of the First World War, Bloch's early philosophy was an explosive mixture of catastrophist anarchism, Marxist materialist premises, and mystical figures of thought. Through an original presentation of the idea of *utopia* as a temporal concept, Bloch absorbed and recreated the prevalent mood of apocalyptic destruction and renewal. For Bloch, reality is inherently unfinished, a world not yet realized in the fullness of its possibility, and therefore it contains the promise of its utopian completion in the future. The anticipatory consciousness of utopia manifests itself in the subjective experience of instantaneity, which Bloch calls the "darkness of the lived moment." The instant is obscure because it is the most immediate experience, too close to be distinctly perceived. This "darkness" involves an inner connection with utopia. The temporality of the instant is a constant experience of the new and unexpected, an intimation of the "not-yet" dimension of reality. In the Weimar era, the exposure to mass culture and avant-garde art would lead Bloch on the search for "traces" of utopia in the ephemeral and transitory aspects of everyday experience and urban reality, as well as to an embrace of montage as a technique charged with a potential for disruption and anticipation. Nazism's political ascent and final access to power impelled Bloch to formulate another concept related to the temporality of the present: the notion of *noncontemporaneity*. Complicating the model of linear, one-dimensional historical time, Bloch was trying to make sense of the fact that large portions of an ostensibly "modern" population had adopted an ideology that championed the most primitive elements of German identity. He concludes that modernization does not necessarily produce a homogeneous social totality, but rather generates a heterogeneous society characterized by the presence of groups that are merely juxtaposed in space, but that exist, both subjectively and objectively, in different historical times. An association between historical temporality and the avant-garde aesthetics of montage is discernible in Bloch's notion of noncontemporaneity. The aesthetics of montage was, in fact, the subject of the Expressionism Debate, Bloch's 1937–1938 dispute with Georg Lukács about the relation between representation and reality from a socialist perspective. Against Lukács' celebration of the uniform time of continuity in a coherent social whole, Bloch passionately defended the avant-garde's temporality of sudden rupture as the privileged repository of aesthetic value and historical content.

Chapter 5 investigates the different conceptualizations of instantaneous temporality in the work of German philosopher and literary critic Walter Benjamin. The chapter first presents Benjamin's preoccupation with the fate of experience in the modern world, which led him to explore the figure of *shock* as the new standard for everyday experience. In his analysis of the effects of the new forms of the "mechanical reproducibility" of art, such as photography and cinema, and in his studies of the cultural manifestations of commodity capitalism in the France of the Second Empire (and, especially, in the poetry of Baudelaire), Benjamin dissects the features of instantaneous shock in the midst of the urban crowd as the "sensation of modernity" par excellence. The chapter then analyzes Benjamin's antihistoricist vision of historiography as the search for "dialectical images": sudden juxtapositions of analogous historical epochs or events. In Benjamin's historical materialist method, past times are not closed entities, accessible only in their own terms, but rather contain a "historical index" that can only be properly deciphered in a future moment: its "now of legibility." The past is, as it were, incomplete, and waiting for the attention of a future present in order to accomplish its full potential. The task of the historian is to interpret authentically historical time as a series of abrupt leaps out of the chronology of linear time—that is, to find those images of the past that have reached their moment of recognizability in the present. Benjamin's radical vision of historiography entailed a conception of history as a discontinuous process punctuated by moments of sudden interruption. His name for these moments outside the progressive continuity of history was *now-time*. For Benjamin, the flashing instant when the past finds its fulfillment in the present is also the moment of radical political action—a now of legibility that coincides with the now of history and politics.

CHAPTER 1

The Instant from Goethe to Nietzsche

The Modern Beginnings of a Concept

The first modern expressions of instantaneity as a form of time consciousness in European thought can be traced back to the end of the eighteenth
and the beginning of the nineteenth centuries. During this time, the motif
of the instant played a significant role in the formation of concepts for the
understanding of subjective perception and historical consciousness. This
chapter focuses on three specific early modern formulations: Goethe's literary treatment of the motif of the *intense moment*; the French Revolution's
historical self-fashioning as *radical rupture*; and the German Romantics'
elaboration of the aesthetic category of *suddenness*. The distinct tradition
of reflection on instantaneous temporality that these formulations put into
motion would crucially influence the instantaneist regime in the twentieth
century. Although each deploys the instant in its own way, they all anticipate
important features of the instantaneity chronotope, such as the distinction
between subjective and the collective perceptions of temporality and the possible interactions between them.

Each formulation addresses instantaneity differently. Goethe's poetry
introduced instantaneity as a category of everyday (but also exceptional) perception. French revolutionaries saw themselves as instigators of a tabula rasa,
initiating a form of ahistorical political consciousness. The German Romantics, in turn, drew upon the German poetic tradition and the political influence of the French Revolution to elaborate an aesthetics of suddenness and
the fragmentary. Later in the nineteenth century, three authors emerged who
presented—under diverse guises and with differing purposes—the first modern theoretical elaborations of instantaneity as a form of time consciousness:
Søren Kierkegaard, Friedrich Nietzsche, and Charles Baudelaire (I discuss

Baudelaire in Chapter 2). These authors primarily involved themselves with
the subjective dimension of temporality, but they also interwove an epochal
consciousness into their thought. Their visions of instantaneous time—especially ahistorical forms of consciousness—would become consequential for
the later deployments of the instant motif.

<h2 style="text-align:center">Two Forms of Instantaneity:
Goethe and the French Revolution</h2>

Although the modern history of the instant could be traced back to René
Descartes, Blaise Pascal, and Jean-Jacques Rousseau, it is the work of Johann
Wolfgang von Goethe that unarguably marks the beginning of a distinctive
era in the conception of the instant as a category for the perception of time.
Goethe was the first modern author to develop a consistent discourse of
instantaneity both as a theme and as a formal feature of his writing. It left an
imprint on the modern conceptions of poetry and the perception of temporality, and it initiated a discussion of the instant that would shape nineteenth-
century treatments of the topic up to Nietzsche. By introducing a secular
understanding of the term, Goethe's instant laid the foundations for suddenness as a philosophical and aesthetic category and for the later development
of forms of historical consciousness predicated on timelessness, untimeliness,
and ahistoricity.

From his lyric poetry to *Faust*, the instant (*Augenblick*) is the temporal
notion most emphatically related to Goethe's literary production. In the German author's work, the instant designates "an experience whose intensity
and significance greatly exceeds the elusiveness of its measurable duration."[1]
Augenblick functions as the key word to indicate those episodes when "in the
flash of the now" (*im Blitzes Nu*) the eternal is revealed in time.[2] Karl Löwith
points out that Goethe sublated Christianity into "humanity" (*Humanität*)
and created a "humanized" version of Lutheran theology.[3] One could accordingly consider Goethe's *Augenblick* as a profane version of theophany (the
appearance of the divine to humans), or as the worldly equivalent of the *nunc
stans* of medieval theology, which perceived time from God's point of view.[4]
Goethe's *Augenblick* thus constitutes the first distinct episode in the history of
the modern conceptualizations of the subjective experience of instantaneous
temporality. It also stands at the beginning of a modern tradition of writing on
secular epiphanies and "profane illuminations." This tradition, which found

its high points in German Romanticism, the philosophy of Kierkegaard, and Nietzsche's doctrine of eternal recurrence, features a common search for the extraordinary experience of the irruption of the eternal within the secular realm of art or the everyday.

In his great dramatic works, such as *Egmont* and *Tasso*, Goethe presents a literary embodiment of what could be termed his personal *theory of moments*. The theory comprises the following premises: (1) truth and fulfillment can only exist as momentary realities; (2) these short-lived experiences of fleeting gratification are, nevertheless, the most important aspect of existence; (3) given their exceptional quality, these moments or instants fall outside the regularity of life and history.[5] Johann Gottfried Herder's work *God: Some Conversations* was of especial importance for the development of Goethe's outlook on the instant. After having read Herder, Goethe concluded "that the moment is everything and that the merit of a rational human being consists only in so conducting himself that his life . . . contains the greatest possible quantity of rational, beautiful moments."[6]

Goethe's theory of moments was also reflected in the poet's understanding of literature as the occasion for the production of such exceptional experiences. As David E. Wellbery has analyzed, in Goethe's early lyric a "new possibility of poetic enunciation" opens up, a possibility that inaugurates a new type of temporality for literature. This new mode is based on the establishment of a phenomenological link between the poem and the now of reading. The "time of the lyric" is a "time of the now" (*Jetztzeit*)—the "temporal actuality of the reader" in the moment of his or her encounter with the text. This lyrical experience aims at reproducing, in its very occurrence, the structure of instantaneity. In Wellbery's words, poetry "presupposes an abruptly discontinuous temporality; the lyric inevitably has an *ecstatic* character, standing out from the rest of time." The "paradox of the lyric" is, then, identical to the "paradox of the instant." The fragile brevity of a moment is, nevertheless, related to eternity as "it seems to efface all linear time." Goethe would, accordingly, have a significant influence on Romantic poetry, an influence that would express itself in the tendency to isolate a single moment "in such a manner that it stands out—ecstatically—from all time."[7]

In *Faust*, his drama published in two parts in 1808 and 1832, Goethe delivers his most significant treatment of the instant. The core of this treatment is Faust's bet that he will never be satisfied with anything that Mephistopheles has to offer and that, if he is, Mephistopheles can take his life. Faust seals the wager with a renowned formulation on the instant: "If I ever say to

the moment 'Linger on, you are so beautiful' . . . Then I will gladly perish. . . .
Let time then be over for me."[8] Faust here condemns himself to permanent
dissatisfaction and the unending striving for the next moment. He makes this
wager, however, because he already knows that these temporary images—
Augenblicke, "moments of vision" in which the absolute can be transitorily
glimpsed—are the only guise under which transcendence can be experienced
in the world. The search for a fulfilling moment amounts to a tantalizing
quest because any satisfaction must vanish at the moment of its appearance.
Goethe's stance in *Faust* is a lament over, and a salutation to, the evanescence
of fulfilled moments. It acknowledges the double, contradictory nature of
such moments, since they are simultaneously glimpses of the absolute and
confirmations that discontent is the default state of the human condition.

The Faustian instant stands for the recognition of the sudden arrival of
a secular eternity into time and for an acknowledgment of the fleetingness
of any form of intense or accomplished experience. *Faust*'s conclusion will
introduce yet another connotation. At the moment of his death, the protagonist pronounces the forbidden words: "Linger on, you are so beautiful." He
does not lose the bet, however, because he is speaking only in anticipation of
the time when his dream of a community of "free people on free soil" will be
fulfilled. The moment of permanence that Faust experiences is, then, nothing
but a dream or, as Mephistopheles calls it, "the last, lousy, empty moment."[9]
These verses present the modern ethos, later elaborated by Romantic authors
such as Friedrich Schlegel, of a permanent (and permanently unfulfilled)
striving for newness, the everlasting frustration with the now, and the belief
that this endless pursuit is, in itself, the only kind of attainable completion.[10]
In the final scene, the Faustian *Augenblick* mutates into an image of a continuous anticipation without achievement or resolution. The concept of the
instant now expresses a tension between the longing for an image of coherence and the temporal principle that disrupts that very ambition.[11]

By stressing the fleeting nature of any semblance of totality, this last
incarnation of the Goethean instant represents an early articulation of what
critics ranging from Walter Benjamin to Jürgen Habermas have identified as
modernity's *temporal mode*—the experience of time as a mania for the new.
This mode is in tension with the understanding of the instant as a form of
worldly fulfillment (even if only fleeting). This contrast represents the origin
of two distinct and opposed styles of thinking about instantaneous temporality. In the first, the instant is conceived as the experience of an extreme, albeit
ephemeral, experience; in the second, the instant is seen as the *semblance* of

this experience that, given its never-ending repetition, becomes the substance of modern time itself.

If Goethe's literary production presented the subjective aspect of modern instantaneity, the French Revolution's historical consciousness articulated its collective dimension. From the early days of the Revolution, the French revolutionaries interpreted their own political action as the enactment of a *new beginning*. Accordingly, in their account of events, the protagonists of the Revolution emphasized rupture and total discontinuity with the past. They construed the Revolution as the founding event of an entirely new era with no connections to the bygone time of monarchies and feudal estates. Among them prevailed the expectation that the Revolution would "deliver happiness, not when it is due but at once."[12] They conceived of the revolutionary event as a distinct one-step process of instantaneous transition from a social reality anchored in tradition to a utopian normativity. The year 1789 was thought to be the moment of an abrupt, almost "miraculous"[13] transformation of the body politic. Consequently, a political rhetoric of the mythic present animated the revolutionaries' determination to break with the past. In the revolutionary imagination, key episodes (such as the Estates General, the Tennis Court Oath, or the storming of the Bastille) were simultaneously "historical and existing outside of time,"[14] thus establishing a sense of temporal dislocation for which an exclusively historicist framework could not account.

Republican revolutionaries gave to this idea of radical beginning a vivid form with their revolutionary calendar. With novel names for the months and days of the year, the calendar proclaimed a new consciousness of time.[15] The Republican calendar—in use from 1793 to 1805—was, according to Sanja Perovic, "a statement of the Jacobins' utopian instincts and regenerative desires."[16] The revolutionaries presented the calendar, which followed the decimal system and was based on the precise measurements of the earth, as the most rational way possible to calculate dates and to organize time. The calendar's abstract but also "natural" time helped constitute a new secular and egalitarian era—"a modern present, separated from the past."[17] "Thanks to the new calendar," Perovic writes, "the Revolution's rupture with the past was to be transformed into a wholly new experience of time, one made according to the joint dictates of nature and reason."[18]

Walter Benjamin provides an instantaneist interpretation of the revolutionary calendar in his "On the Concept of History." There he identifies the introduction of the calendar as a powerful sign that the French revolutionaries knew that they were about "to make the continuum of history explode."[19] The

Republican calendar provides for Benjamin a formidable historical example of the phenomenon of "revolutionary interruption," the moment when radical political action suddenly introduces a "standstill" in the flow of time:[20] "What characterizes revolutionary classes at their moment [*Augenblick*] of action is the awareness that they are about to make the continuum of history explode. The Great Revolution introduced a new calendar. The initial day of a calendar presents history in time-lapse [*Zeitraffer*] mode. And basically it is this same day that keeps recurring in the guise of holidays, which are days of remembrance [*Tage des Eingedenkens*]."[21]

If for Reinhart Koselleck *experience* and *expectation* are the two categories of historical time, and what we call *modernity* is the historical condition characterized by the increasing differentiation between the two,[22] then the French revolutionary consciousness could be interpreted as the radical will of suddenly collapsing this widened gap between experience and expectation, not through the mediation of gradual, progressive unfolding of historical reason but through the instantaneous performance of revolutionary action. In this self-image, the Revolution believed itself to have thrown out all historical gradualisms or mediations and brought about the immediate social realization of a utopian program based on absolute equality. As Mona Ozouf has documented, the organization of revolutionary festivals constituted a sort of commemoration of that irreversible discontinuity in the flow of historical time.[23] This modality of historical consciousness was also evident in the practice of ritual oaths that celebrated "the instant of creation of the new community."[24] Through these celebrations, the moment of the irruption of a utopian normativity preserves itself as a ritual re-creation. This irruption was the *eternal present* of equality in which the people of France lived after the storming of the Bastille. Hegel's interpretation of the events of 1789 emphasized this instantaneist reading of the Revolution. According to Rebecca Comay, Hegel believed that the subject of the Revolution was characterized by a certain autarkic quality, which expressed itself in an attachment to the "immediacy of the moral now-point."[25] This subject had to continually recreate this moral now-point in order to maintain the effect of immediacy, or "the fantasy of an incessant, ex nihilo beginning."

The perception of the French Revolution as the sudden abolition of an unjust past and the immediate enactment, here and now, of the values of equality and freedom created a new kind of historical consciousness: that of revolution as an instantaneous "framework of political action."[26] After 1789, revolutions present themselves—at least during their early stages and in the self-image of their own agents—as absolute beginnings, incarnations of an *absolute present* outside the flow of history. The extent to which the French Revolution actually constituted this far-reaching disruption in the continuity of French history has been vehemently debated.[27] But the fact remains that, in the realm of political imagination, it produced a true break in "the ways of legitimating and representing historical action."[28]

It must be noted, however, that the French Revolution mobilized not only one, but several (often conflicting) forms of the experience of time.[29] If the revolutionary period featured instantaneity as a modality of historical consciousness and political action, it also represented one of the high points in the development of a historicist understanding of historical time. According to François Hartog, the Revolution constitutes, in fact, the beginning of the modern—or "futurist"—regime of historicity. In this regime, a particular version of the experience of time prevails in which events gradually unfold in order to accomplish, in the future, a predetermined *telos*, or goal, such as "the Nation" or "Progress."[30] The lessons that arise from the pursuit of the goal, and the ensuing acceleration of events rushing toward its realization, become the basic framework for the organization of the experience of time in a given community. Hartog's thesis follows the ideas of Koselleck, who had identified the period between 1750 and 1850 as the "saddle" or "transitional time" (*Sattelzeit*) for the creation of the modern concepts of temporality, which feature a linear, progressive, and future-oriented philosophy of history.

The French revolutionaries situated their historical consciousness somewhere between the two conflicting temporalities of instantaneity and progress, but it is possible to distinguish an *instantaneist moment* of the Revolution from its more historicist conceptions. This instantaneist moment postulates the instant of *sudden rupture* as the fundamental category for the organization of historical temporality. This instant posits an *ahistorical* temporality, a moment "outside of time" that obliterates both the past and the future in the name of an absolute present. The instantaneist moment rejects all ties with the past. It presents itself as a form of creation ex nihilo; and it also rejects the future, because it assumes itself as the realization of liberty and equality, not in an upcoming time, but in the here and now. This instantaneist moment coexisted with the interpretation of the Revolution as the gradual unfolding of a certain historical reason, and soon it was entirely conflated with it. But the prominence of the French Revolution in the formation of historicist conceptions of time should not prevent us from noticing the existence of the Revolution's instantaneist dimension. This instantaneist moment of revolution would be subsequently repeated, albeit as an ephemeral phase, in other instances of revolutionary upheaval, such as the Paris Commune of 1870, the early stages of the Russian Revolution in 1917, or the short-lived Soviet Republics of Munich and Hungary (1919). In this sense, the instantaneist moment of the French Revolution prefigures the years of the Weimar Republic in Germany, when the ahistorical consciousness of instantaneity would become the foundation for a general regime of historicity that pertained an entire era's experience of time.

If the Goethean instant was born alongside its own critique—the Faustian acceptance of the moment as a never-ending striving—the revolutionary moment, on the contrary, was born along with its own self-mythologization. Both of them can be construed as the outcome of a process of secularization, understood as the *reoccupation* of a position previously held by religion.[31] The Goethean moment, for example, is a *secular theophany* in the sense that, while it preserves the abstract structure of transcendence, it is divorced from any explicit reference to the language of Christianity. The revolutionary break, for its part, responds to a form of historical consciousness that has endowed earthly human agency with the (formerly divine) power of enacting an ex nihilo creation in history.

The German Romantics and the Aesthetics of Suddenness

By the end of the eighteenth century, Goethe had introduced into the German aesthetic the category of the instant as a moment of perceptual intensity, and the French Revolution had attuned European opinion to the notion of sudden political change. It was within this intellectual atmosphere that some of the early German Romantic authors developed a vigorous notion of the instant, in which one can easily trace the influence of the Goethean and French revolutionary articulations of the concept. Romantic poets and writers commonly referred to the experience of an "unsustainable moment" at the intersection of time and eternity.[32] They thus contributed to the elaboration of the concept by developing a sophisticated treatment of the figure of suddenness as the basis for an original form of aesthetic consciousness.

The theological writings of Friedrich Schleiermacher are characteristic in this respect. In opposition to dogmatic and moral theories of religion, Schleiermacher—who belonged to the original early Romantic circle—championed an experiential interpretation of the sacred based on the immediacy of intuition and the interiority of feeling. In his work *On Religion: Speeches to Its Cultured Despisers* (1799), the German theologian portrays the instant as a privileged condition for the experiencing of religious emotion, which he defined as a "sensibility and taste for the infinite."[33] The instant is the moment in which the highest principle is revealed as transitory and inexpressible; it is "that first mysterious moment that occurs in every sensory perception, before intuition and feeling have separated, where sense and its objects have, as it were, flowed into one another and become one."[34] The instant for Schleiermacher is not only that event in which an "image of the universe" is manifested in the particular; it is also the decisive experience in the life of an individual. In each individual existence, Schleiermacher writes, "There is some moment, like the silvery flash in the melting process of baser metals, when, be it through the close approach of a higher being or through some sort of electrical shock, it is, as it were, raised out of itself and placed on the highest pinnacle of what it can be. For this moment it was created, in this it attended its definition, and after it the exhausted life force sinks back again."[35] In this passage, Schleiermacher seems to be desecularizing the Goethean profane instant, claiming the existential overtones that the concept had acquired in the work of the German poet only to place them back into a religious framework. But what stands out in the end is his continuation of the Goethean motif of the instantaneous as a category of everyday experience. Importantly, in his translation of Plato's *Parmenides*, Schleiermacher renders the Greek philosopher's notion of the sudden (*exaiphnes*) as *Augenblick*—a foundational gesture that would later influence Søren Kierkegaard's conception of instantaneity.[36]

As discussed earlier, the self-image of the French Revolution introduced the notions of sudden rupture and absolute present into the consciousness of historical time. Karl Heinz Bohrer has argued that, in their literary treatment of the "anticipatory moment" as a leap into the unexpected, the early German Romantics represented the first attempt at giving an aesthetic cast to this new structure of historical time. The early Romantics shared the French revolutionaries' rhetoric of destruction, novelty and spontaneity, as well as their notion of the now as the place for an "explosion of renewal."[37] Romantic literature was in this sense *revolutionary*, not so much due to its political content, but as a result of its mode of poetic consciousness. In their use of language, Romantics intended to represent a form of sudden irruption in itself, a sort of poetical "event."[38]

Schlegel's theory of literature is one example of this Romantic embrace of suddenness as an aesthetic and historical category. Schlegel interpreted

the French Revolution in line with the revolutionaries' self-understanding—
that is, as a radical historical rupture or a sudden break that had forced the
appearance of a new time. Accordingly, Schlegel designated the Revolution
as "the first true age,"[39] the beginning of modern history as such. Due to its
nature as "an almost universal earthquake," Schlegel considered the Revolution "the prototype of revolutions" and "the absolute revolution *per se*."[40] But
Schlegel's did not limit his reception of the revolutionary event to historical
commentary, as his literary vision extrapolated some of the key aspects of the
revolutionary historical consciousness to the realm of aesthetics. For Schlegel,
the superiority of modern Romantic literature over classical literature resided
in the former's instantaneous, fragmentary character, which embodies an
incessant struggle for the realization of beauty. In the Romantic perspective,
poetry "eternally becomes and can never be completed,"[41] or, in other words,
poetry, as modern history itself, is always thrown into the "unknownability"
of what is forthcoming. In his essay "On Incomprehensibility," Schlegel insists
that there can be no final expression of truth. The individual's inner happiness
depends on something that "must be left in the dark."[42] Romantic aesthetics,
then, relies on a notion of the poetical as an instantaneous reality that is con-
tinuously exposed to the undecided possibilities of the unforeseen.

In Schlegel's perspective, one of the most telling manifestations of Romantic aesthetics was the new prominence of the *fragment* as a literary form in
modern times. "Many of the works of ancients have become fragments. Many
modern works are fragments as soon as they are written,"[43] he writes in his
own *Athenaeum Fragments* (1798). This new prominence of the fragment, in
fact, evinced significant connections to the revolutionary mood of the era. As
Rebecca Comay has argued, there is a link between the Romantic aesthetics
of the fragmentary and the French revolutionary notion of a historical *Null-
punkt*—or "ground zero"—of an absolute present. The connection resides in
their shared positing of an "absolute beginning," either in the space of history
or in the realm of art and literature. Every episode or absolute beginning is,
because of its origin in sudden rupture, inherently *unfinished*. Thus, all acts
of creation or instances of a radical break can only result in the production of
fragments, which mark "a return to the *tabula rasa*." The Romantic fragment
represents, in this sense, a repetition of the revolutionary gesture, a way of
"formalizing its essential incompletion."[44]

Heinrich von Kleist's essay "On the Gradual Production of Thoughts
Whilst Speaking"—written around 1805–1806 and published in 1878—is
another example of the Romantic elaboration of the revolutionary event

from the perspective of aesthetics.[45] In the essay, Kleist introduces a thesis that prefigures the surrealist experiments on automatic writing. He posits that ideas tend to be the result not of previous rumination but of impulsive, thunder-like verbal eruptions during conversation. Kleist's main illustration for his theory is, suggestively, the comte de Mirabeau's dismissal of the king's master of ceremonies during the last meeting of the Estates General under the Ancien Régime. At the master of ceremonies' order to dissolve the Estates, Mirabeau hesitated, then unexpectedly came up with a thoroughly new political idea. The Estates could not receive orders from the king for they were the authentic representatives of the nation. Mirabeau's affirmation contributed to the transformation of the Estates into the National Assembly and thus to the further radicalization of the revolutionary process. In Kleist's account, a single, instantaneous witticism marks the before and after of the Revolution.

However, it was Friedrich Hölderlin's series of late hymns that provided the most multifaceted interpretation of instantaneity in early German Romanticism. Written around 1800, Hölderlin's hymns present a vision of poetry and history in which the notions of the now and the event are the protagonists. At the time, Hölderlin held the double conviction that the world was about to suffer a radical transformation and that poetry was to play a decisive role in this change. A new age was coming, which would be marked by the recognition of nature's divinity and the reappearance of the long absent gods of classical antiquity. Accordingly, a tone of anticipation characterizes Hölderlin's poetry from this period, which Michael Hamburger has called Hölderlin's "prophetic phase."[46] The atmosphere in Hölderlin's hymns is one of imminence, expectation at the impending return of the gods after a long season of absence. In this mood of anticipation, time itself acquires the features of a dynamic presence. The epiphany of the return is particularly accentuated in one of Hölderlin's hymns from 1799, "As on a Holiday," where he heralds an epochal dawning: "*Jetzt aber tagts!*" (But now day breaks!).[47] Likewise, "Bread and Wine," another hymn from the period, expresses the feeling of the coming fulfillment of prophecy and the "organic consummation of time."[48]

In his hymns, Hölderlin explores another aspect of the romantic motif of suddenness: the figure of *nearness*. Nearness is the facet of instantaneity that corresponds to the premise of an imminent return, which dominates this phase of his work. Take, for example, the opening lines of "Patmos": "*Nah ist / Und schwer zu fassen der Gott*" (Near is / And difficult to grasp, the God).[49] For Hölderlin, the more intense the divine presence, the more difficult it is to perceive and comprehend—and the more threatening, or even more dangerous, it becomes. Hölderlin took the French Revolution and the European wars that followed to be signs of the long-awaited reawakening of Nature and the coming of the gods.[50] In "As on a Holiday," for example, he writes: "*Die Natur ist jetzt mit Waffenklang erwacht*" (Nature has now awoken amid the clang of arms).[51] Hölderlin considered revolution and war—what he called the "deeds of the world"—occasions for new poetical illumination, and he gave expression to it throughout his hymns in the motif of *Jetzt*— an "emphatic now." [52] In the text's paratactic literary style, Hölderlin established a dialogue between historical rupture and the formal sudden break. In Theodor W. Adorno's description, parataxis lines up unconnected elements in a sequence and suspends "the traditional logic of synthesis" by encouraging "artificial disturbances that evade the logical hierarchy of subordinating syntax."[53] Hölderlin's paratactic style foreshadows the twentieth-century avant-gardes' "aesthetics of juxtaposition": the mixing of disparate fragments with the intention of producing a "shock," as in Dadaist collage or surrealist automatic writing. Hölderlin fashioned modern poetry as an event in its own right, an authentic, historical *Augenblick* that corresponded to the sociopolitical transformations of the era.[54] His hymns constituted a crucial early attempt to codify the experience of historical rupture and to enact that very experience by means of literary form.

Despite its political implications, Martin Heidegger's reading of Hölderlin offers estimable insights concerning the role of temporality in the German poet's hymns. His interpretation remains significant because it focuses on Hölderlin's expression of a poetico-historical consciousness.[55] For Heidegger, Hölderlin's *now* stands against the abstract time of the calendar. As in Goethe, this now is the now of poetry, the instant in which the poetic act happens and determines time itself. In this instant, the poetic act invests time with a qualitatively temporal substance. The time of the now is "itself a date—that is to say, something given, a gift."[56] Therefore, this now not only names the poet's chronological period but, more essentially, the uniqueness of an age that was living in a state of expectation for the coming of "the holy"—the time of "the gods who have fled *and* the god who is coming."[57] For Heidegger, this naming is "historical in the highest degree, because it anticipates a historical time."[58] To use another of Hölderlin's concepts, the effect of the now of poetry on temporality is the introduction of a *caesura* in time. In his reflections on tragic poetry, Hölderlin defines the caesura as "the pure word, the counter-rhythmic rupture" that precipitates the appearance of "the representation itself." These are the moments when "man forgets himself because he exists entirely for the moment" and "the god [forgets himself] because he is nothing but time." The moment of caesura is a self-containing instant. In it, time is "reversed categorically . . . no longer fitting beginning and end."[59] One might also say, using yet another key term from Heidegger, that Hölderlin's now of poetry is what founds historicity as such.

Another dimension of Heidegger's reading is his examination of Hölderlin's motif of nearness. When Hölderlin writes in "Homecoming," "*Was du suchest, es ist nahe, begegnet dir schon*" (What you seek, it is near, already comes to meet you), the image of closeness presents a perplexing paradox that what is near is also what is kept at a distance. Elsewhere, the gods are absent but at the same time "so near" or even "too near." His poetry never dispels the essential ambiguity of this nearness, which, on the contrary, he deliberately presents as a mystery. Accordingly, in Hölderlin's hymns the gods' absence emerges as their way of being actually present. The gods are present in the poem itself, which anticipates their return.[60] Hölderlin's treatment of nearness as a feature of the present foreshadows Ernst Bloch's "darkness of the lived moment," or the present moment's obscurity because it is too near to be properly grasped (see Chapter 4).

A particular structure of the present can be deduced from Hölderlin's poetry. In these poems, the now does not coincide with itself. Rather, it is as if a deferment were inherent to the internal configuration of the present. The now is revealed essentially as anticipation, a mere prelude to presence that turns out to be, in fact, the only possible way of experiencing that presence. The poems suggest not only that the implied event will not actually take place but also that it is, in a certain way, impossible. What constitutes the event then is its own poetic anticipation. In other words, the actual event is the poem itself. Hölderlin originates the modern tradition of identifying the text with the event, a tradition that implies the mutual entanglement of History and the representation of history. This tradition would inform certain aspects of the instantaneist historicity regime, especially in Bloch's and Benjamin's writings on reading and writing as prefigurations or actual enactments of a utopian vision.

The Hölderlinian motif of nearness, of the difficulty of grasping "the God," also fits within the genealogy of another important category of instantaneity: the notion of *the contemporary*. If, as Giorgio Agamben has stated, "the contemporary is he who firmly holds his gaze on his own time so as to perceive not its light, but rather its darkness,"[61] then Hölderlin's effort in grasping "the God" can be read as a primordial image of this form of appropriation. The early German Romantic circle developed this sense of the contemporary,

perhaps precisely as a response to the impression of being juxtaposed in time to the Revolution, but only as external spectators. The experience resulted in the sensation of being both close to and far away from the event. In contrast to Hölderlin, the French revolutionary attitude toward the present did not entail a preoccupation with the contemporary. The notion of a *distance* from the event was absent from the historical self-awareness of the revolutionaries. Rather, they thought of themselves as *enacting* the present without any mediation. Hölderlin brought the French revolutionary consciousness of rupture to a new level of self-reflection. The question he postulated was: What does it mean *to be in the present*, to be attuned to the actuality of the now? Hölderlin's "God" can be read as an allegory of the present moment and of the difficulties that it poses as a form of historical consciousness.

In forging a sensibility for the instantaneous, the Romantics were creating one of their most enduring ideas. Perhaps, as the Schlegel fragment goes, Goethe and the French Revolution were indeed, at least with respect to the conceptions of sudden temporality, "the greatest tendencies of the age."[62] Goethe devised a new aesthetic based on the emphatic now, and the French Revolution created a grammar of historical rupture, but the German Romantics combined both dispositions into a sensibility that inaugurated a tradition of reflection on instantaneity. In the twentieth century, this tradition would become one of the foundations of a regime of historicity based on the phenomenon of suddenness.

Søren Kierkegaard and Decision

The first modern thinker to develop a wide-ranging philosophical conceptualization of the instant was Søren Kierkegaard (1813–1855), who approached instantaneous time from the point of view of individual subjectivity. In *Philosophical Fragments*[63] and *The Concept of Anxiety*[64] (both published in 1844), the Danish philosopher presents the instant as an entirely unique concept, which poses new and exceptional problems to philosophy. Kierkegaard's treatment of the instant was a momentous philosophical move that, according to Heidegger, transformed the horizon of thinking. With Kierkegaard's instant, Heidegger wrote in 1929, "the *possibility* of a completely new epoch of philosophy has begun for the first time since antiquity."[65] Although Kierkegaard's idea of the instant exhibits parallels with earlier formulations—such as Goethe's glimpse of the absolute, or the Romantics' sudden rupture—it distinguishes itself by including the embodied, existential dimension of instantaneity in *decision*. Kierkegaard provided a further refinement of the language of instantaneity, many of whose features would reappear in the approaches of Jünger, Bloch, or Benjamin in the twentieth century.

In *Philosophical Fragments*, his study of the contrast between Christian and Greek modes of thinking, Kierkegaard provides two definitions of the instant: (1) the instant as the "once and forever" moment when God became flesh and assumed a human form in the *Incarnation*; and (2) the instant as the decisive moment of personal *conversion*. The first definition is, essentially, a theological category.[66] It denotes the act by which God made himself present in the world in the person of Christ, designating the irruption of an eternal divine into the finite human. This intersection of time and eternity represents for Kierkegaard the primary instant—the concept's very prototype. But the Incarnation also introduces a primordial paradox because it means that the eternal can have a beginning in time. Kierkegaard's second definition of the instant is that moment when the eternal truth of the divine reveals itself in the subjective life of an individual. In this singular moment, a radical conversion or "turning around" takes place, which amounts to a spiritual leap from nonbeing to being. This instant of conversion is brief as any other instant, but also eternal and thus decisive as no other. Kierkegaard refers to this second instant as "the fullness of time," following Saint Paul's designation of *kairos* as the adequate moment for an event to happen.[67] The instant for Kierkegaard is the propitious time for the birth of eternity in time.[68]

Another fundamental Kierkegaardian concept, *contemporaneity* between Christ and the believer, derives from his understanding of the instant. Contemporaneity does not allude to simultaneity in time, but to the believer's absolute relationship with the eternal no matter what time the believer inhabits. This relationship collapses the historical time gap that separates Christ from the disciple. To have been converted means to belong to the eternal present of truth such that faith allows one to share the same present as Christ.[69] Disciples are authentic contemporaries of God because they have accepted the Incarnation as the historical event that signals the origin of an affiliation of time with eternity. The disciple knows that personal redemption is at stake precisely in the relationship with that moment of history—that instant—when, in Kierkegaard's words, "the eternalizing of the historical and the historicizing of the eternal" takes place.[70]

In the moment of the encounter of the individual with the divine, Kierkegaard tells us, human understanding confronts the unknown; reason enters into a paralysis that only an act of the will can undo. This act of will is a *leap of faith* that happens outside of time, in an instant. The leap cannot be accounted for in terms of previous events, and it is impossible to explain it within the laws of causality or logic, as it constitutes a form of qualitative transition that rejects continuity.[71] Conceiving of it otherwise would amount to a negation of free choice as a spontaneous act of the will. The Kierkegaardian leap is conceptually in debt to the Platonic notion of *exaiphnes*, which Plato introduces in the *Parmenides* as a definition of instantaneity. A particular mood—anxiety—precedes the leap. (Anxiety would later become crucial for Heidegger's phenomenology). In contrast to fear, which is always fear of something concrete, anxiety does not relate to anything in particular. Rather, it is the "dizziness of freedom,"[72] the open-ended feeling that the individual experiences before possibility itself. Kierkegaardian freedom is dependent on the notion of *spirit*—that dimension where the experience of interiority occurs. Ignored by the ancient Greeks, this notion of spirit reflects the preoccupation with the self that Christianity introduced in its belief that eternal salvation or damnation confers to the individual a new radical freedom. With this new freedom, the individual determines his or her fate for eternity through existential decisions made in time.

Kierkegaard's analysis of the instantaneous leap, moreover, presents the problem of *decision* as the distinctive moment of spontaneous choice. The instant is that "new decision," the existential "decision of eternity"[73] that revelation opens up to the individual as a possibility. In his psychological reflection on the mental states of the self, *The Concept of Anxiety*, Kierkegaard explains that the instant, as a moment of transcendental choice, occurs at the intersection of the temporal and the eternal, where the content of eternity is decided within the fleeting interval of a privileged now. He finds the prototype for the decision as leap in Abraham's sacrifice of Isaac. By following God's unfathomable command to turn Isaac into a victim, Abraham made "the great trampoline leap"[74] into infinitude. The decisive moment that Abraham raised his knife to murder his son, Abraham "fulfilled" himself by suspending his relationship with God and the realm of the ethical. God had subjected Abraham to the paradox of faith,[75] wherein the exception of a single individual is greater than the universal rule of the ethical because it stands in a nonmediated "absolute relation to the absolute."[76] In the twentieth century, the Kierkegaardian notions of decision and exception would play a fundamental role in Carl Schmitt's political and juridical theory, especially in his formulations of sovereignty and the "state of exception."[77] Kierkegaard found in the term *the instant*[78] a powerful means of expressing decisive existential situations: "Nothing is as swift as the blink of an eye, and nevertheless it is commensurable with the content of the eternal."[79]

Kierkegaard's temporality is a new formulation of a Pauline concept. In his First Epistle to the Corinthians, Saint Paul offers a poetic paraphrase of the instant when he writes that the end of the world will take place in "the twinkling of an eye."[80] For Kierkegaard, the moment of destruction also announces the advent of the eternal.[81] Consequently, the instant should not be considered the "atom" of time but rather "the atom of eternity." The instant's connection to eternity is fundamental to the experience of temporality. If time lacks these sudden instances of alignment with the eternal, it is nothing but an infinite sequence of irrelevant moments, and the present is reduced to a merely mental limit that, strictly speaking, does not exist. It is simply the abstract transition between the past and the future, just like Aristotle's now.[82] Abstract visions of time are able to artificially maintain the division between past, present, and future only because they represent time as space—that is, as an unending flow that is a "parody of the eternal" in which the present is perpetually vanishing. In contrast, in the moment of decision, time acquires its most explicit signification. In this moment, the eternal is incorporated into the temporal, and the abstract now turns into an instant, the concrete now that, precisely because it is charged with existential content, postulates temporality.

Thinking in terms of past, present, and future from an existential point of view is possible only after the moment of decision establishes itself as the point of orientation. Kierkegaard even declares: "Only with the moment does history begin."[83] He means that qualitative historical time—what Heidegger would later call *historicity*—is possible only through the postulation of the now as the propitious moment of kairos.[84] Even if Kierkegaard focused mainly on the individual and subjective dimensions of time, his philosophy provides powerful insights for analyzing the collective dimensions of temporality. Kierkegaard's main contribution to the conceptual basis of instantaneity is to have illuminated the connection between a form of ahistorical consciousness of time (i.e., the irruption of eternity in time) and historicity proper (i.e., historical time's existential condition).

Toward the end of his life, Kierkegaard unambiguously underlined the link between his discourse on instantaneity and a more explicit commitment to the political situation of his own time. In 1855 (the year of his death), Kierkegaard wrote and circulated *The Moment*, a self- published pamphlet intended to address the Danish Church's most pressing concerns. In the publication's first issue, Kierkegaard explains that, after having written all of his previous work from an attitude of intellectual detachment, the urgency of criticizing Denmark's religious establishment had now compelled him into writing "in the moment."[85] By writing in the moment, he declares his intention to achieve something eternal. In his draft of the pamphlet's last issue, Kierkegaard offers a suggestive, more politically committed, definition of instantaneity: "The moment[86] is when the man is there, the right man, the man of the moment . . . only when the man is there, and when he ventures as it must be ventured . . . then is the moment."[87] Kierkegaard explicitly frames the meaning of the word (øjeblik) in terms of kairos. The moment is a "venture"—a resolute decision and a wager on his own fate. In the same draft, Kierkegaard insists on the impossibility of reducing the moment to its circumstances: "The moment is precisely this (which is not due to circumstances), the new thing, the woof of eternity—but at the same instant it manages the circumstances to such a degree that it illusively (calculated to make a fool of worldly sagacity and mediocrity) looks as if the moment emerged from the circumstances."[88] It is as if Kierkegaard had realized, in the last year of his life, a transformation of his philosophical notion of spiritual contemporaneity into something closer to Agamben's historical (and implicitly political) definition. He sketches this transformation as an effect of historical nearness. The historical "moment" may seem to be nothing else than its circumstances. But to authentically grasp it amounts to realizing that in its center resides the uncanny alterity of the eternal.[89]

Kierkegaard's treatment of the instant—either as an expression of the sudden apparition of eternity in time, or as the sign of a historical nearness—adds another dimension to the concept, which twentieth-century authors take up in several ways. This additional dimension is the distinction between the abstract present of mental time and the concrete instant of existential temporality. In his account, the present is nothing but the mediated representation of an instant—an actual event—which, because of its intensity, cannot be experienced directly. This distinction delineates the cohabitation of two different dimensions of time in what we usually name simply as *the present*. It therefore points to a basic *disimultaneity*, or "delay," at the heart of temporality—a characteristic that could be defined as proleptic, in reference to the rhetorical figure of prolepsis, or anticipation. Instantaneity's effect of nearness is related to this sudden nature that is irreducible to whatever precedes or surrounds it. The instant does not coincide with what we habitually understand by the present, because, insofar as it manifests itself as a sudden irruption, it is always "too soon" or "too late" with respect to the regular perception of

time. The instant is that rupture that comes before or after the present.[90] What
we call the present, then, is either a representation of a past instant or the
anticipation of an instant to come. The instant is always "no longer" or "not
yet." This elaboration is something akin to what Hölderlin had perceived as
the ungraspable nature of "the God" in its nearness. It is also comparable to
what Bloch would name the "darkness of the lived moment." Paradoxically,
the instant (and, with it, the contemporary) depends upon this fundamental
noncontemporaneity.

Friedrich Nietzsche and the Eternal Return

Thirty years after Kierkegaard's death, Friedrich Nietzsche (1844–1900)
developed his own discourse on instantaneous temporality as a form of ahistorical time consciousness. Nietzsche's ideas on the instant feature both a subjective and a historical dimension. Twentieth-century authors such as Jünger
and Benjamin would elaborate on them as a way to make sense of the crisis,
rupture, and danger that characterized their epoch. Despite the considerable
differences between Kierkegaard and Nietzsche—one working from Christian premises, the other professing to destroy them—both men granted crucial importance to the notion of the *eternity of the instant*. Nietzsche's first
treatment of the concept appears in his essay "On the Utility and Liability of
History for Life," the second of his *Unfashionable Observations* from 1876.[91]
In this essay, Nietzsche denounces the "historical sickness" that he believed
was plaguing his time: the apparent inability to forget the past. As a remedy
for the sickness of "the historical," Nietzsche prescribes the antidote of "the
ahistorical": the vital attitude of forgetting the past and living only in the present moment. Such an attitude is possessed by animals and children, who are
always immersed in the instantaneous now.[92]

Nietzsche's later work presents a more complex treatment of the instant
as the central temporal dimension of the ahistorical, where it is interwoven
into his doctrine of the eternal return. *The Gay Science*, Nietzsche's book of
aphorisms and fragments from 1882, contains the first mention of eternal
recurrence in his published works. There the eternal return is postulated by
the words of a demon in a passage titled "The greatest weight": "The life as
you now live it and have lived it, you will have to live once more and innumerable times more; and there will be nothing new in it, but every pain and
every joy and every thought and sigh and everything unutterably small or

great in your life will have to return to you, all in the same succession and sequence."[93] Later, Nietzsche assumes that the default reaction to the hypothesis of recurrence would be to curse the demon. But he also contemplates the possibility of experiencing "a tremendous moment when you would have answered: 'You are a god and never have I heard anything more divine.'"[94] The idea of eternal return is the "greatest weight" because, if laid upon every action, it would "change you as you are or perhaps crush you."[95] It thus poses the question: How do people need to live their lives so that all of their actions receive *eternal confirmation*?

These early insights would converge in *Thus Spoke Zarathustra* (1883–1891), Nietzsche's late lyrical fiction on the life and deeds of an imaginary prophet. In this work, the instant is presented as the metaphorical "gate" where the two eternal "roads" of the past and the future collide. The road of the past runs backwards from the gate, and in it everything that could happen has already happened innumerable times. Everything that has happened will cross the gate of the instant to enter the road of the future, where everything will happen again and again, eternally repeating itself.[96] As in Aristotle's conception of time, the present instant is, for Nietzsche, the point of encounter between the past and the future. But even if he is in some way recovering the Aristotelian notion of the now as the threshold between the future and the past, Nietzsche's instant is not a mere abstract limit—it is the concrete moment in which the eternal return of the same actualizes itself. In *Thus Spoke Zarathustra*, the instant is then presented as the specific temporality of eternity, the only experience in which ceaseless recurrence can actually be grasped as a concrete experience.

Like Kierkegaard, Nietzsche endows the instant with a decisive existential dimension. The eternal return, far from creating a feeling of indifference to events, turns the instant into something fundamental: the juncture in which a universal affirmation takes place. In the Nietzschean pattern of time, to say yes to one aspect of reality or the self—in other words, to say yes to a single instant—amounts to an affirmation of the entire cosmos. A posthumous fragment from *The Will to Power* expresses this view: "If we affirm one single moment, we thus affirm not only ourselves, but all existence. For nothing is self-sufficient, neither in us nor in things, and if our soul has trembled with happiness and sounded like a harpstring just once, all eternity was needed to produce this one event—and in this single moment of affirmation, all eternity was called good, redeemed, justified, and affirmed."[97] In recurrence, "everything is affirmed in a single moment."[98] The assertion of a single moment leads to the affirmation of the totality of time because "such an instant cannot exist without implying all the others."[99]

Repetition transforms the instant into a principle of ethical selectivity. In every moment, we will desire only what we can bear to be repeated forever. As with Kierkegaard, Nietzsche's instant involves a decision ("a choice, an act of the will").[100] In eternal recurrence, every instant repeats itself eternally, but this repetition contains a dimension of freedom because we are capable of choosing every instant's content and of deciding what will happen again and again. This aspect of eternal recurrence serves as a practical ethical formulation: "Whatever you will, will it in such a way that you also will its eternal return."[101] Nietzsche, like Kierkegaard before him, is offering a new version of Pascal's wager, arguing that decisions made in time have eternal reverberations. In Nietzsche, the eternal outcome is that every single act of an individual is essential to who that individual is. As Alexander Nehamas has explained, eternal recurrence is, in the end, not "a theory of the world but a view of the self."[102] In his seminars on Nietzsche from the late 1930s, Heidegger emphasizes this aspect of the instant in his reading of recurrence from the point of view of decision: "Not only must the thought emerge out of the creative moment of decision in some given individual, but, as a thought that pertains to life itself, it must also be a *historical decision—a crisis*."[103]

Accordingly, despite depending on a temporal structure of repetition, the Nietzschean doctrine on the eternal return does not exclude, but rather privileges the notion of the instant as an exception or "peak" in experience. These exceptional moments appear not only under the form of decision but also under something akin to revelation—something that the individual does not decide upon but receives purely as a gift of knowledge or vital intensity. In *Thus Spoke Zarathustra*, for example, Nietzsche discusses the impending coming of a "great noon." It is difficult not to associate this notion with the Greek kairos and, more specifically, with Saint Paul's "propitious moment" or instant of redemption. Zarathustra's "great noon" is inextricable from a transfigured (or trans*valued*) apocalyptic temporality: "The day is coming, the transformation, the judgment sword, *the great noon*: then much shall be revealed!"[104]

What Zarathustra announces as the great noon is the overcoming of the merely human and the coming of the overman, the "man of the future" who will redeem humanity from nihilism. This new kind of redemption consists in turning the "it was" into the "I wanted it so"; this turning creates a new "type of life that is strong enough to be able to will the eternal recurrence."[105] Only the strong could assent to the eternal return, for only they could lead a life that would deserve eternal repetition. The highest moment—the moment of the overman's arrival—is when the "reactive forces" that will not withstand recurrence's test self-destruct. Nietzsche's philosophy both affirms the recurrence of the same and exalts the overman as the one who creates a new form of existence. Zarathustra's great noon thus reconciles the eternal return with the instant as an exceptional moment.

In the Nietzschean understanding of temporality, the structure of the moment of exception pertains, at least potentially, to all moments. This understanding grows out of the "suprahistorical outlook," which, like the aforementioned ahistorical point of view, represents another antidote to the "historical sickness" of being unable to forget the past. In "On the Utility and Liability of History for Life," Nietzsche writes that, with a suprahistorical perspective, one "does not seek salvation in a process, but . . . instead the world is complete and has arrived at its culmination in every individual moment."[106] This attitude reappears when Zarathustra says: "Everything breaks, everything is joined anew; the same house of being builds itself eternally. . . . In every Instant being begins."[107] The eternal return's temporality is, in this sense, suprahistorical. Past, present, and future are affirmed as constituted in every moment, for in every moment all time is reevaluated.[108] For Nietzsche, every instant is a complete whole in itself, significant for its own sake, and entirely independent from any other instant. There is no static being, only instants in the process of becoming that are continually arising and perishing, and which do not end in the horizontal flux of time but in the vertical interruption of eternity.[109] Only the experience of these autonomous, self-contained instants with no finality beyond themselves allows us to have knowledge of the eternal. Each of these instants is an eternity of its own. Nietzsche's grasping of temporality thus precludes *duration*. It constitutes a categorical reversal of any idea of time as a continuous, uninterrupted flow. Consequently, it also precludes teleology. If every instant holds an eternal value, if no instant is "for the sake of another," this means that there is no finality, no teleological goal with which to make sense of the overall process of time and history.

Nietzsche's rendition of the instant evokes Kierkegaard's paradox of eternity as a moment in time. As with Kierkegaard, Nietzsche's instant is not identical with the traditional present. The present is a moment in time, but the instant occurs outside of time—in eternity. The instant is a disturbance of the continuous duration in which the present takes place. Eternity is reachable only through instantaneous temporality; that is, the suddenness that comes before and grounds the present. To duration's unbroken flow of being,

Nietzsche opposes the disruption of the instant. The instant is the radical foundation of the cosmos and the self at every moment. In it, being is constituted in the eternity of an abrupt, eternally self-repeating interruption.[110]

The concepts of the instant and eternal return form the basis of Nietzsche's response to nihilism. Nihilism is the attitude of devaluating the "here and now" of life in the name of some immaterial transcendence.[111] Eternal recurrence does not mean the eternal return of nothingness, as if it were itself a form of nihilism. Heidegger wrote that eternal return, understood in terms of instantaneity, implies an affirmation of "the temporality of independent action and decision."[112] Eternal return is the opposite of a desire to flee from the world and thus represents the overcoming of nihilism. Something essential—what Nietzsche calls a *creation*—takes place in the moment of decision. This moment is the recoining of *becoming* as *being* and brings together the two fundamental determinations at the origins of Western philosophy: the doctrines of Heraclitus and Parmenides. The conceptual synthesis of Nietzsche's metaphysical position—amor fati, or the "love of necessity"—is unveiled "in the awestruck moment of an eternity, an eternity pregnant with the Becoming of being as a whole."[113] Nietzsche's position, Heidegger estimates, represents the end of metaphysics because it reverts philosophy to its beginning and thus closes the cycle of Western thought.

Nietzsche expresses the ahistorical and suprahistorical outlooks through a particular understanding of the notion of the *historical event*. In "On the Utility and Liability of History for Life," Nietzsche presents the ahistorical condition as the womb to every significant deed.[114] He thus confronts us with the paradoxical nature of the historical event, which is that authentic historical action is possible only outside the consciousness of the historical. François Dosse surmises that Nietzsche believed that the individual who was in love with history was a conservative, a slave to the past, and that only the irruption of events, as the source of a will to affirmation, enabled the individual to be creative and to escape history. From this belief in the value of discontinuity, every historical event is born.[115] Nietzsche's belief in ahistoricity and suprahistoricity leads him to critique the linear, progressive understanding of historical time and to insist on the role of singularity in history. Additionally, because the suprahistorical standpoint entails the awareness that action is blind,[116] it represents another instance of the Hölderlinian experience of the contemporary as an ungraspable nearness. It also prefigures both Bloch's intuitions about "the darkness of the moment" and Benjamin's eventist philosophy of history.

One would be tempted to cite the French Revolution as the quintessential example of an ahistorical or suprahistorical action. The revolutionaries were, in a sense, entirely "cured" of their "historical sickness." They acted (or believed themselves to have acted) with the steady conviction that the past had to be violently rejected. Nietzsche himself, however, was much warier of the deep historical significance of sociopolitical transformations.[117] In *Thus Spoke Zarathustra*, his protagonist has lost faith in "great events." He disdains revolutionary changes, "overthrowers of statues" and "inventors of new noise."[118] What Nietzsche deemed to be an epoch-changing event of world-historical consequence was, rather, the moment in which the idea of the eternal return was *thought*—both in the history of humankind and in the life of the individual. In *Twilight of the Idols*, he wrote: "Mid-day; moment of the shortest shadow; end of the longest error; zenith of mankind; INCIPIT ZARATHUSTRA."[119] To Nietzsche, the overcoming of nihilism and the coming of the overman represent this "high point of humanity"—a high point that Heidegger later characterizes as a true *Ereignis*, or "propriative event."[120] Nietzsche devotes the same passion to the individual reception of the eternal return. In *Ecce Homo*, for example, he describes the moment of his own recognition of the doctrine of recurrence as an instant of revelation, of the perfect "being-outside-yourself" when "you take, [and] you don't ask who is giving."[121]

Nietzsche no longer expects, as Hölderlin did, the return of the gods. He proclaims instead that "all gods are dead" and announces the overman, whose arrival will be a sort of "noon" in the history of mankind. Despite their differences, Hölderlin and Nietzsche share a common attitude. They both think of the occurrences in the life of the mind—either poetical or philosophical—as events in themselves. The antecedents and models for this attitude are probably Kant, who described his critical project as a "Copernican revolution," and, especially, Hegel, who alludes to his own system as a high moment in the self-consciousness of the universal Spirit. It is perhaps not a coincidence that both Hegel and Kant wrote their works during the immediate aftermath of the French Revolution. It is as if after the end of the eighteenth century, the history of thought had come to be seen as part of history in its own right, and the formulation of theoretical categories for thinking the event came into being as events in and of themselves.

Considered from the perspective of the history of temporality, Nietzsche's instant can be read as a response to the Goethean interpretation of instantaneous time. In *The Gay Science*'s fragment "The greatest weight," a demon plays the role of Mephistopheles as the provocateur who offers the "bet" of the eternal return. The demon asks: "Do you desire this once more and innumerable times more?" His question is Nietzsche's version of Faust's wager. But whereas Faust condemns himself to always say, "No, do not linger," to every moment, Nietzsche persuades us to say yes to anything that the instant may bring. In *Thus Spoke Zarathustra*, the reference to Faust is more explicit, so that the final pages of the book can be read as an ecstatic reversal and rejoinder to Goethe: "Have you ever said Yes to one joy? Oh, my friends, then you also said Yes to *all* pain . . . —if you ever wanted one time two times, if you ever said 'I like you, happiness! Whoosh! Moment!' then you wanted *everything* back!— . . . For all joy wants—eternity!"[122] Zarathustra is convinced that every instant is worthy of affirmation, as is the totality of phenomena that the instant entails. If the instant for Goethe is a glimpse of the absolute, the instant for Nietzsche is the overjoyed assertion of everything that is. Goethe's instant is a wager on the failure to embody the ideal, a celebration of a fleeting now of aesthetic integration and of the moments of exception in the midst of a chaotic world. The instant for Nietzsche is the embrace of everything that is just as it is, in all its confusion and contradiction. From the exaltation of the finitude of the present moment to the celebration of the instant as the all-encompassing affirmation of being, Goethe and Nietzsche established the foundations for a lineage of reflection on instantaneity in modernity.

CHAPTER 2

The Instant of the Avant-Garde

As we have seen so far, aesthetic ideas since German Romanticism have served as a laboratory for modern time consciousness.[1] In the first decades of the twentieth century, the historical avant-gardes continued this tradition with a significant reelaboration of the temporal category of the instantaneous present. The accomplishment of this critical work—in artistic productions or in ideological statements—had momentous effects in the realm of modern aesthetics, and beyond. Futurism, Dadaism, and, especially, surrealism together form an essential chapter in the modern history of the notion of the instant. The historical self-understanding of the avant-garde manifested itself in a particular aesthetic sensibility and in a set of creative techniques that, based on the notions of *the new* and *the unknown*, resulted in a series of influential articulations of the figure of suddenness. Karl Heinz Bohrer has noted that the "consciousness of the modern age . . . came into its own in the avant-garde."[2] In this coming of age, the role of instantaneity was substantial.

Alongside the lineage that grew between Goethe and Nietzsche, the avant-garde represents the culmination of the other great genealogy in the modern history of instantaneity and its rhetorical deployments. Charles Baudelaire's poetic musings on the life of city crowds and his ideas about the nature of aesthetic modernity mark the beginning of this genealogy. The avant-garde contributed two new crucial elements to instantaneity: first, the perception of discontinuity and the experience of the ephemeral in the conditions of urban modernity; and, second, an aesthetics of the sudden juxtaposition of dislocated fragments. The avant-garde's ideas about time represent, in many ways, a continuation or reelaboration of Baudelaire's original undertakings. In particular, they engage with his postulation of the *transient* as a legitimate category of authentic temporality and his concomitant praise of the "fleeting moment" as a substantive temporal reality in its own right. The avant-garde thematization of suddenness had fundamental consequences for the aesthetic formation of an *ahistorical* form of the consciousness of time. When they elaborated the instantaneity chronotope, Ernst Jünger, Ernst Bloch, and Walter Benjamin took up certain elements of this time consciousness, especially the vanishing distinction between *ordinary* and *extraordinary* (or *everyday* and *limit*) experience. The avant-garde represents something more than a period in the history of literature or the arts; it represents a mode of historical consciousness that recognizes the instantaneous present as the site of an encounter with the unknown.[3] It offers a temporality of imminence in which the *anticipation* of experience is itself the event.[4]

The Idea of the Avant-Garde:
A Messenger from the Unknown

As an aesthetic stance, the main feature of the avant-garde was a feverish cult of the new. Essential to the avant-gardist ethos of newness was its belief in the obsolescence of all of previous artistic practice and convention, as well as its ensuing demand for the annihilation of tradition.[5] An impulse toward the violent renewal characterized this spirit, with calls for a tabula rasa or "blank space" of aesthetic creation from which art could be utterly regenerated. Dadaism's nihilistic compulsion to demolish all established artistic practices and negate the idea of art itself was one archetypal expression of this antagonism to tradition. As Tristan Tzara wrote in his "Dada Manifesto 1918," the Dadaist avant-garde held one belief: "There is great destructive, negative work to be done. To sweep, to clean."[6]

Another representative example of this hostility to artistic convention was Italian futurism's "antitraditionalist principle,"[7] which found its most daring articulation in "The Founding and Manifesto of Futurism," published by Filippo Tommaso Marinetti, the movement's leader and founder, in 1909. Marinetti relishes futurism's intention of tearing down libraries and museums, its celebration of all anarchical gestures of destruction, and the vital activism of movement, modern technology and speed. The manifesto calls for finishing with the "useless contemplation of the past" in order to engage in breaching "the mysterious doors of the Impossible." For Marinetti, "to admire an old painting is the same as pouring our sensibility into a funerary urn, instead of casting it forward into the distance in violent spurts of creation and action."[8]

Futurist self-understanding arguably belongs within the historical consciousness that the revolutionary tradition created. Reactivated in different
ways by the outbreak of the Great War in 1914 and the onset of the Russian
Revolution in 1917, the spirit of 1789 seems to be at work in the temporality
that futurism's self-assertion implies, particularly its claim to constitute a new
historical beginning. In its attempt to establish a mythic present or moment of
absolute self-creation, the futurist attitude can be construed as a reenactment,
in the field of aesthetics, of the historical consciousness characteristic of the
French Revolution. In a similar spirit, Alain Badiou considers the avant-garde
notion of tabula rasa as "parallel to the revolutionary political idea in its most
tightly drawn form."[9] Badiou defined the event as that "something that brings
to light a possibility that was invisible or even unthinkable," and it is possible
to interpret the avant-garde notion of an aesthetic absolute in these terms. At
the same time, futurism and Dadaism's celebration of deliberate destruction
and renewal echoes some of the main motifs—such as activism and resoluteness—of the decisionist style of thinking that characterized certain currents
in European philosophy and politics after the First World War. It is revealing
that Tzara published the "Dada Manifesto"—a text in which the experience of
destruction and the will to regeneration are the protagonists—in 1918.

Another aspect of the avant-garde's fascination with novelty was its sense
of itself as leading an aesthetic exploration of the unknown. The metaphor's
military origin comes to light again here. To belong to the "avant-garde" of an
army (or of a culture or a society) is to be ahead of the rest, the first traveler
to unmapped regions of reality. In a similar vein, the 1911 "Manifesto of the
Futurist Painters" declares that art must draw inspiration from the "spasmodic
struggle to conquer the unknown."[10] The futurists inserted an especially disruptive element in this association between the unknown and the new: the
principle of violence, both real and symbolic, and therefore an exaltation of
risk, danger, and war. Marinetti had already expressed his views on combat
as a form of renovation in his 1909 manifesto: "We intend to glorify war—
the only hygiene of the world—militarism, patriotism."[11] It is impossible to
dissociate this glorification of violence from Italian futurism's embrace of an
ultranationalism and militarist right-wing political stance, which led some of
its members to an involvement with fascism. Within a few years after the end
of the war, a similar fusion of modernism and conservatism was going to be
featured in Ernst Jünger's early writings.

The convergence of the belief in the significance of "action for action's
sake" and the absolute value of the new constitutes what Renato Poggioli has

identified as the "futurist moment": an attitude of vital activism and ecstatic projection onto the future that characterizes not only futurism itself but all the other avant-gardes. According to Poggioli, this moment refers to that "prophetic and utopian phase, the arena of agitation and preparation for the announced revolution." None other than Leon Trotsky appraised Russian futurism in the same terms. In Trotsky's words, "futurism was the pre-vision of all that (the imminent social and political crises, the explosions and catastrophes of history to come) within the sphere of art."[12] The avant-garde spirit thus became synonymous with an exalted estimation of its own historical significance as the anticipatory enactment of a profound historical transformation.

The futurist moment entailed a belief in art and literature as acts of decisive anticipation. Insofar as avant-garde artists were persuaded that their activity constituted an event—an unexpected rupture in the regular flow of time that creates a new possibility[13]—they were reenacting Hölderlin's faith in the poetic act as a form of advent in its own right. The anticipation of the event in the poem or artwork *was* the event. The same premonitory spirit animates Arthur Rimbaud's series of letters known as the "Letters of the Seer," in which he presents the poet's vocation as an endless striving for the new and the unknown—a mission "to explore the invisible and to hear the unheard." For Rimbaud, the poetry of the future will reclaim as its own the status of event; it will "no longer beat *within* action; it *will be before* it."[14]

The avant-gardes' powerful rhetoric around "the future" contrasts significantly with a properly "futurist" or future-oriented temporality. Rather than a historicist celebration of the future as the primordial category of time, from which all historical meaning would be derived, the futurist moment constitutes an affirmation of the present as the privileged moment of irruption, rupture, or action. Despite its linkage to a sense of anticipation, the avant-garde's "future" represents in the end not a subservience of the present to an abstract moment to come, but a celebration of the consciousness of the present *as such*. François Hartog has argued that Marinetti's futurist manifesto had itself already demonstrated that "futurism was also (already) a presentism." Hartog continues: "When Marinetti declared: 'Time and Space died yesterday. We are *already* living in a world of the absolute, since we have *already* created eternal, omnipresent speed,' the present became 'futurized,' or, equally, there was already nothing but the present. Speed transformed the present into eternity and Marinetti, at the wheel of his racing car, could imagine himself to be God."[15] The words of Marinetti show that the present, not the future, is the central category of avant-garde time consciousness. But, in rebuttal to

Hartog, I argue that the regime of historicity to which this centrality of the present belongs is not exactly presentism (a regime characterized by a passive sense of the present and a feeling of historical stagnation), but rather, instantaneism. It is more accurate to say then that in the time consciousness of the avant-garde the present does not become "futurized," but rather that the future becomes "presentized" in the form of an ecstatic affirmation of the instantaneous quality of the present.

The Origins of the Avant-Garde Present: Baudelaire and the Instant of Modernity

The temporality of the futurist moment exposes the complex interactions between the notion of an avant-garde and the idea of progress. On the one hand, the present instant matters only as anticipation or as an announcement of what is to come. Devoted entirely to the future, the instant lacks any particular substance. Because it appears to involve the temporal certainty of living "ahead of one's own time" and of being "closer to the future" than the rest, the notion of an avant-garde depends inescapably on a progressive view of history. On the other hand, however, the present instant bears a specific historical meaning as it embodies the now of rupture and of the irruption of the new—a gesture that assumes its own significance, regardless of what is to come. In continuation with Romanticism, the instant supposes that art is an endless quest, the pursuit of a goal that will never be entirely accomplished. The result of this incomplete quest is that, as the Romantic aesthetics of the fragmentary attests, each historical moment can attain its own autonomous historical significance.[16] The fundamental aspect of the logic of instantaneity is not the aftermath of rupture but rupture itself. Jürgen Habermas has argued, in this sense, that these two distinct dimensions of instantaneity—"anticipation of an undefined future and the cult of the new"—constitute two faces of a single attitude toward temporality—"the exaltation of the present." In consequence, art's self-understanding as "invading unknown territory, exposing itself to the danger of sudden, of shocking encounters, conquering an as yet unoccupied future" results not so much in a devaluation of the present moment as in the attribution of a new importance to the values of "the transitory, the elusive, and the ephemeral."[17]

The foundations of the avant-garde's approach to temporality are to be found in the work of Baudelaire, whose art criticism represented the first far-reaching enunciation of the nature of beauty in modern times. In his essay

"Salon of 1846," published that same year, the French poet refers to the existence of a specific "modern beauty" that is always composed of two different elements: one "eternal" or absolute; and other "transitory" or particular.[18] Baudelaire's analysis introduced a radical break with conventional understandings of aesthetics. Against all neoclassical definitions, Baudelaire asserts that the beautiful is neither absolute nor unique, but historical. A work of art can be said to be more or less in tune with its own times, that is, more or less modern, and such modernity represents a critical index of the work's degree of aesthetic accomplishment. Baudelaire would continue his reflections on "modern beauty" in his poetry. *The Flowers of Evil*—his volume of poems from 1857—concludes by establishing a compelling association between newness and the unknown:

Only when we drink poison are we well—
we want, this fire so burns our brain tissue,
to drown in the abyss—heaven or hell,
who cares? Through the unknown, we'll find the new.[19]

In these verses, beauty, mortality, and the spirit of modernity's poetic quest are all recognized as belonging to a single system of symbolic and existential correspondence. Theodor W. Adorno would later identify Baudelaire's poetry as the original embodiment of aesthetic modernism precisely because of the French poet's visionary connection between the new and the indeterminate, the cryptic, and the unknown.[20]

Baudelaire further deepened his ideas on the historicity of beauty in his celebrated essay "The Painter of Modern Life" from 1863. "The pleasure which we derive from the representation of the present," Baudelaire writes, "is due not only to the beauty with which it can be invested, but also to its essential quality of being present." In his outline of beauty as a double reality—one absolute, one circumstantial—Baudelaire underscores the latter. The circumstantial is "the ephemeral, the fugitive, the contingent," and it comprises "the age, its fashions, its morals, its emotions."[21] The modernity of a work of art resides in this element of circumstance and particularity. It is, moreover, the work's only possible way of historical existence. For Baudelaire, there is no such thing as an abstract, timeless beauty. The beautiful can be reached only through the historical mediation of the ephemeral.

Baudelaire's modern artist is "the painter of the passing moment and of all the suggestions of eternity that it contains." Such an artist "makes it his business to extract from fashion whatever element it may contain of poetry within history, to distil the eternal from the transitory."[22] The ephemeral, for Baudelaire, is accordingly the site of an intriguing dialectical mediation. If the present is to be seized from the perspective of continuous renewal, Habermas writes, then "the authentic work is radically bound to the moment of its emergence; precisely because it consumes itself in actuality, it can bring the steady flow of trivialities to a standstill, break through normality, and satisfy for a moment the immortal longing for beauty."[23] The fleeting is the opposite of the eternal, but at the same time it is the only guise under which eternity can be grasped. Following this dialectic, the present moment—that creative tension between the ephemeral and the eternal—becomes its own focus of orientation and its own unit of understanding; it dissociates itself from any progressive interpretation of history. This is why, contrary to the notions of tradition and progress, Baudelaire believes that "the artist only stems from himself."[24]

What results from Baudelaire's analysis of modernity is a new paradigm for the instant's aesthetic structure and moral signification. This paradigm simultaneously echoes, and differs from, the model of instantaneous temporality as presence represented by Kierkegaard and Nietzsche. In one aspect, Baudelaire's analysis reiterates Kierkegaard's and Nietzsche's insight about the instant as an interaction between time and eternity—the finite as the only doorway of access to the infinite. But these two thinkers dismiss the hollowness of the merely transient moment in favor of the existential authenticity of the instant of decision (Kierkegaard) or of saying yes to everything that exists (Nietzsche). In contrast, Baudelaire seems rather to proclaim the primacy of the fleeting over the eternal and to celebrate the fleeting *qua* fleeting, and to assert, ultimately, that eternal signification resides in the ephemeral itself.

Romanticism introduced the artistic obligation of "belonging to one's own time" and elevated this initially aesthetic demand to the status of a moral commitment, but Baudelaire's theory of modernity took this Romantic exaltation of the present to a new level of articulation, based on his view of the role of instantaneity in the consciousness of temporality. In Baudelaire, the present moment exhibits a sort of ontological autonomy, a temporal autarchy in respect to all other moments from the future or the past and, consequently, an absolute detachment from all forms of historical teleology. Matei Calinescu has suggested that the meaning of Baudelaire's vision was actually an identification of modernity with the present "in its purely instantaneous quality." In my view, Baudelaire exposed an unexpected affinity between modernity and instantaneity in their opposition to historical time.

In Calinescu's words, "modernity, then, can be defined as the paradoxical possibility of going beyond the flow of history through the consciousness of historicity in its most concrete immediacy." In a prefiguration of Nietzsche's ahistorical and suprahistorical outlooks, Baudelaire celebrated the instant as an *ahistorical* moment—ahistoricity being the very condition under which creative imagination is possible. "The proper functioning of imagination," Calinescu writes, "seems to imply for Baudelaire a forgetful immersion in the 'now,' the real source of 'all our originality.'"[25] The present instant, in particular the instant of artistic creation, is a moment of Nietzschean ahistoricity, a space where a fusion of the now of timeless contemplation and the timely now of history takes place. Baudelaire's poetics of temporality thus establishes the existence of an aporia inherent to the concept of modernity. Modernity as a notion is meaningful only within the framework of historical time—linear and irreversible—but, at the same time, modernity is also identical with instantaneous ahistoricity, so that the modern presents itself as simultaneously historical and ahistorical.[26] This aporetic understanding of temporality would become the foundation of avant-garde time consciousness and, during the years of the Weimar Republic in Germany, it became one of the basic elements of the instantaneity chronotope.

The Aesthetics of Juxtaposition

Instantaneity plays a central role in the avant-garde not only in its attitude of radical renewal and affirmation of the present but also in the formal features of the avant-garde style. The imprint of the instantaneous is apparent in what Roger Shattuck has called the "aesthetics of juxtaposition"—the method of artistic creation based on the "setting of one thing beside the other without connective."[27] In the first decades of the twentieth century, avant-garde production opposed this aesthetics of juxtaposition to the classical "art of transition,"[28] namely, the inclination to place, in works of art and literature, one formal element harmoniously after the other. Antagonistic to the predictability of classical art, the avant-garde embraced an aesthetics of suddenness, discontinuity, and shock expressed through the abruptness of unexpected formal connections. In the visual arts, for example, the formal chaos of cubist collages and Dadaist photomontages replaced the visual stability of previous painting and sculpture, and eventually turned into an emblem of avant-garde aesthetic sensibility.

Juxtaposition's foremost technical device was *montage*:[29] a "construction" or assemblage of isolated fragments in which the unforeseeable effects of aesthetic mishmash are actively encouraged and incorporated into the work. In contrast to the organic relationship between part and whole that prevailed in traditional works of art, the elements of an avant-garde montage do not support the work's general sense of structure; as fragments, they are explicitly contingent and stand as if emancipated from the whole.[30] The perceptual space in which the act of aesthetic reception takes place is no longer the unitary, absorbed, self-forgetting context of the classical piece of art. Rather, montage turns it into a theatrical, disjointed now of contrasting times and places, integrated only by a disruptive synchronization. In his discussion of this technique's significance for aesthetic modernism, Adorno affirms that, insofar as avant-garde "constructions" subordinate fragments of incoherent materials to an "imposed unity," they actually lack composition understood in any organic, traditional way. Montage's shocking appearance and its incorporation of "art-alien objects" thus destroyed the notion of the artwork as a "nexus of meaning."[31]

As with other key elements of the avant-garde outlook, the sensibility for sudden juxtaposition finds one of its main precedents in the work of Baudelaire. The French poet first sketched an aesthetics of discontinuity, irregularity, and imperfection in 1851 in a fragment from his intimate journal: "The unexpected, surprise, and astonishment are an essential part and the characteristic of beauty."[32] A decade later, the notion of suddenness would present itself as the structuring element of "To a Passerby" ("À une passante"), one of *The Flowers of Evil*'s most compelling poems. An enigmatic woman in mourning is fleetingly sighted by a passerby in the midst of the urban crowd:

A lightning flash . . . then night! Fleeting beauty
By whose glance I was suddenly reborn,
Will I see you no more before eternity?[33]

This unexpected vision leaves the speaker of the poem in a state of perplexity and awe. Such bewilderment is the *shock*—a notion that Walter Benjamin would elaborate on in the late 1930s as representative of the everyday aesthetic experience of the modern metropolis. Baudelaire would further develop this aesthetics of "fleeting beauty" in an urban setting in his 1869 volume of prose poems, *Le Spleen de Paris*. In that book's foreword, Baudelaire states his ambition to achieve a description of modern life by means of a poetic prose adapted to the "*soubresauts de la conscience*" ("the twists and turns that consciousness takes"), an abrupt style of writing whose inspiration would be born out of "*la fréquentation des villes énormes*" ("[the] frequenting [of] vast cities") and of "*du croisement de leurs innombrables rapports*" ("the intersections of their infinite connections"). One typical example of Baudelaire's experiments is "Perte d'auréole," the story of a poet's sudden "loss of his halo" due to the "abrupt movement" of the crowd.[34]

Benjamin identifies Baudelaire as the first author to recognize exposure to shock as the fundamental experience of modernity and to connect this exposure to contact with city crowds. Frenetic urban traffic, modern advertisements, and the proliferation of situations in which "a single abrupt movement of the hand triggers a process of many steps," such as the "snapping" of the photographic camera, the lifting of the telephone's receiver or the lighting of a match—all of these experiences support his case that sudden shock is the archetypical "sensation of modernity."[35] Benjamin, however, would probably not have attributed a "shock" quality to Baudelaire's poetry if he had not already been influenced by surrealism's ideas on "convulsive beauty," as interest in the avant-gardes of his own time considerably determined his reading of Baudelaire.[36] Benjamin's interpretation was a retroactive attempt to make sense of his own cultural world, the search for an allegorical image that contained clues for illuminating the present.

As suggested by Benjamin's reading of Baudelaire, suddenness and shock as aesthetic categories were historically inscribed in capitalist urban modernity. By the time of the avant-garde's appearance in the artistic landscape, the developments that had historically conditioned the emergence of these perceptual categories had accelerated. The demands that urbanization, industrialization, and new means of transportation and communication pressed on individual sensory capacities had reached an unprecedented level of intensity. In the modern metropolis of the early twentieth century, Georg Simmel observed in 1903, the proliferation of sudden shifts of intense stimuli—"the rapid telescoping of changing images, pronounced differences within what is grasped at a single glance"—was beginning to dislocate the mental life of the city dweller. Violence perpetrated on the human sensorium was something that could happen "at every crossing of the street."[37] The First World War, with its processes of mass mobilization and the experience of shell shock, together with the economic crisis and political instability of the interwar period, further increased the disruption of everyday life through the exposure to violent, unexpected stimuli.

Understandably, the avant-garde's techniques of juxtaposition and montage became the aesthetics of the era. The experience of shock and its depiction in art and literature provided an "interface"[38] for the mediation between sensory overload and individual perception, a principle of organization that could echo "the pace, the multiplicity, the disorientation, the thrill, and of course the fragmentation of modern everyday life."[39] In Weimar Germany, for example, the production of photomontages by artists such as John Heartfield and Hannah Höch was emblematic of attempts to explore fractures in subjectivity. These experiments relied, precisely, on the absorption and manipulation of materials from mass media, one of the very sources of these fractures. The German Dadaist poet Richard Huelsenbeck provided a theoretical formulation of this stance in his "Dada Manifesto" from 1918: "The highest art will be that which in its conscious content presents the thousandfold problems of the day, the art which has been visibly shattered by the explosions of last week, which is forever trying to collect its limbs after yesterday's crash."[40]

Bloch and Adorno understood montage as a historically significant principle of artistic organization. For Bloch, the disjuncture and fragmentation of the technique were vehicles for the development of an "anticipatory consciousness" for a better future. Bloch believed that there was something about the contrast of dissimilar images, sensations, and emotions characteristic of avant-garde "constructions" that stirred the imagination of utopia by evoking the "noncontemporaneity" of a historical "not-yet."[41] For Adorno, the emergence of assemblage techniques represented nothing less than a change in the status of the relationships between art and reality—a change compelled by the new forms of social experience. Montage's integration of the unforeseen as an element of the artwork, Adorno thought, was more than a mere formal effect. It was also an "objective dimension" through which the loss of power suffered by the alienated subject in modern technological society was turned into an aesthetic program, an attempt to tame what the individual could not control. In montage, art, by acknowledging its own powerlessness to reconcile heterogeneous material, protested against existing society.[42]

Along these lines, the avant-garde's experiments in montage and juxtaposition coined a formal language and radical style that re-created, in the very artwork or text, the continuous feeling of shock representative of modern life. Symptomatic of this cultural trend was Guillaume Apollinaire's essay "The New Spirit and the Poets," from 1918, which merges Baudelaire's poetics of the ephemeral, Rimbaud's insight of the artist as seer, and the futurist praise of modern technology into one single theoretical framework. In the essay, Apollinaire presents the poets of his era as the embodiment of what he labels the "new spirit": a novelty specific to modern times that manifests itself in the phenomenon of *surprise*. "Everything," writes Apollinaire "is in the effect of surprise. . . . *Surprise is the greatest source of what is new*. It is by surprise . . . that the new spirit distinguishes itself from all the literary and artistic movements which have preceded it."[43] The historical emergence of surprise as an aesthetic effect was the result of a rich symbolic interaction between the visionary powers of poetry and the astonishing feats of the most advanced technology. He saw modern technology as a creative force that had brought about what earlier poets had imagined: "Insofar as airplanes did not fill the sky, the fable of Icarus was only a supposed truth." The modern poets are called to imagine new fables that the inventors can, in turn, materialize. They are expected to be the creators of new surprises and the bearers of new prophecies, and the sudden happenings that take place in the everyday provide these surprises: "a dropped handkerchief can be for the poet the lever with which to move an entire universe."[44]

Simultaneist Poetry

The new spirit of surprise found one of its representative manifestations in the formal practice of poetic *simultaneism*. A literary technique and stylistic device common to many writers of the avant-garde, such as Marinetti, Blaise Cendrars, and Apollinaire himself, simultaneism is the artistic method of collapsing different times and places in the now of the poem. As the futurist Umberto Boccioni wrote in 1912, this practice aims to portray "the simultaneousness of states of mind in the work of art," that is, "the synthesis of *what one remembers* and of *what one sees*."[45] Roger Shattuck provides a telling description of this praxis: "The aspiration of simultaneism is to grasp the moment in its total significance or, more ambitiously, to manufacture a moment which surpasses our usual perception of time and space."[46] Simultaneism's ambition is indeed the construction of an artificial moment that replicates the sensorial context and temporal structure of a particular instantaneous situation— and, accordingly, of the revelatory potential of the ephemeral—by means of words and images. Simultaneity and the aesthetics of juxtaposition would come to play a fundamental role in the thought of Bloch and Benjamin, particularly in Bloch's notion of the noncontemporaneity of disparate historical temporalities and Benjamin's *dialectical image* that juxtaposes different historical nows in a flashlight vision.

Cendrars' poem "Contrastes," written in 1913 and published in *Nineteen Elastic Poems* in 1919, illustrates the simultaneist tendency in poetic form. Following the procedure of juxtaposition, the poem recreates the parallel occurrence of conflicting sights and sounds in Paris city life:

> The windows of my poetry are wide open onto the boulevards and in
>   its shop windows
> Shine
> The jewels of light
> Listen to the violins of the limousines and the xylophones of the
>   linotypes
> The stenciler washes up in the washcloth of the sky
> Everything is splashes of color
> And the women's hats going by are comets in the burning evening
> . . . .
> At the Chamber
> They're wasting the marvelous elements of raw materials
>
> At the bar
> The workers in blue overalls drink red wine
> . . . .
> It's raining light bulbs
> Montrouge Gare de l'Est Métro Nord-Sud Seine omnibus people
> One big halo
> Depth
> Rue de Buci they yell *L'Intransigeant* and *Paris-Sports*
> The aerodrome of the sky is now, all fiery, a picture by Cimabue
> And in front
> The men are
> Tall
> Dark
> Sad
> And smoking, factory stacks[47]

As exemplified in Cendrars' poem, simultaneism and the aesthetics of juxtaposition in general represented a sort of subtle realism, a more sophisticated kind of mimesis. By rejecting harmonious transition and embracing conflict and shock—the perceptual categories for making sense of modernity's social and cultural reality—they put forward an idea of art as the imitation of modern life in the context of boisterous metropolises. The now of simultaneist poetry comprehends then not only the time and place of the act of reading, as in the Romantic lyric, but the complex coordination of a number of dislocated time and places. By displaying the coexistence of past, present, and future in individual perception, as well as in the collective psyche of city life, simultaneist works of literature displayed the intricate interplay between private and public time. Simultaneism comprehended not only poems, but also larger narrative works. One example is *Berlin Alexanderplatz*,[48] wherein Alfred Döblin has recourse to different methods of narrative simultaneity, such as montage, for reproducing "the multiplicity of the city as instantly and totally present."[49]

The phenomenon of avant-garde juxtaposition makes sense only within the particular evolution of the aesthetics of instantaneity. To Heinrich von Kleist's motif of suddenness, the avant-garde adds the Baudelairean receptiveness to the "shocks" of urban life. The art of juxtaposition not only engages with the leaps of consciousness characteristic of the Romantic self, but also with the unexpected happenings in the streets of modern-day metropolises, for the kind of extreme encounters that the comte de Lautréamont famously alludes to in *Les Chants de Maldoror*—"Beautiful as the accidental encounter, on a dissecting table, of a sewing machine and an umbrella"[50]—could only take place within the mass-culture, commodity-intensive context of an industrial urban society. In terms of form, juxtaposition echoes the aesthetic effects that the rhythm of modern capitalist economy and technology impose on the subjectivity of an individual. It is also the realization of Rimbaud's call for the creation of "new forms" that contain an unfamiliar newness. In this sense, juxtaposition embodies both a principle of formal composition and a cultural trait of modernity.

Another way to view juxtaposition is as the deployment of a sort of Kierkegaardian aesthetics of the leap in that it extrapolates his philosophy to the realm of artistic creation. Avant-garde's aesthetics share Kierkegaard's emphasis on discontinuity as a major pattern of thought and as the foundation of an ahistorical time consciousness. As discussed in Chapter 1, in Kierkegaard's works, the irruption of the eternal into time's regular flow brings about the effect of discontinuity. But in the avant-garde works, it is the juxtaposition of fragments originating from contemporary mass culture and previous eras in art history that produces this effect. In the end, however, the temporal structure of both relationships is the same. The two share the notion that time's most authentic experience—either from a theological or aesthetic point of view—is not related to linearity, continuity, accumulation, or progress, but to sudden interruptions that underline a certain form of juxtaposition of disparate realities or fragments. If, in Kierkegaardian thought, this juxtaposition concerns the encounter of time and eternity, in avant-garde collage, it pertains to the simultaneity of dislocated time and spaces.

As a cultural phenomenon, the simultaneist tendency inscribed itself within broader changes in cultural perceptions of temporality. These broader changes represented, as Charles Taylor argues, a displacement of the "center of gravity" of modern culture from the unitary "I" of Romanticism to the fragmented ego of modernism, or, in aesthetic terms, from a subject based in expressivity to a self grounded in language and experience, particularly the subjective experience of time.[51] Henri Bergson's philosophy epitomized this change by calling for a radical turn in the interests of philosophical inquiry from the concern with abstract, scientific time to a renewed attention to concrete temporality as it was actually experienced by human subjectivity. To this concrete time, which took the form of a continuous temporal flow, Bergson gave the name *duration* (*durée*).[52] Simultaneist literary experiments proved to be a natural dwelling place for this new prominence of lived temporality. However, although the avant-garde time consciousness did belong, in general terms, to this philosophical tendency, it also embodied a different variety of this turn, which represented a fracture within its conceptual universe. Duration assumes the experience of lived time as flow, but the avant-garde involves itself with an exploration of temporality as sudden rupture. In the avant-garde, the aesthetics of juxtaposition and the new perception of temporality concurred in an extension of the present as a perceptual field and in an expansion of instantaneity's significance as a cultural category. In aesthetic productions, such as the works of simultaneist poetry and literature, this new sense of the instantaneous present found a crucial and lasting formulation.

Surrealism and Suddenness

Of all the historical avant-garde movements, surrealism arguably made the most intensive use of the aesthetic of suddenness in all its creative derivations. Adorno wrote that montage had "reached its acme in surrealism" and that surrealism itself had to be understood in terms of the montage technique and its formal principle of the "discontinuous juxtaposition of images."[53] Surrealism was born as a theory and practice of the art of sudden literary associations. In his *Manifesto of Surrealism* (1924), André Breton endorsed cubist poet Pierre Reverdy's doctrine of the poetic image as the result of the coming together of two realities far removed from each other. "The more distant the two realities, the stronger the image" became the surrealist standard for the assessment of literary accomplishment. In the *Manifesto*, Breton announced another central characteristic of the surrealist aesthetic: openness to the irruption of unexpected verbal utterances. The paradigmatic model for this kind of phenomena occurred to Breton one night, when he overheard the "distinctly articulated" phrase: "*Il y a un homme coupé en deux par la fenêtre*" ("There is a man cut in two by the window").[54]

Verbal disruption was the logic behind surrealism's most distinctive literary practice: automatic writing. The supreme aspiration of automatism was, according to Breton, to achieve speech delivered as quickly as possible without the intervention of critical judgment, so that it became a sort of spoken thought (*pensée parlée*).[55] Breton believed, in Kleistean fashion, that the accelerated rhythm of language created the space for verbal surprise. Automatic writing represented a further step in the Kleistean mode of speech production, because it forced the technique to its extreme. Verbal abruptness was no longer about "the gradual production of thoughts while speaking." It was about the sudden manifestation of ideas while doing nothing else, in order to generate as many startling images as possible. What Breton theorized in the *Manifesto* in 1924, he and Philippe Soupault had already put into practice in *The Magnetic Fields* (1920), the first work of automatic writing.[56] One of the two poets would write a sentence as quickly as possible, and the other composed a response "without thinking, at that very instant."[57] This poetic endeavor resulted in the generation of disconcerting images in the style of the shocking encounters of Lautréamont's *Les Chants de Maldoror*: "*Les accidents de travail, nul ne me contredira, sont plus beaux que les mariages de raison*" ("Work accidents, no one will ever contradict me, are more beautiful than the marriages of reason").[58] Breton and Soupault followed instantaneous temporality as a deliberate method for retrieving the materials of the unconscious mind. The aim of automatism was to devise, then, an unlimited chain of literary instants or "events" of literature, in order to generate an art form that recreated the leaps and movements characteristic of dream and wit.

The history of surrealism's relationship to the aesthetics of juxtaposition was not limited to the dimension of verbal creativity. It extended itself to everyday life through the attention paid to phenomena such as chance encounters and sudden revelations. In the late 1920s and throughout the 1930s, Breton would turn his attention from the inner movements of the mind to the correspondences of subjective imagination with objective reality. Two paradigmatic examples of this shift were the practice of city strolls, as depicted in his *Nadja* and further articulated in *Communicating Vessels*, and the cult of the *objet-trouvé*, as exemplified in his *Mad Love*.[59]

The first and most expressive example of this shift is *Nadja*, Breton's narrative work from 1928. The subject of *Nadja* is, in Breton's words, to narrate: "The most decisive episodes of my life *as I can conceive it apart from its organic plan*, and only insofar as it is at the mercy of chance—the merest as well as the greatest—temporarily escaping my control, admitting me to an almost forbidden world of sudden parallels, petrifying coincidences, and reflexes peculiar to each individual, of harmonies struck as though on the piano, flashes of light that would make you see, really *see*, if only they were not so much quicker than all the rest."[60] In *Nadja*, Breton fashions himself as a sort of twentieth-century flaneur in search of the "marvelous" element in the everyday experience of a modern metropolis. This element repeatedly arrives in the form of instantaneous phenomena. Sometimes this takes place as *coincidence* (the juxtaposition of subjective perception and objective reality), sometimes as *divination* (the moment in which subjective perception anticipates the manifestation of objective reality), as when the character of Nadja accurately foresees that a window's curtains will turn from black to red just before it happens. Coincidence and divination appear to Breton as two instances of the subjective dimensions of instantaneity. Breton calls these occurrences the "decisive episodes" that stand apart from life's "organic plan" because, in the narrative of *Nadja*, the awareness of the instantaneous is opposed to the belief in a coherent narrative of validation for the events in the life of an individual. The logic that imposes itself is, rather, the arbitrary antilogic of chance. Breton's *Nadja* represents, as it were, both the negation and fulfillment of Baudelaire's "To a Passerby." In Breton's text, the *passante* is not only seen but also *met* by the flaneur. Baudelaire's "blinding flash" at the sudden sighting of the woman in mourning transforms itself into Breton's *encounter* with Nadja.

The exposition of an aesthetics of surprise occupies the closing pages of *Nadja*. For Breton, the main feature of the aesthetics of surprise (or shock) is the identification of beauty not as a qualitative condition, as in conventional aesthetics, but as an *impulsive movement*.⁶¹ Suddenness is articulated as an aesthetic modality based on the explosive value of discontinuity. Surrealist beauty consists, Breton writes, of "jolts and shocks, many of which do not have much importance, but which we know are destined to produce one *Shock*, which does." Breton's stance on violent revelation is synthesized in his well-known maxim: "Beauty will be CONVULSIVE or will not be at all."⁶² The aesthetics of such a "convulsive" beauty was further formulated in his *Second Manifesto of Surrealism* (1930), where Breton states that "the simplest surrealist act" consists in, armed with a revolver, arbitrarily shooting at a crowd.⁶³

The French literary theorist Maurice Blanchot coined a concept to name the philosophical dimension of instantaneity as depicted in Breton's *Nadja*: the *encounter*. The encounter is, above all, an episode in discontinuity—"interruption, interval, arrest, or opening." The experience of an encounter—for example, the sudden first appearance of the character of Nadja in the novel—has a seismic effect on subjectivity because it defies the established grounds of regular thinking. An encounter is an interval of disorder that, displayed through either chance or play, represents the irruption of something so unfamiliar and strange that it opens up the door for "the impossible" (the new, the surprising, the unexpected) to arrive. The broader philosophical signification of surrealism lies then in representing a revolt against what Blanchot called the *ideology of the continuous*—the tendency to identify reality with continuity and seamless harmony. Against the ideology of the continuous, surrealism presented a series of methods for introducing the random elements of play into artistic creation and everyday life, such as automatic writing and chance.⁶⁴ Such surrealist receptiveness to the encounter thus worked as an existential counterpart to the more formal techniques of juxtaposition.

Breton would continue to explore the motif of instantaneity in his literary works from the 1930s. In *Communicating Vessels* (1932), for example, he further analyzes the experience of sudden encounters in the everyday. Contact with the unexpected, Breton writes, urges the individual to reconsider the meaning of *causality* so that it can account for the uncanny phenomenon of *coincidence* in daily life. Breton resorts to the concept of *objective chance*, an alternative causality in which random facts are endowed with an inner necessity, so that they can be interpreted as both fortuitous and foreordained at the same time. Such chance occurrences that conform to the laws of objective chance realize surrealism's most genuine intention: the casting of a "*conduction wire* between the far too distant worlds of waking

and sleep, exterior and interior reality, reason and madness."[65] In *Mad Love*
(1937), Breton narrates his personal experiences with the phenomenon of
the *trouvaille*, the "found object" discovered by chance in a flea market or
on the street and in which one can "recognize the marvelous precipitate of
desire." In the *trouvaille*, the secret mechanisms of the unconscious establish
a linkage between the interiority of the human psyche and the outer reality
of the material world. The finding of this object produces at first a disturbing
epiphany of "*panic-provoking* terror and joy," but has as its final outcome an
"enlarging [of] the universe."[66] The encounter with the *trouvaille* cannot take
place unless individual perception is set to a state of vigilant expectation and
openness to chance, a state that Breton calls *disponibilité* (availability). *Nadja*,
Communicating Vessels, and *Mad Love* constitute a literary trilogy on the surrealist notion of *the marvelous*. Through its emphasis on the sudden nature
of perception, this notion signals a traumatic rupture in the natural world by
negating the identity of the rational with the real.[67]

The surrealist notion of shock might be interpreted as the result of Breton's
distinctive interpretation of Hegel's philosophy. According to such an interpretation, the surrealist thematization of shock—the astonishment triggered
by unexpected encounters—would constitute an appropriation of the Hegelian dialectic.[68] However, although the structure of some core surrealist ideas
belongs to an intellectual space shaped by Hegelianism, the shock concept in
the end fits better within the lineage of an anti-Hegelian attitude. The surrealist
shock is, in this sense, essentially the example of an unresolved dialectic of
sorts—the standing still of two contrary images, states or ideas that generate
meaning out of their very divergence and conflict, excluding reconciliation on
a higher level. In surrealism, the collision of two contradictory states does not
generate a sublation or dialectic resolution, which would in turn become the
ground for further contradiction and resolution. Collision is not a moment
within a larger process of teleological unfolding, but rather an instantaneous
event that constitutes a category in and of itself. The sudden temporality of surrealism features—just like Kierkegaard's paradox—a distinctive denouement
for contradiction, different from its dissolution in a higher level of expansion
or growth. It constitutes a conceptual alternative to the dialectic. This observation can even be extended to the avant-garde aesthetics of juxtaposition in
general. Adorno seems to confirm this interpretation when he states that in
montage "the negation of synthesis becomes a principle of form."[69]

Another idea that can contribute to understanding the conceptual implications of the surrealist interest in discontinuity and shock is Blanchot's

limit-experience. According to Blanchot, a limit-experience occurs whenever an individual is capable of "grasping himself as a whole" within the time lapse of a "privileged instant."[70] Limit-experiences—like Goethe's privileged moments or the Romantics' encounters with suddenness—belong therefore to the fragmentary in that they represent fleeting revelations of totality and a feeling of incompleteness that, nevertheless, discloses an abundance of meaning. The surrealist limit-experience represents a twentieth-century variation of Hölderlin's motif of nearness, that infinite remoteness of what is closest to us. The fragmentary revelation of the limit-experience is situated, Blanchot writes, "where the proximity of the remote offers itself only in its remoteness" and is seized "only insofar as it is beyond reach."[71] In the surrealist limit-experience, the experience of the present is assumed to be an experience of incompleteness—a form of negativity intrinsic to temporality itself.

Surrealism is the most emblematic discourse on subjective instantaneist experience in the twentieth century. Surrealist texts present the sudden revelation—whether on the page or on the crowded urban street—as the model for experience at large, as if every perception were, at its core, a possible repetition of the prototypical surrealist moment of rupture. If in the nineteenth century Kierkegaard had affirmed that the rule should be understood in terms of the exception,[72] in the twentieth century surrealism proposed that the "exception" of *shock*—the abrupt tearing apart of the regularity of the everyday—unveiled a fundamental aspect of temporal reality that pertained to all forms of experience.

The Ephemeral and Modern Mythology

Another way to approach to the nature of surrealist instantaneous temporality is through comparison with mystical experience. Albert Camus saw surrealism's central aim as the achievement of a moment of fusion between dream and reality, reason and unreason, through the "concrete irrationality" of "objective chance." The point where this fusion is accomplished is for Camus a "*sommet-abîme, familier aux mystiques*,"[73]—that is, a state of mind analogous to the "abyssal climax" of religious mysticism. Benjamin adopted a similar outlook when he defined the surrealist undertaking as a revolt against Catholicism consisting in the "overcoming of religious illumination" through a "profane illumination" based on a "materialistic, anthropological inspiration."[74] To the traditional spirituality's sacred states of contemplation surrealism opposed a secular and explicitly profane mysticism based on earthly human experience such as the convulsions of perception in modern city life and the shocking surprises hidden in the materials of the everyday. For Benjamin, the surrealist text that most lucidly represents this experience is—besides Breton's *Nadja*—Louis Aragon's *Paris Peasant* (*Le paysan de Paris*).

Published in 1926, Aragon's *Paris Peasant* is a hybrid literary text—half novel, half prose poem—that initiates the reader into a universe of secular revelations and "profane illuminations." Aragon himself introduces the book as "a modern mythology" or a "mythology of the modern" in which the urban experience of promenades in the metropolis provides, in typically surrealist fashion, the timely landscape for a return of the irrational and the source of unprecedented fables and symbols: "New myths spring up beneath each step we take."[75] In *Paris Peasant*, the Baudelairean flaneur turns into an allegorical figure, and his activity—the random roaming around crowded or empty streets and *passages*—becomes the unexpected foundation of a new, secular "sense of the marvelous."[76] Michael Löwy has called this the practice of *dérive*: purposeless wandering in the city that breaks away from the laws of rationality.[77] Aragon presents the flaneur as the priest, and walking as the rite, of these modern myths that are constantly being created out of the second nature of city life.

According to Aragon, the new divinities have abandoned the traditional dwellings of the sacred and they now manifest themselves in the newfangled temples of modern urban spaces. They do so in accordance with a specific category of temporality: the *ephemeral*. The "poetic deity" of urban modernity can "become palpable" only abruptly.[78] The *passages* or "arcades" of Paris constitute one of such unusual settings for the appearance of the sacred. As Philip Nord has pointed out, the Parisian arcades were originally built during the first half of the nineteenth century as a "daring innovation in commercial architecture" featuring gaslight and the new construction materials of iron and glass.[79] The arcades' popularity survived the Second Empire (1853–1870) and Georges-Eugène Haussmann's large-scale renovation of Paris (a "commodity utopia or a utopia *tout court*") but declined toward the turn of the century.[80] By the 1920s, the surviving spaces of this kind had already become the relics of an outdated modernity. But for Aragon it was then, right when the arcades had turned into the symbols of bygone eras, that they transformed themselves into "the true sanctuaries of a cult of the ephemeral"[81] and theaters of supernatural visions of a mythological version of modernity.

In the "twilight of the gods" brought about by modern times, the only "divinity" that has retained its authority, Aragon explains, is *chance*, the most obvious manifestation of which is the random encounter with the unknown. The purpose of surrealism as an aesthetic position, Aragon explains, is to capture this new mythology of the sudden as it expresses itself in the modern city's frantic processes of destruction, transformation, and renewal. Surrealism is the original sensibility attuned to this new universe—an "entrance to the realms of the instantaneous, the world of snapshot." The stakes for Aragon are nothing less than the *reenchantment* of modern time itself: "I began to understand that their kingdom [of urban life's "disparate elements"] derived its nature from their newness. . . . So they appeared to me in the guise of transitory tyrants, and in a sense the agencies of chance in relation to my sensibility."[82]

Aragon's most striking insight is his association between modernity— understood as never-ending social transformation and change—and *the sacred*: "These gods live, attain the zenith of their power, then die, leaving their perfumed altars to other gods. They are the very principles of every transformation of everything. They are the necessity of movement. . . . I set about forming the idea of a mythology in motion. It was more accurate to call it a mythology of the modern."[83] For Aragon, modernity's accelerated pace of continual disruption contains a marvelous substance, a deity in itself; the ephemeral is a "god," a "polymorphous divinity." Aragon aims at a redivinization of time, in this case the specific form of modern time, similar to that envisioned by Hölderlin more than a century before.[84] For both Aragon and Hölderlin, this redivinization can be accomplished through the formation of a contingent notion of the sacred, the essence of which is molded by history and temporality; it is a divinity conceived of *sub specie temporis*, not *sub specie aeternitatis*. But whereas Hölderlin was concerned with the absence and imminent return of "the gods," Aragon believes that the movements of history are divine in and of themselves. By narrating city life using the transitory as a vehicle for the revelation of the sacred, Aragon's *Paris Peasant* constitutes a new version of Baudelaire's poetics of modernity in a "supernatural" key.

CHAPTER 3

Ernst Jünger and the Instant of Crisis

Ernst Jünger (1895–1998) was an officer in the German Army during the First World War, a renowned chronicler of the "front experience" (*Fronterlebnis*), a publicist with a nationalist and militarist orientation during the Weimar years, and an author of ambitious interpretations of modern urban and industrial society. He ranks among the most representative authors of German intellectual life during the first decades of the twentieth century. His writing ranges from war diaries and political journalism to poetic prose and treatises on social theory, but despite its formal diversity, his entire oeuvre shares a set of aesthetic and historical concerns that revolve around instantaneous temporality. This time category provided Jünger with an intellectual framework with which to portray and analyze the experiences of *crisis* and *sudden rupture* that characterized both the collective space of historical consciousness and the personal realm of subjective perception during the First World War and the Weimar Republic in Germany.

After participating in the War—first as a volunteer soldier, then as an officer—and receiving the German army's highest distinction (the order *Pour le Mérite*), Jünger began his writing career with a series of works that addressed his era's prevailing sense of a historical break. In his first Weimar writings, Jünger explored the extreme conditions of perception on the battlefield. Rooted in the immediacy of his experience, his descriptions of war rendered discontinuity and crisis as embodied realities. In his later work, devoted to social and cultural issues, he distilled the elements of the *Fronterlebnis* into a vision, both critical and utopian, of contemporary society. The formulation of this vision was Jünger's attempt both to make sense of the crisis-ridden interwar world and to promote an ideal form for this new society—a form that would incorporate the new reality of extreme and sudden experiences into the core of its cultural values and social dynamics. In both aspects of his Weimar intellectual production, Jünger turned to a series of figures of instantaneity in order to give concreteness to a general feeling of rupture.

In Jünger's Weimar literary and political production, the notion of instantaneity unites his representations of key moments in early twentieth-century German history—from the mood of frantic expectation and enthusiasm that greeted the First World War in 1914 to soldiers' traumatic experience of shock on the battlefields and the postwar sense of catastrophic crisis due to political breakdown, social revolution, and economic collapse. As a "seismograph" of the times,[1] Jünger framed these moments within a series of perceptual and historical categories stemming from instantaneous temporality. Accordingly, in this chapter I read the first stage of Jünger's intellectual trajectory—from the publication of his war memoirs, *Storm of Steel*, in 1920 to the appearance of *The Worker*, his treatise on modern technological society, in 1932—with the aim of showing the author's contribution to the formation of an instantaneist regime of historicity.

It is my contention that Jünger's recourse to the motif of instantaneity played a critical role in the constitution of this new chronotope. By situating the concept of the instant at the center of his intellectual production, Jünger—like his contemporaries Walter Benjamin and Ernst Bloch—helped to demarcate *suddenness* as an alternative paradigm for the organization of the experience of historical and individual time. This paradigm is central to understanding the historical consciousness in Germany during the first decades of the twentieth century. Essential to it was a revisiting of the modern traditions of the instant, from Romanticism to Kierkegaard and Nietzsche, and from Baudelaire to the historical avant-gardes. Like Bloch and Benjamin, Jünger exhibited significant affinities with these literary and philosophical genealogies of instantaneity.

In particular, Jünger's Weimar writings reveal a defining feature of the instantaneity chronotope: its simultaneous operation on the individual level of personal subjectivity and on the collective level of political and historical consciousness. As Jünger's reflections on terror, total mobilization, and danger attest, the concept of the instant brings these two different levels together within a single conceptual framework. Introducing suddenness as a unifying category of experience, Jünger's work proves the relevance of instantaneity for the intellectual representation of historical crisis and for the emergence of a new concept of experience as a counterpart, in individual subjectivity, to the period's sense of historical rupture.

The Great War and the Consciousness of Crisis

Because of its use of new technological means and mass mobilization for belligerent purposes, and because of the unprecedented destruction that it brought about, the First World War was generally experienced in Germany as an unparalleled moment of rupture in historical continuity. This sensation was first discernible in the euphoric belief in the liberating possibilities of war, which Detlev Peukert has called the "mythology of 1914." For a few months, in the summer of 1914, the German people expected that the war would break the Reich's international isolation, create a hoped-for united *Volksgemeinschaft* (national community) and regenerate the nation.[2] Modris Eksteins has even interpreted the 1914 German outlook as a sort of political expression of the aestheticist ideal of the fusion of life and art; in this reading, national enthusiasm for violence and destruction as forms of creation was the equivalent of the primitivist postures of the avant-garde but in the sphere of historical action. During these months, a feeling of urgency seized the German nation, radicalizing its perception of time and sharpening its reception of sudden phenomena. According to Eksteins: "The moment became supreme. Hours, years, indeed centuries, were reduced to moments."[3]

By contrast, 1918—the year of Germany's military defeat—brought a sense of disappointment and political collapse, which created the conditions for another kind of experience of temporal discontinuity. Eventually, this period of general breakdown and radical disenchantment would leave a lasting sense of rupture in German collective memory. The war's catastrophic conclusion, not the rapturous moment of its outbreak, gave rise to the perception of the First World War as an unmistakable break in historical continuity. Norbert Bolz refers, in this sense, to the great "caesura of 1918."[4] The early years of the Weimar Republic, with their intense succession of revolution, civil war, political assassinations, failed putsches, foreign occupation, hyperinflation, and general disappointment, did nothing but confirm this feeling of "almost uninterrupted crisis."[5] This series of fierce convulsions and violent changes were not incidental but at the core of the political and cultural debates of Weimar Germany. It is no surprise, then, that a deepened self-awareness of living in a time of crisis defined the epoch's historical consciousness from its inception.[6] Oswald Spengler's *The Decline of the West* (1918) and Karl Barth's *The Epistle to the Romans* (1919) represent two influential intellectual embodiments of this prevalent spiritual disposition.

As a result, after the end of the First World War, the notion of crisis pervaded the Weimar Republic's political and cultural discourses. The experience of the caesura of 1918 demolished optimistic narratives of progress and
brought about a mood, alternatively pessimistic or ecstatic, in which thinking about crisis thrived.[7] The diagnoses and cultural critiques that alluded
to a crisis, either in politics, economics, or the arts, proliferated.[8] Weimar
contemporaries tended to deploy crisis as a means of structuring and drama-
tizing the "life world" of the era. Rüdiger Graf points out that, between 1918
and 1933, more than 370 published works used the term *crisis*.[9] Reinhart
Koselleck has argued that the Weimar intellectuals' use of the concept of crisis never went beyond the historicist outlook of nineteenth-century philosophies of history. They saw crisis as a mere "transitional stage" within a larger
coherent narrative.[10] Although Koselleck's observation is correct about some
of the period's deployment of *crisis*—such as in the Marxist interpretations
of economic crises as intermediate phases in processes of social development—many other Weimar applications of the term do indeed transcend the
historicist perspective. In the minds of many Weimar observers, the experience of crisis was one of radical discontinuity, comparable to a gap in the
flow of historical events or even to the irruption of a moment outside of
time and history. Among these observers, the representations of crisis as a
rupture, break, or renewal were more widespread than its interpretations as
a prospect of "continuous development."[11] Behind this consciousness of crisis
as a moment of ahistorical temporality was the event of the First World War,
a catastrophe so exceptional and profound that it shattered all points of reference and all criteria for the meaningful organization of historical experience
or the anticipations of the future. The message that the war left imprinted
in the collective awareness was, as Michael Makropoulos writes, "that the
unimaginable had occurred and that nothing could be excluded."[12] In the
war's aftermath, the relationship of the present with either the future or the
past became problematic. On the one hand, the standards from the past—
such as the nineteenth-century idea of modernity as an age of security—had
been revealed as illusory and vanished. On the other, the war had destroyed
the identification of the future with progress and, therefore, deprived the
horizon of expectation of any coherence.[13]

In the new condition of crisis, one came into contact with the present as
if it were a form of timeless temporality, an experience so radical and absolute that it could not be integrated into any consistent historical narrative or

comprehensive frame. This properly antihistoricist sense fostered an ahistorical time consciousness that was, in turn, conducive to the appearance of *decisionism,* the philosophical attitude that identifies the instantaneous "moment
of decision" with an experience irreducible to reason and charged with a
fundamental existential role.[14] Decisionism defined the present as the time
of decision and became the predominant ethical stance among the Weimar
era's radical authors (both from the left and the right). In this cultural mood,
the future was no longer an ideal image situated at the end point of a historical process, but rather a fragment that, sometimes in hidden form, already
existed in the present. The recognition of this fragment depended on *activity.*
Weimar intellectuals of all ideological inclinations had an "activist tendency,"
which caused them to construct "radical dichotomies" and to believe in the
existence of pressing either-or alternatives.[15] Jünger shared with this group
of Weimar authors a decisionist understanding of the present and a vision
of the years of the First World War and the birth of the Weimar Republic as
an unprecedented rupture in historical continuity. But Jünger was different
from many of his contemporaries in his conviction that the war's profound
sense of discontinuity had been closely mirrored by an analogous break in
subjectivity. This break in the continuity of experience manifested itself in the
irruption of multiple instances of sudden perception, first on the battlefield,
and then in everyday life. Jünger's literary examination of this break was the
beginning of his Weimar intellectual production. He would later elaborate
specific aesthetic categories (such as terror and danger) to name these new
experiences, as well as to enlarge his analysis into a general theory of modern
technological society.

The Break in the Continuity of Experience:
War and Suddenness

Walter Benjamin was among the most important observers of this rupture
in the stability of perception. Looking back to the Weimar era, he diagnosed
a vast crisis in the very notion of experience (*Erfahrung*) as a result of the
First World War. "Experience has fallen in value amid a generation which
from 1914 to 1918 had to experience some of the most monstrous events
in the history of the world. . . . Wasn't it noticed at the time how many people returned from the front in silence? Not richer but poorer in communicable experience?"[16] For Benjamin, the war experience had had a powerful

impact on the perceptual faculties of a whole generation. Life on the front had imposed exhausting sensory demands on combatants. It drained their minds and bodies through the irruption of a previously unknown sense of urgency stemming from the war's technologized, industrial-scale combat. As a result, the risk of being wounded, mutilated, or killed on the front had intensified. The battles of the First World War were indeed, as Dorothée Brill has pointed out, "the paradigmatic breeding ground" for experiences that exceeded the individual's ability to anticipate them.[17] Furthermore, action on the front exposed combatants to an expanded sense of the present as an instantaneous experience disjointed from past and future. An extreme isolation of the present instant from the regular course of time characterized temporal perception on the battlefield. This new experience of time tangibly refuted some of the contemporary philosophical propositions (such as Husserl's and Bergson's) that rendered time as a continual, uninterrupted flow.[18]

Jünger's first literary work, *Storm of Steel*, the memoir of his service on the battlefront published in 1920, was an ambitious attempt to give a firsthand account of this break in the stability of perception and its concurrent sense of an intensified present. According to Jünger, the most salient attribute of perception under the new conditions of technological modernity was the element of suddenness. Consequently, in his autobiographical exploration of the "objective" or more exterior manifestations of combat, Jünger posits that the proliferation of sudden experiences and shocks on the battlefield entailed a rupture in the continuity of perception. This rupture in subjective continuity paralleled the war's rupture in historical continuity. Throughout the book, Jünger narrates the emergence of suddenness as the predominant sense experience at the front. He sets the tone from the very first page: "Grown up in an age of security, we shared a yearning for danger, for the experience of the extraordinary. We were enraptured by war. . . . Surely the war had to supply us with what we wanted; the great, the overwhelming, the hallowed experience."[19] In the battlefield, where the soldier lived with the ongoing possibility of his unexpected demise, he learned to make an automatic association between any interruption of regularity and the possibility of his own death. The soldier's heart "would stop with a sense of mortal dread," and he would jump at any sudden and unexpected noise. "The experience hit so hard in that dark country beyond consciousness," Jünger writes, "that every time there was a break with the usual, the porter Death would leap to the gates with hand upraised, like the figure above the dial on certain clock towers, who appears at the striking of the hour, with scythe and hourglass."[20]

In *Copse 125: A Chronicle from the Trench Warfare of 1918*, another of his war memoirs, published in 1925, Jünger evokes the everyday experience of having to be "night and day without a breathing space, always on the alert."[21] During the First World War, invisibility took on a new tactical function. As Anton Kaes explains, in war "the enemy seems . . . to have disappeared; what was once a physical encounter between bodies is transformed into a pervasive *fear* of an unexpected and sudden attack. A heightened perception now seeks to detect the slightest sign of an impending assault."[22] The soldier on the front had to learn "to listen to the unexpected" in order to recover a primal sense of survival: "I know well these moments when the unexpected happens. One is concerned with quite other matters and the ear seems scarcely to hear the rush of the iron cylinder that describes its arc above the level ground. . . . We were brought up in such security that at first we heard this voice indistinctly as a confused though urgent call; but we have learned to listen for it."[23]

In Jünger's memoirs, the *Fronterlebnis* becomes an object of detailed methodical attention. He dissects the decisive moments of battle when the experience of vulnerability presents itself as a sort of "profane illumination." In these limit-situations, the exceptional discloses some aspect of the truth that, were it not for the "instant of danger," would have remained hidden behind the veil of average normality. In the *Storm of Steel*, he proclaims: "You can't say you really know a man if you haven't seen him under conditions of danger." Jünger himself experienced one of these secular epiphanies when a bullet left him in a state of suspense between life and death. At that moment, he writes: "I understood, as in a flash of lightning, the true inner purpose of my life."[24]

Jünger interpreted these moments of extreme perception as representing a deep qualitative change in the nature of sensory experience. After the First World War's epic battles, "death has been given a more frightful aspect than in the days of black powder and round bumbling cannon-balls. . . . To-day the fever of battle is more like a delirium, and its impressions so violent that there is no room left for observing them." The sensory stimuli the soldiers were exposed to at the front were so radical that the emotions the previous generations had felt in battle "were nothing but literary sentiments, effusions at second hand, mere reflections of genuine feeling that could not warm the blood, nor make the heart stand still."[25]

Jünger's account echoes Benjamin's proposition that the First World War's soldiers had returned speechless from the front because they had undergone an unprecedented fracture in "communicable experience."[26] However, it must be noted that, notwithstanding Benjamin's interpretation, Jünger did not return speechless from the front. Rather, Jünger made the fracture Benjamin refers to—the crisis in the continuity of tradition—into a key theme of his writing. His memoirs, as much as his journalism and literary pieces, were an attempt to communicate that fracture—that, during the war, "the hazardous, unknown, and exceptional became for four years the ordinary."[27] In later writings, Jünger would give the name of *terror* to the unprecedented experience that this fracture had brought about. The latest military technology had heightened the intensity of danger, and, with that, it also fractured the space of subjective experience. But the moment of rupture in the continuity of experience began to be perceived as a new, historically shaped *space of perception*. The consequence of the historical fracture was not, as Benjamin claimed, the reticence of its survivors but, rather, the transformation of the *moment of interruption* into a new form of experience in and of itself.

War and the Concrete Experience

Jünger's *Battle as Inner Experience* (*Der Kampf als inneres Erlebnis*), a controversial 1922 meditation on the spiritual meaning of warfare, and his *Storm of Steel* form a powerful diptych. Together, the two works cover the subjective and objective aspects of the war experience, respectively.[28] An intellectual elaboration of Jünger's days on the front, *Battle as Inner Experience* constitutes a sort of manifesto in which the author attempts to recover a form of direct, unmediated perception. His fundamental intent is to construe war as the supreme incarnation of authentic *Erlebnis*. *Erlebnis* means "isolated experience" or the immediate, intuitive response before intellectual abstraction. It is the radical opposite of bourgeois *Erfahrung* ("continuous experience").[29] Jünger's cult of *Erlebnis* decrees that dangerous situations, such as warfare, represent the highest form of living. It equates combat with a state of intoxication and excess and envisions the battlefield as a situation where long-dormant animal instincts return. The naked experience of battle, Jünger believes, infuses the soldier with a feeling of ecstasy, a sensation of being between life and death that reactivates the primordial drives that bourgeois civilization represses.[30]

Jünger's book belongs to the spirit of what Robert Wohl has called "the generation of 1914."[31] By 1914, Wohl explains, "youth" had become a symbol of the attack on the older Wilhelmine institutions and of the renewal of

German society. A cohort of junior officers had returned home convinced of "the creative and renovating force" of their combat experience, and, together, they wove individual perception and historical collective memory into the shared point of view of a "generation." After Germany's defeat, the pre-1914 enthusiasm for violent regeneration survived to play a role in the cultural atmosphere of the Weimar Republic. Radically transformed by the disastrous outcome of the war, it became gloomier in nature and more virulent in intent. As Anson Rabinbach has shown, this transformation in the meaning of regeneration is related to the emergence, after 1918, of *catastrophe* as a new intellectual category in German culture and thought.[32] Jünger wrote his Weimar works from the point of view of a new horizon that the "destructiveness of total war" had defined.[33]

Jünger's engagement with the war's catastrophic aftermath accounts for his affinities with a group of Weimar authors characterized by their right-wing nationalist politics and collectively known as the "conservative revolutionaries."[34] Authors such as Oswald Spengler, Werner Sombart, Hans Freyer, and Carl Schmitt shared a fascination with soldierly heroism, a rejection of republicanism, and the condemnation of the capitalist economy's individualist spirit. The conservative revolutionaries conceived of themselves as a new type of conservatism: rejuvenated by the experience of the war; willing to embrace rather than condemn the social and cultural consequences of modern technology; and committed to taking the idea of revolution from the left in order to reformulate it in a nationalist key.[35] Products of the 1918 defeat, the conservative revolutionaries longed to reconstruct the lost community of German soldiers on the front through the creation of a new national order.[36] They believed in the moral renewal of society through a doctrine of action for action's sake that privileged life and feeling over analysis and abstract reason. Their "activist logic" and "thought of the act" represented a sort of "political existentialism" of decision that derided mere opinion and affirmed resolute action as the only possible exit from a situation of crisis.[37]

Unmistakably influenced by Nietzsche, *Battle as Inner Experience* presents a version of this activist logic. Jünger's meditations imagine war as the unleashing of powerful antinihilistic energies, a passionate saying yes to the world, and an aesthetic interpretation of the world that defies conformity and boredom.[38] Self-realization through violent sacrifice constitutes war's inner meaning. Battle is, beyond its final outcome or the rightness of its purpose, an end in itself.[39] Such was the prevalent mood among German war veterans who, deprived of the recognition of victory, turned to an apology of sacrifice and a celebration of war as "inner experience" to redeem their experience of defeat.[40] Since they had been vanquished, the veterans had to vindicate action itself, regardless of its consequences or results. In his essay "Fire," Jünger wrote: "The warriors' spirit, the exposure of oneself to risk, even for the tiniest idea, weighs more heavily in the scale than all the brooding about good and evil. . . . We want to show what we have in us; then, if we fall, we will truly have lived to the full."[41]

A few years later, in *Copse 125*, Jünger would insist on combat's "supernatural" aspects. War, he tells us, is not only a "material matter," but also, and more primordially, a "spiritual experience" that situates the soldier right at the center of a radical moment of decision: "It was plain to us that it was all or nothing."[42] With his aestheticized love for war and danger, Jünger represented a powerful incarnation of the transgressive ethos of the avant-garde. As he attempts to create an aesthetics with certain avant-garde attributes—a modernist discourse of war as the source of "the new" and an expressionistic literary style[43]—Jünger emerges from the pages of *Battle as Inner Experience* as a sort of hero of transgression (and perhaps a predecessor of later thinkers devoted to the subject, such as Georges Bataille and Michel Foucault).

Terror and the Phenomenology of the Sudden

The limit-experiences that the war imposed on combatants also put the limits of language to the test. After the war, the usual categories for describing experience were no longer valid, and if they were expected to render what had actually taken place on the battlefield, they had to be changed. Jünger's fascination with suddenness, for example, compelled him to coin a specific aesthetic category for this type of perception: the notion of *terror* (*Schrecken*). In *The Adventurous Heart* (*Das abenteuerliche Herz*), his volume of short narrative and poetic prose pieces (originally published in 1929, and later substantially revised for a second edition in 1938),[44] Jünger refined his approach to instantaneous temporality from the point of view of terror. As Karl Heinz Bohrer has argued, Jünger's idea of terror indicates his affinity with the surrealist aesthetics of the marvelous and the convulsive.

In *The Adventurous Heart*, battlefield epiphanies become Jünger's raw material for his aesthetics of terror, which he builds around the concepts of *commotion* (*Erschütterung*) and *surprise* (*Überraschung*).[45] Take for example his primal scene of "demonic impression": the experience when something believed to be dead suddenly turns out to be alive (or vice versa). This terrifying instant "when life and death change places" escapes all rational explanation—and, moreover, it recalls Plato's definition of instantaneity.[46] Another example is that of the unexpected appearance of an enemy soldier. It horrifies not because the enemy is present but because of "the surprise of suddenly seeing him in flesh and bone coming out of a dead landscape."[47]

An equally important structural principle of terror is what Jünger calls "the other" (*das Andere*), naming the critical moment when two different phenomena collide with each other. Unleashing an effect similar to that of the aesthetics of juxtaposition and montage, the collision triggers the irruption of the unexpected as a doorway into the realm of "the demonic." (Kierkegaard had introduced the category of the demonic in relation to instantaneity in *The Concept of Anxiety*.[48]) At the appearance of the other, the ground beneath one's feet is suddenly replaced by the sensation of an utter void into which one is vertiginously falling. Near-death incidents are such moments. These occasions forever leave in the mind of the soldier the memory of having "almost crossed the threshold of death." They are moments in which all the events of a life are shown in reverse so that the last moment to appear is the instant of birth, "the instant of the most intense obscurity."[49]

Building on this typology of terror, Jünger describes in *The Adventurous Heart* the contents of consciousness at the encounter with unexpected events, or what I will call a *phenomenology of suddenness*. He starts by characterizing terror as a distinct form of mood. If Kierkegaard had already outlined the distinction between *fear* and *anxiety*—fear is always fear of something in particular, whereas anxiety, having no concrete object at all, is a general state of disquiet before existence itself[50]—Jünger now in turn locates the specificity of terror as a mood in its connection with instantaneous temporality. The phenomenon of terror is the space "that extends between the recognition of the downfall and the downfall itself."[51] Terror is, then, that sudden, uncanny sensation of eternity that takes place in the fleeting time lapse between the terrifying event and the moment in which the subject becomes aware of what is happening.

Jünger narrates his own experience of terror after having been wounded in the battlefield. He writes that the "greatest revelation" occurs within an "inconceivably short moment."[52] While lying injured on the ground, he experiences an abrupt transition from a state of impulsive will to one of contemplation. It is "as if there existed within the space of the battlefield an even deeper space, a chamber more secret." What happens in these brief moments of vision is not a mere return of images from the past, but rather the coming to the surface of these images' deeper content, their "meaningful source," so that "one thinks of everything that has taken place as absolutely necessary, as good, as pious, as just."[53] Mortally wounded, and almost crossing the threshold of death, Jünger experiences a Nietzschean moment: the instant of one's death as a realization of amor fati.

In another episode, Jünger undergoes a similar moment of revelation just after a storming of the trenches when, amid the cries of the wounded, he has the sensation that he and the men under his command "had participated, as improvising extras under the laws of a higher stage direction, in a spectacle during which we could not think and whose image, frozen before us, we only now gathered into our awareness." The second just after the peak of the battle—that moment after an event—is a moment in which "the world spirit perhaps shifts its wrappings a little too vigorously, a little too hastily, so that what had been veiled appeared for a moment to the blunted senses." These are moments, Jünger tells us, when "fissures appear through which we are able to divine architectural secrets normally concealed from us."[54] If in *Battle as Inner Experience* the unleashing of impulsive energies is a "deeper reality than that of victory,"[55] in *The Adventurous Heart* it is the knowledge brought about by experiences of sudden temporality.

In direct continuity with Goethe and Nietzsche, Jünger outlines a philosophical stance—*intuitive skepticism (anschaulicher Skeptizismus)*—to make sense of these fractures within ordinary perception. The term refers to the "form of insight far removed from the norm" that arises in states of perceptual exception, such as pain and danger. In these states, "a level of astonishment . . . drives away fear" and the "fine veil that nearly always shrouds the world is lifted."[56] Intuitive skepticism reveals that the experience of the instantaneous present is always inherently delayed, because the experiencing subject can realize that an event has taken place only after the event.

The Adventurous Heart is Jünger's ambitious attempt to reach the core of what the *Fronterlebnis* had meant in spiritual and perceptual terms. In some passages of the book, Jünger suggests that the battlefront's imposition of suddenness on the individual sensibility had philosophical implications in that it clarified heretofore obscured aspects of human perception. *Fronterlebnis* had brought about new knowledge and a sharper understanding of the workings of the mind not only in extreme situations of danger but in general. In other passages, however, Jünger explicitly maintains that the new insights into the nature of perception are fundamentally historical in that they brought about a new sensibility attuned to "a new kind of terror."[57] He declared terror to be "the style of our times," a style of "volcanic precision" characterized by the "coexistence of tremendous unchained power with an unflinching boldness of view."[58]

In this last sense, *The Adventurous Heart* ends up also offering penetrating reflections—in a literary key—on the peculiarities of historical consciousness during the Weimar era. Jünger's earlier war writings had echoed the prevalent sense of historical discontinuity by exploring its subjective counterpart in the categories of individual perception, but in the poetic prose pieces of *The Adventurous Heart*, it is the reverse. Here, it is the depiction of the general feeling of historical breakdown that sheds light on the crisis in subjectivity. As Bohrer points out, the references to emotions of terror and fear in *The Adventurous Heart* typically correspond to contemporary political events, such as the rise of German fascism in the 1930s.[59] The recurring allusion to the "fall" metaphor, for example, not only stands as a representative image of Jünger's theory of aesthetic perception, but also contributes to the identification of an "epochal sign"[60] with historical and political connotations. Wars and revolutions are consequently presented as the alleged "epochal conditions" for terror,[61] since they establish, Jünger believes, the most favorable circumstances for experiencing the kind of emotions that allow entrance into the "decisive zones of the soul."[62] Jünger's category of terror can be interpreted, then, as an attempt to conceptually name a widespread sensation of ahistoricity, which expresses itself both in individual experience and in a general feeling of historical discontinuity that abandons any notion of history as a gradual and coherent process.

Jünger's reflections on ahistorical forms of consciousness are embedded in *The Adventurous Heart*'s literary style as well. According to Bohrer, its style is illustrative of the modernist literature because it features a significant correspondence between narrative construction and the time-structure of convulsive historical periods. *The Adventurous Heart* denies narrative continuity; instead, it emphasizes the "event-character" of what is narrated. Focused on the "dangerous moment," among other formal decisions, it depicts historical time as a "sequence of unanticipated events."[63] Jünger's category of terror echoes, in particular, Walter Benjamin's "shock" and the surrealists' "convulsive beauty." In Bohrer's interpretation, André Breton's *Nadja* and Louis Aragon's *Paris Peasant*—the two surrealist pieces on the urban marvelous and sudden encounters—could be listed as the sources for this aspect of Jünger's style. Bohrer thus situates Jünger's involvement with instantaneous temporality within the context of the literary avant-garde, advancing an interpretation of the German author as a modernist writer in his own right. Jünger's formulation of terror as an aesthetic category places him among modernist authors such as James Joyce, Virginia Woolf, and Marcel Proust, who aspired to portray the phenomenon of "secular epiphanies" in their work.[64]

Because of his phenomenological analysis of experience, Jünger participates in the broader intellectual search for a new form of existential relation to time within the conditions of modernity. A central feature of the modern condition, since the last decades of the nineteenth century, was the attribution of the "homogeneous, empty time" of science, technology, and the capitalist economy to all spheres of life. Most participants in this search for a new relation to time, such as Bergson, Husserl and Heidegger, shared a common ambition: to displace the concerns with the rational self in favor of the recovery of lived, immediate experience.[65] These authors usually responded to the new conditions by establishing dichotomies between quantitative or qualitative, or between common and authentic forms of temporality, but Jünger sought a new concept of temporal experience that did not disavow but assumed as a point of departure the realities of mass technological modern society. Jünger's exploration—notably influenced by Nietzsche—revolved around the observation of, and engagement with, the phenomenon of sudden rupture in the realm of perception. For Jünger, the conditions of technological society had not suppressed the occasions for these experiences of suddenness; it had multiplied them.

Jünger and Weimar Suddenness: Affinities and Genealogy

Jünger was, in fact, only one among several significant authors of the Weimar era who embraced a form of thinking shaped by instantaneous temporality from a conservative political stance. Heidegger, also writing under the aegis of Nietzsche, examined the temporality of suddenness, and his treatment exhibits significant correspondences with Jünger's ideas. Both authors shared an antagonism to the formalistic conception that had, from Aristotle to Hegel, favored an abstract idea of time over the concreteness of lived temporality. In *Being and Time* (1927) Heidegger saw concrete lived time as the ground for resolute, authentic existence, and most precisely, in the *Augenblick*, he saw the "moment of vision" when the realities of finitude and contingency are revealed to individual awareness.[66]

Karl Jaspers' notion of "limit-situation" also bears a significant affinity to Jünger's aesthetic category of suddenness. Jaspers, another contemporary influenced by Nietzsche, had already offered one of the first twentieth-century philosophical formulations of the *Augenblick* in his *Psychologie der Weltanschauungen*, published in 1919, where he defined the instant as "the impenetrable, the infinite, that which is absolutely filled, the medium of crisis and creations."[67] Jaspers would later develop another influential philosophical concept: the notion of limit-situation (*Grenzsituation*). Limit-situations are those states of extreme anxiety, suffering, guilt, or proximity to death that the individual cannot escape or master through knowledge. They can only be grasped existentially. In his *Philosophy*, from 1932, he writes: "We become ourselves by entering into the limit situations with open eyes."[68] While under a limit-situation, we undergo our pure, naked existence. For Jaspers, the act of thinking amounts to taking into consideration these exceptional moments when a "limit" is experienced. As he writes in *Reason and Existenz* (*Vernunft und Existenz*, 1935), to think is "to philosophize in view of the exception." Opening up to the "truth of the exception," the individual can access a state of permanent questioning, of new possibilities, even of those possibilities that speak "in despair, in suicide, in the passion for the night-side of life, in every form of negative resolve."[69] Jüngerian terror is the aesthetic equivalent of Jasper's limit-situations.

Yet another Weimar author influenced by Nietzsche, the jurist and political theorist Carl Schmitt, presented important affinities with Jünger. Like Jaspers, Schmitt celebrated the epistemological and moral value of the *exception* as a sudden event that evades reason because it cannot be anticipated.[70] For Schmitt, the exception is different from a simple anomaly or an inharmonious irregularity; it is the moment when the deeper truth of the general is manifested. This phenomenon is evident even from an aesthetic point of view: "The exception," Schmitt writes in *Political Theology* (1922), "is more interesting (*interessanter*) than the rule."[71] As an example, he identifies the constitutional "state of emergency"—when a sovereign suspends all individual rights—as the structural equivalent, in politics, of the *miracle* in theology. In a similar vein, Jünger emphasized the role of apparently marvelous events during moments of danger. In the extreme conditions of the battlefield, it is useless to look for causes and logical connections because soldiers actually experience situations in which they are brought "into touch with the miraculous."[72] Similarly, Schmitt's glorification of war in *The Concept of the Political* (1932) presents a significant parallel with Jünger's assertion of combat's existential meaning.[73] Schmitt's thought, like Jünger's, represents a variation of decisionism. According to Schmitt, decision, not deliberation, was the only proper way of responding to intense, all-or-nothing confrontations with an enemy.

Total Mobilization as the Source of New Dangers

During the 1920s and the early 1930s, Jünger expressed his views on the war and its outcomes for German society and culture not only as a memoirist and literary essayist, but also as a journalist and political writer. His political essays appeared as forewords, as volumes of essays, but especially as contributions to right-wing periodicals such as the *Völkischer Beobachter, Deutsches Volkstum, Widerstand*, and *Die Standarte*.[74] The latter, published by the Stahlhelm, Bund der Frontsoldaten (Steel Helmet, League of Soldiers from the Front), maintained unambiguous political links with nationalist and militarist organizations that played a significant role in the formation and expansion of fascism in Germany.[75] In tune with this political mood, Jünger's journalistic pieces typically called for the renewal of German politics in the spirit of the soldiers from the front.[76] In this sense, Jünger's journalism constituted an emblematic example of the activist *Front-Denken*: the extrapolation of the attitudes of martial combat to the field of social and political commentary during a time of peace.[77] This political renewal sought a "new nationalism" founded on the war experience of ex-combatants, for whom defeat represented nothing less than the birth of a new Germany and the beginning of a new historical time. In this spirit, Jünger conceived of nationalism as "the unlimited will to the deployment of a Nation," and of "the Nation" itself as the most fundamental value, a universal principle naturally leading to rivalries and enmities between peoples, and thus to the rejection of internationalism and pacifism.[78] Jünger's "Nation" was a metaphysical rather than biological concept, which he drew from the "integral nationalism" of the French writer and ideologue Maurice Barrès. Barrès expounded on the reality of the nation as an all-encompassing force capable of determining human existence and countering the effects of modern individualism.[79]

The charges against Jünger's nationalism rightly include his irrationalism and fundamentalism, as well as his hostility to peace and the "(pre)fascist character" of his image of state and society.[80] However, Jünger's Weimar political writings also featured, in addition to his "new nationalist" stance, the outline of a theory of modern technological society. For Jünger, the contemporary world's main characteristic was its "total invasion" by technology.[81] The origin of this social mutation was modern warfare, and, more specifically, the experience of the First World War, an event larger in magnitude than the French Revolution given its momentous historical outcomes. Because it had foreshadowed a process that would soon dominate the entirety of the social world, the war epitomized for Jünger the unlimited expansion of modern technology during the first decades of the twentieth century. Modern technology multiplied the moments of risk and danger, and, as a result, the instantaneous sense of the present typical of the war experience now pervaded all spheres of life, even in times of peace. The disruption of regular perception, characteristic of the battlefield, had been transposed to everyday existence in modern industrial metropolises. The experience of the war, along with its transposition to everyday life, had put an end to one of the main tenets of bourgeois ideology: the identification of security with progress.

Against this political and intellectual background, Jünger expanded his reflections on suddenness into the new areas of social theory and cultural criticism. His most important writings from this period—notably *The Worker* (1932) and the essays "Total Mobilization" (1930), "On Danger" (1931), and *On Pain* (1934)—analyze the broader social and cultural consequences brought about by the rupture in historical continuity and in the stability of perception, which he had described in his earlier literary works. Among these consequences was an entirely new conception of the individual and society. In this new conception, *danger* became the standard category for the study of perception as well as the defining cultural sensibility of the era.

The concept underlying Jünger's analyses of technological society is that of *total mobilization*. Jünger had introduced the notion in a piece of the same title[82] included in *Krieg und Krieger*, a 1930 collection of essays by nationalist authors, which he himself edited.[83] "Total Mobilization" is Jünger's cultural manifesto for the postwar society. The concept of total mobilization refers to the extensive deployment of the sum of a society's resources for war purposes, a process so encompassing that it ends up erasing the distinction between combatants and civilians, as well as that between warfare and everyday life. In a totally mobilized collectivity, every individual human being becomes a "worker"—that is, a component in a never-idle machine that constantly conveys the "densely veined power supply of modern life towards the great current of martial energy."[84] "Total Mobilization" presents the first articulation of the notion—so prevalent in Jünger's writings from the 1920s and 1930s—that the experience of the war had constituted a sort of elemental blueprint of the society to come, not only in terms of individual subjectivity, but also in terms of social and political organization. For Jünger, the war had represented a sort of avant-garde of world history. Military mobilization had been the prelude for the permanent mobilization of society, and the frontline soldier was the model for the worker as a new social type.

A prominent critic of the *Krieg und Krieger* volume was Walter Benjamin. "Theories of German Fascism," his review of the collection of essays—published in 1930 in *Die Gesellschaft*—reveals the attention Jünger incited in the German political left. Although Benjamin praises Jünger's characterization of contemporary social reality as a form of total mobilization, his assessment overall condemns the volume's plan and ideas. For Benjamin, the authors' celebration of warfare as a primordial event represents an "immoral mysticism" lacking any respect for the victims of the war.[85] Moreover, the notion of "the warriors"—consecrated in the volume's title—as the model for the reconstruction of German society embodies, Benjamin believes, the very image of fascism, as well as an ideologization of the war experience intended to support the ruling bourgeois classes.[86]

For Jünger, the First World War had in fact realized the apocalyptic call to radical renewal of 1914, albeit in a bleaker and unexpected way. In "On Danger," Jünger writes that the process of total mobilization, triggered by the war, inaugurated a new social condition marked by permanent crisis and the constant upheaval of collective existence and individual perception. The advent of a totally mobilized society entailed the end of the era of bourgeois liberalism and, more specifically, the expiration of the bourgeois understanding of war, conflict, and danger as mere "historical errors" waiting to be eventually suppressed by the inevitable expansion of progress.[87] Against all liberal formulas, the totally mobilized society was characterized by a new, universally present possibility of danger in the form of accidents, disasters, warfare, and revolutions.[88] This persistent possibility was a symptom of the irruption, in the modern condition, of a primordial reality that the bourgeois ethos of safety had pretended to contain without any success—that is, fate. As a result of the new technological order—its pervasive presence in not only industrial production but also in the social organization of every aspect of life—ubiquitous danger affirmed fate for modernity. Therefore, contrary to the commonplace liberal expectation, a technological society should not be expected to materialize a dream of comfort, security, and peace, but to completely repudiate it: the creation of a world plagued with *more*, not less, sources of danger.[89] Jünger's "On Danger" represents, in this sense, an early version of Horkheimer's and Adorno's "dialectic of Enlightenment" thesis, which holds that reason, when expressed as modern technology, ends up defeating itself. In Jünger's account, the paradoxical end result of the Enlightenment project to protect humanity from risk through the advancement of technical progress had been the intensification of risk. Intellectuals failed to realize that modern technology constitutes, inescapably, a vehicle for danger and an incarnation of the primal materiality of fate.

The rise of a technified and totally mobilized society incited changes so radical that they permanently altered the meaning of the "human." Jünger identified the creation, after the war, of a new postbourgeois and postindividualistic humanity that ushered in a new relationship toward the collectivity. The treatise *Der Arbeiter* (*The Worker*), from 1932, includes the theoretical exposition of this new humanity and represents the culmination of Jünger's journalistic work.[90] In *The Worker*, Jünger formulates three new key concepts: the figure (*Gestalt*); the type (*Typus*); and the worker (*Arbeiter*).[91] Marcus Paul Bullock explains the relationships among them: "Jünger presents the term *Gestalt* as an idea, or an abstract essence arising from the world of technological power and giving the form of human life that is expressed on an individual level by the *Typus*, or type, also called the *Arbeiter*."[92] Jünger's worker represents that new form of human existence that responds to the fusion of man and technology. In this social formation, the purpose of human interaction is the accomplishment of a "higher unity" between the individual and the community. The "human" that participates in this process can no longer be said to have "human rights" in the liberal sense; rather, it is a "worker" belonging to a larger, all-encompassing, and totally mobilized "work-state."[93] Jünger's ideal typification of a highly technologized and all-involving community of workers was emblematic of what Jeffrey Herf has termed the "cultural paradox of German modernity." The simultaneous embrace of modern technology and rejection of Enlightenment reason characterized the previously discussed "conservative revolutionary" thinkers, who combined "political reaction" with "technological advance," and "political irrationalism" with "industrial rationalization" as the unlikely formula to revitalize the German nation.[94] His embrace of modern technology was what distinguished Jünger's stance from more traditionalist political postures. In contrast to conventional conservatism, Jünger—like other "conservative revolutionary" authors—did not condemn, but rather accepted the technification of society as an irreversible process that had to be integrated into the defense of hierarchical and communitarian values.

Danger Between Ordinary and Extraordinary Experience

In the totally mobilized world of the worker, the possibility of danger is no longer at the margins but right at the center of individual experience and social organization, and it marks a new form of normality.[95] The transformation is striking. The extreme existential and sensory conditions that soldiers had undergone on the battlefront had become the new general standard of perception and the human condition. In the modern world, the "moment of danger" is no longer separated from everyday life or secluded in the narrow limits of the frontline. Rather, "the real contemporary zone of danger is the technological realm itself,"[96] a realm that now encompasses the totality of social life. In Norbert Bolz's words, "the *Gestalt* of the worker . . . normalizes the state of exception," and as a result, "the extraordinary becomes the defining element of order."[97] The consequence of this new sweeping technological dominion is, for Jünger, "a situation in which catastrophe appears as the a priori of a transformed thought."[98] Jünger's allusion to Kant contains an illuminating insight: that in modern times, danger has become another universal a priori category of perception, at the same rank as time and space. What Jünger achieved in his series of pieces devoted to total mobilization and danger amounted, then, to a systematization of his own *Fronterlebnis* into a wide-ranging vision of culture, society, and the state.

Nowhere was this universalization of danger more patent than in the landscape of modern metropolises. In this setting, the realities of industrial production, mass politics, and urban transportation multiplied risk, as if the ever-present danger typical of the battlefield had been relocated to the city.[99] This is a subject Jünger deals with not only in his writings on social and political subjects, but also in his literary works. In *The Adventurous Heart* in particular, Jünger sets out to find occasions for the experience of terror in the seemingly peaceful course of everyday existence. The book's most representative passages are literary extrapolations of the front's shock-sensibility to urban life.[100] It is significant, however, that in Jünger's work the relationship between the battlefield and the cityscape is a two-way interaction. Not only did Jünger want to project the front's sense of peril into his depiction of modern city life but, as Anton Kaes points out, Jünger's speculations on warfare and perception were already situated within a larger discourse on urbanism. Jünger believed that an "urban spirit" animated the extreme visions of the battlefield landscape.[101] His ideas on sudden danger not only implied an extension of the war experience into civilian life, but also recognized the presence of an urban element in war itself. With Simmel, Benjamin, and Baudelaire, Jünger shared the conviction that the modern city was the primordial landscape of shock.

The work of Jünger, along with that of Benjamin and Bloch, represents a different stage in the construction of instantaneity as a category of perception. These three authors, in varying ways, distance themselves from the idea of the instant as a unique occurrence (as in the more conventional Goethean or Nietzschean accounts). Rather, they approach instantaneity, in its incarnation as shock, as a new standard of perception. The identification of this new standard is one of the main components of the instantaneity chronotope typical of the Weimar era. Jünger's main contribution to this aspect of the chronotope is, precisely, his description of the blurring of the distinction between *extraordinary* and *everyday* experience. The French philosopher Michel Foucault later labeled these two kinds of experience *phenomenological experience* and *limit-experience*, respectively. Whereas phenomenological experience is a way of organizing the conscious perception of daily occurrences in order to grasp their meaning, limit-experience—as sketched by authors such as Nietzsche, Bataille, and Blanchot—represents the endeavor to attain a maximum amount of intensity, reaching at the same time "that point of life which lies as close as possible to the impossibility of living, which lies at the limit or extreme."[102] So, while regular experience tries to make sense of the flows of everyday sensory perception, limit-experience tries to collapse the categories of standard sensibility, overloading it so that it transgresses its boundaries. A limit-experience is transgressive because it undermines the foundations of the rational subject and breaks the "limits of coherent subjectivity as it functions in everyday life."[103]

The genealogy of Foucault's notion of limit-experience can be traced back to Jünger himself. One of Foucault's main sources for his ideas about transgression and experience was Bataille, who for a time exhibited a certain Jüngerian influence. The concept of inner experience connects Bataille and Jünger. As Alexander Irwin has pointed out, Bataille, in the first draft of the chapter "War" for his unfinished project *La limite de l'utile*, draws on Jünger's war imagery from *Der Kampf als inneres Erlebnis*.[104] Martin Jay has called attention to the fact that Bataille was captivated by Jünger's language of ecstatic sacrifice on the battlefield. Even though Bataille's position was at odds with an activist stance such as Jünger's, in the end both authors considered the ultimate limit-experience to be death and the proximity of death.[105]

However, in Jünger's account of the conditions of subjectivity in modern technological society, the contrast between limit-experience and everyday experience transcends itself into new categories that revolve around the notion of instantaneity, such as the categories of danger and terror. A notable precedent for this intellectual operation is surrealism's "convulsive beauty" of sudden encounters in the modern urban landscape. Its aesthetic accepted "the marvelous" as a phenomenon that could take place amid commonplace objects and situations. But, because Jünger provided a detailed articulation of the role of instantaneous perception in the mediation between the limit and the everyday, his work more thoroughly accomplishes the transcendence of the opposition between the two notions of experience. In a sense, Jünger's notion of danger represents a secularization of the temporal structure of eschatological expectation based on imminence. In the eschatological mode of expectation, each moment is potentially the last. Jünger's account offers an analogous model, in which each moment potentially is the moment of accident or death. Additionally, Jünger's treatment of instantaneity accounts for another form of mediation between categories: the coupling of individual, subjective perception with collective, historical, and political experience. As both an aesthetic category and an expression of an "epochal" historical consciousness, Jünger's instantaneity represents a key element of this articulation between the individual and the collective.

In this context, it is important to note another of the charges Benjamin raised against Jünger in his review of *Krieg und Krieger*: that of aestheticism. To Benjamin, Jünger's "mysticism of war" represented the "uninhibited translation of the principles of *l'art pour l'art* to war itself," and, therefore, a relativization of the concrete sufferings experienced by victims in the war. But, although it is undeniable that Jünger's writings from this period feature an ethically dubious elevation of warfare into a form of aesthetics, this elevation does not encompass the full extent of Jünger's social criticism. In particular, Benjamin's accusation does not account for Jünger's reflections on the conditions of modern perception and the concomitant transformation of experience in a technological society. In fact, some of Jünger's ideas—such as the importance he gives to the category of suddenness—stand in a very close relation to some of Benjamin's own reflections on the fate of experience in

modernity, such as his analysis of shock—an alternative designation for terror—as a central category of perception.[106]

Jünger's aestheticism can, in this sense, be interpreted as an attempt to
create an alternative model of experience, one that could make sense of the
new circumstances of sensory perception after the traditional model of experience as continuity or uninterrupted transmission had been disrupted. A
fundamental aspect of this new model was the creation of an imaginary distance through language with respect to shock—a project analogous to that
of Benjamin in his writings on the Paris of Baudelaire. Indisputably, Jünger's
polemically mythologizes his own combat experience, but at the same time
he conceptually articulates those states of constant exposure to the proximity of death. Throughout his Weimar writings, Jünger transformed "trauma
into theory,"[107] thus helping to create a critical language for the description
and analysis of sudden and potentially disturbing experiences. Like Benjamin, Jünger attempted to construe the "destruction of experience" brought
about by modern warfare and urban life not as mere decline but, rather, as
the ground for an altogether new formulation of the concept of experience.[108]
In this new formulation, the "inexperiencible" became the new generalized
condition of experience, and shock—in Jünger's versions of instantaneity as
danger and terror—became a basic premise of the everyday.

Photography and the Representation of Danger

The birth of the worker as a new human type constituted another phase in the
crisis of individual perception that the historical rupture of the war brought
about. The worker had a productive aspect as the creation, out of the catastrophe, of a new subjectivity adapted to the peculiarities of a totally mobilized
world and its aesthetics of terror and danger. Jünger believed that embracing
these new categories as the "a priori of a transformed thought" would prepare
human sensibility for the extreme conditions of daily life in a technological
society.[109] These propositions, presented in essays such as "On Danger" and *On
Pain*, constitute the "sensory" counterpart to *Der Arbeiter*, insofar as they help
to articulate the features of a new sensorium for the worker. Jünger was convinced that one of the most salient expressions of this new sensibility of total
mobilization was photography, and that this fact accounted for the cultural
prominence that it had acquired during the Weimar era.[110] Photography was
the medium best suited to the emergence of the new subjectivity of the worker,

because it synthesized "the style of the era"[111]—that convergence of unbridled instinct and technical precision that resulted from approaching "the elemental" without sacrificing "the acuity of our consciousness." The photographic format of the snapshot captured the immediateness of the instantaneous with mysterious accuracy and spontaneity. It also had the power to record "the bullet in mid-flight just as easily as it captures a man at the moment an explosion tears him apart," and, as such, it was a telling sign of the confluence of the civilized and the barbaric. Such unheard-of capacity for uncannily detailed documentation was modern man's "peculiar way of seeing."[112]

In Jünger's analysis, photography's significance was not exclusively historical; it was both the cause and the symptom of a deeper change in the nature of human perception. Surprisingly in line with Benjamin's reflections on photography and cinema, Jünger asserted that the formal and technical characteristics of the medium were the model for a mutation in the perceptive faculties of humanity. Photography gave expression to the struggle of human perception to adapt itself to the new reality of ubiquitous danger. At the same time, it also confirmed that this metamorphosis had, in a way, already taken place.[113] In the process of molding the new sensorium of the worker, photographs constituted "instruments of a technological consciousness."[114] The type that had emerged from the war was expected to have a gaze analogous to the structural patterns of photography, imitating its precision, discipline, and detachment even in the face of the most extreme pain. Jünger predicted that the result of the adoption of this new kind of gaze as a "second, colder consciousness" would be the domestication of terror.[115] By bringing the "dangerous moment" to the level of consciousness and allowing the observer to adopt a distanced attitude toward risk, photography would "normalize" danger by avoiding the traumatic effects of shock.

In the early 1930s, Jünger was involved in the publication of a series of photobooks on social and political themes. He contributed texts and edited a number of such volumes, which explored crisis-related topics through the juxtaposition of texts and photographic images. Examples of such photobooks were *Luftfahrt ist not!* (*Aviation Means Trouble!*, 1928); *Das Antlitz des Weltkrieges. Fronterlebnisse deutscher Soldaten* (*The Face of the World War: German Soldiers' Experiences at the Front*, 1930), edited by Jünger himself; and *Die veränderte Welt* (*The Transformed World*, 1933), edited by Edmund Schultz, with an introduction by Jünger.[116] The photobooks—a sort of "visual companion pieces to *Der Arbeiter*"[117]—presented snapshot photography as the privileged form for the visual representation of historical experience during the Weimar period. They provided, moreover, a graphic complement to the prevailing language of crisis and in their own way performed shock through their very content and form.[118] Perhaps the most emblematic of these photobooks, *The Dangerous Moment* (*Der gefährliche Augenblick*), edited by Ferdinand Bucholtz in 1931, featured Jünger's essay "On Danger" as prologue. *The Dangerous Moment* represented a conscious effort to examine the "symptomatology" of a dangerous era by presenting snapshot images of accidents involving new technical inventions (e.g., car crashes, airplanes on fire), natural disasters, and scenes of political instability and war.[119] The photobook was a perfect example of Jünger's belief in the "therapeutic effects" of photography as a means for neutralizing traumatic experience. As Daniel Magilow points out, the photobook functioned as a sort of "training manual for dealing with the shock experiences of the modern world."[120]

Photography's "domestication of terror" had further implications. Because of the snapshot's "demoniacal precision," which exceeded the regular limits of human perception, the new relation of humanity to danger became "visible in an exceptional fashion."[121] The medium provided for the first time the possibility of an examination of that misty region of experience that he called terror, the zone that "extends between the recognition of the downfall and the downfall itself," and which coincides with instantaneity. Photography's technical precision presented a vicarious way to perceive what was hitherto impossible to perceive. If we are never able to experience the instant itself, and if what we call *the present* is something else taking place before or after the event, the promise of the snapshot, as interpreted by Jünger, would be entry into the blind spot of experience—that immediateness of lived temporality that Walter Benjamin called "the photographical unconscious" and that Ernst Bloch named "the obscurity of the lived moment."[122]

Instantaneity and the Reenchantment of the World

Contrary to other twentieth-century authors preoccupied with the fate of experience in modernity, Jünger, as mentioned earlier, did not simply oppose the "reified" temporality of industrialism to the "authentic" temporality of lived experience. In his interpretation, modern technology was not synonymous with the degeneration of humanity's perceptive faculties, but in fact constituted the ground for the creation of a sensorium for a new human type. Rather than lamenting the decline of experience in the modern world, the German author identified in the technological realm the formation of a space for a new type of experience. Jünger thus integrated the theme—shared by many of his contemporaries—of a "crisis of experience" with the possibility of an entirely new form of perception in the setting of technified, urban modernity.

Therefore, although Jünger's fascination with sudden temporality represented a search comparable to that of those authors who, in the first decades of the twentieth century in Europe, attempted to find a new kind of experience of lived temporality in reaction to the abstract, mechanized time of modernity—for example, Husserl, Heidegger, and Bergson—his thinking constituted, in the end, a critical turn away from these thinkers' original intentions and scope. Like these authors, Jünger explored the experience of lived time as an alternative to the disenchanted world of modernity, but, in contrast to them, he wanted to find this alternative precisely in the new possibilities implied by that radically mechanized setting. For Jünger, the machine-like universe of total mobilization did not represent the end of authentic experience; it was rather the environment that would promote the creation of a new *Erlebnis* based on unheard-of moments of extreme sensibility.

There is, consequently, also a significant contrast between Jünger's position and Max Weber's classic diagnosis of modernity. For Weber, the processes of modernization had brought to an end the belief in "mysterious, unpredictable forces" as agents in nature and society, with the implication that, in principle, everything could be controlled "by means of calculation."[123] The expansion of these social methods of rationalization had brought about the "disenchantment of the world."[124] For Jünger, on the contrary, the processes of rationalization carried out by a totally mobilized society implied the return of those primal energies, with renewed power, to the center stage of social life. The comeback of these forces, within new conditions, supposed a transformation of collective organization and individual perception that, by means of the creation of new forms of instantaneous experiences, "reenchanted" the world. As in Aragon's *Paris Peasant*, Jünger's reenchantment takes place through the deployment of the same cultural energies that had brought about the disenchantment in the first place: modernity, technology, and progress. Jünger embraced the "iron cage" of urban and technological modernity as the territory from which, out of the processes of disenchantment themselves, a new type of reenchanted culture and sensibility could be created.

In sum, the motif of instantaneity is, in Jünger's account, the means for a reenchantment of personal experience and social life. His concern with this temporal modality in its many variations—from the experience of shock on the battlefield to the dangerous moment of modern city life; and from the literary rendition of terror to the examination of photography as the medium for the recording of danger—defined the contents and tone of his Weimar writings. What Jünger's early writings introduce is, then, a dialectical understanding of modern time, based on the interweaving of technology and myth in fate and danger, which expressed itself through instantaneous forms of atemporal time consciousness. This reenchantment took place through a "transvaluation" of the main agent of the original disenchantment: the advancement of modern technology. But, in the end, what is transvalued in Jünger's early work is the ideology of progress itself. Originally a form of historicist time consciousness, progress, in Jünger, reveals itself to be, after the careful evaluation of its practical effects, nothing other than the vehicle for its antithesis. The antithesis to progress is an ahistorical form of the consciousness of time, which expresses itself in an awareness of crisis as a rupture of historical continuity and in the unheard-of proliferation of moments of instantaneous perception.

For Jünger, life in modern technological society presents itself as the perplexing juxtaposition of the most archaic and the most advanced. As crises open up gaps and holes in historical continuity, they inevitably produce fragments of historical temporality and the unexpected association of dissimilar historical formations, such as the sudden connections between technology and danger. In this *noncontemporaneity*, or juxtaposition of different historical times, the historicist consciousness of progress as a coherent process is disavowed; what prevail are the ahistorical energies of fate materialized in instantaneity.

CHAPTER 4

Ernst Bloch and the Temporality
of the Not-Yet

The philosophical oeuvre of Ernst Bloch (1885–1977) spanned several decades and encompassed an extensive range of intellectual questions and perspectives, from medieval thought and the problem of materialism to the question of atheism and the philosophy of art and music. The common issue that tied all these subjects together was Bloch's lifelong concern with the temporality of utopia. His work can be seen then as a series of variations on the single theme of utopian expectation and its ramifications in the fields of philosophy, theology, aesthetics, and politics. Among these variations, one stands out: his preoccupation with the temporality of the present moment—the instant, the now—as an expression of a utopian consciousness.

In this chapter, I analyze Bloch's contribution to the formation of the instantaneist regime of historicity by focusing on the evolution of Bloch's conceptions of instantaneous temporality during the crucial early stage of his intellectual trajectory—the twenty years between the publication of his first work, *The Spirit of Utopia*, in 1918, and his escape from Nazi Germany in 1938.[1] The era's shifting intellectual mood—from the catastrophic and simultaneously hope-inspiring atmosphere that reigned in the aftermath of the First World War and the Russian Revolution to the establishment and consolidation of the National Socialist regime in Germany and the imminence of another devastating war—would prove fundamental to Bloch's understanding of collective and individual temporality. Moreover, as in the case of Ernst Jünger, Bloch's conceptions of temporality can be seen as a series of reactions to the crises in historical consciousness and individual perception that the experiences of war, revolution, the Weimar era, and Nazism had brought about in German society.

Within this larger phase of Bloch's writing (1918–1938), I discern smaller discrete phases that generally correspond to episodes in German history during this same period: the aftershock of war and revolution; the agitated years of the Weimar Republic; and the rise of Nazism to power. In the first phase, Bloch published *The Spirit of Utopia*'s two editions (1918 and 1923) and *Thomas Münzer als Theologe der Revolution* (1921). Then Bloch turned to an experimental literary treatment of his philosophical concerns in *Traces* (1930). Next, he published *Heritage of Our Times* (1935), in the shadow of the political and cultural success of National Socialism. Additionally, Bloch's abiding interest in the phenomenon of avant-garde art, and its philosophical and social repercussions, culminated in the Expressionism Debate between himself and Georg Lukács in the late 1930s. In each of these phases of his work, Bloch formulated a particular version of the concept of instantaneous temporality that contributed to the conceptual framing of historical experience and individual perception in terms of the temporality of suddenness.

The Spirit of Utopia and the Darkness of the Lived Moment

Bloch's initial treatment of instantaneous temporality is found in his first work, *The Spirit of Utopia*, written between 1915 and 1916, published in 1918, and published again in 1923 in a second, revised edition. When Bloch described *The Spirit of Utopia* as a "*Sturm und Drang* book . . . against the War," characterized by its "revolutionary Romanticism" and its engagement with a new "revolutionary gnosis,"[2] he succinctly laid out the main contexts and traditions that informed his writing. It was a work written with war as its historical background and with revolution as its theoretico-political horizon. Framed amid the catastrophic aftermath of the First World War and messianic hopes sparked by the Russian Revolution, a temporality born out of the confluence of the instant with utopia predominated in this first stage of Bloch's thinking. After the outbreak of the war in 1914, Bloch was compelled to make sense of the secular apocalypse that seemed to be taking place before his eyes. Then, after the end of the war, Bloch again had to make sense of the German Revolution of November 1918, a conjuncture for the realization of socialism.[3]

In this historical setting, two major traditions acquired particular significance and became the main intellectual sources for *The Spirit of Utopia*. First, Bloch drew upon the lineage of anticapitalist Romanticism that critiques bourgeois civilization from the point of view of premodern premises, such as attacking money and profit and resisting the rationalization of individual and social life. In the work of Bloch (and Lukács, his close friend and colleague), this current of thought transcended its contradictions—its apparent tendency to adopt a reactionary position—and disclosed its full revolutionary potential. This is particularly the case in *The Spirit of Utopia*'s second edition of 1923, in which the young Bloch states a political stance closer to Marxism that clearly distinguishes his own radical Romanticism from the reactionary varieties.[4] Second, *The Spirit of Utopia* was a product of what Anson Rabinbach has called the "German-Jewish generation of 1914," that group of intellectuals who in the first decades of the twentieth century revived the politics of messianism. Based on belief in a coming renewal of the world after the total destruction, the messianic outlook implies a redemptive vision of fulfillment that is necessarily utopian. It supposes, too, an apocalyptic idea: that salvation will not come from any expression of historical immanence (such as the gradual change of evolution or reform), but from the manifestation of a revolutionary event coming from *outside* of history that will therefore disrupt its regular flow.[5] As early as 1908, when, along with Lukács, Bloch participated in Georg Simmel's seminar in Berlin,[6] he had begun reflecting on the "not-yet" (*noch-nicht*) concept that would become the key aspect of all his future work.[7] But it was the outburst of the war in 1914 that brought about the apocalyptic element in his thinking. Bloch's recourse to messianism was an attempt to make sense of the war's actual destruction. In Rabinbach's words, *The Spirit of Utopia* "announces the messianic redemption that awaits at the end of the war. . . . [For Bloch,] a redeemed world without death and suffering could only be found in the ruins of the old order."[8]

The defining characteristic of Bloch's involvement with Jewish messianism was an acute *antihistoricist* form of historical consciousness that expressed itself in an instantaneous vision of time. In a messianic vision the expectation of a sudden "apocalyptic event" prevails. It will disrupt history through the insertion of a caesura or radical division between a new present and the past. The redeeming event, Rabinbach writes, "can appear either as the *end of history* or as an event *within* history" but "never as an event produced by history." The revolutionary calendar of 1793 offers a secularized representation of that "decisive and total break"—a complete destruction of the past as the precondition for historical redemption.[9] Given the sudden nature of its occurrence, redemption is not "the product of immanent developments"[10] and is at odds with any vision of history as evolution or progress. Since neither individual will nor collective forces can call for its arrival, the messianic element "remains otherworldly," outside of time. Because messianic temporality represents a form of ahistorical time consciousness—sudden, unpredictable, and independent from the causality of history—it is visibly distinct from all the historicist forms of secularized eschatology, such as history or progress, which are predicated on immanent, linear, and continuous visions of time.

Bloch's thought, moreover, drew upon another defining dimension of Jewish mysticism: the belief in the connection between the messianic idea and everyday phenomena. As a result, during the war years—which he spent mostly in exile in Switzerland—Bloch began to associate aspects of individual cognition with the will to a radical transformation of the sociopolitical world.[11] The original form of this link was established through the discovery of an analogy—grounded on the notion of instantaneity—between the experiences of subjective temporality and collective historical time. *The Spirit of Utopia*'s underlying thesis represents a version of this analogy, as it affirms the existence of a relationship between instantaneous temporality and utopian thinking. Bloch supposes a close correlation between the experience of internal time and the utopian promise of a superior form of collective existence; that is, between the individual "self-encounter" in the "darkness of the lived moment," on the one hand, and the "problem of the We" (the external fulfillment of utopia), on the other. For Bloch, this correlation implies a two-step operation, in which the subjective interiority of the self-encounter expands toward the outer realm of utopian realization, which is the space of collective social life.[12]

The first step in this cognitive and existential process is what Bloch called the darkness of the lived moment (*das Dunkel des gelebten Augenblicks*), meaning the subjective involvement with instantaneous temporality. He described the concept more fully in the book's second edition in 1923. The instant is for Bloch an experience of "obscurity," a blind spot. The darkness of the moment depends on its abrupt "slipping away." The lived moment is what stands *too near* the subject; it can be recognized "only immediately afterward"—that is, after it actually happens. What we call the present moment is, then, something always already "gone by" once the perceptive faculties can grasp it: "When does one really live, when is one consciously present oneself in the vicinity of one's moments? As urgently as this can be felt, however, it always slips away again, the fluidity, darkness of the respective moment."[13]

In his phenomenology of the instant, Bloch thus emphasizes *nearness*.[14] Just like the motif of darkness, the recourse to nearness exposes Bloch's connection to mysticism. For Bloch, existence and identity themselves are forms of this obscurity, a kind of ontological "mist." This existential darkness constitutes the starting point of philosophy: the space where the self-encounter takes place. The self-encounter posits the fundamental philosophical problem of knowing the self, from which all the other philosophical questions derive. Bloch embraces, as Kierkegaard and Jünger did, a vision of temporality that establishes a distinction between *the instant* and *the present*. The instant itself cannot be fully and consciously experienced; it is merely the "blind darkness," the pure immediateness of the self. What we call the present is the mediated remembrance of an experience of instantaneity already vanished—the memory of what has just happened. We can thus affirm that, in Bloch's thinking, darkness occupies a place analogous to that of terror in Jünger's critical vocabulary: "We have seen that only just after it passes can what was experienced be held up in front of oneself, and it is organized spatially, in the intuited form of its simultaneity, which diverges from the flow, so to speak: half still just experientially real, and half already a juxtaposition of inactive content."[15] In this passage, Bloch takes the premises of Edmund Husserl's phenomenology of internal time consciousness[16] to a different level of signification, in which the regular experience of time reveals itself as the expression of a mystical and utopian message.

Bloch's notion of the darkness of the lived moment had a variety of sources. First, one can situate Bloch's early thought in the context of twentieth-century German social philosophy, in particular that of Simmel, who talked about life as a "dark substantial being."[17] This notion influenced Bloch's development of his concept of the darkness of the moment.[18] (It also influenced the young Lukács, who in *Soul and Form* states that "life is an anarchy of light and dark: nothing is ever fulfilled in life, nothing ever quite ends."[19]) Friedrich Wilhelm Joseph von Schelling's account of consciousness as an opaque phenomenon that results in the blind spot of the moment provides another inspiration.[20] Even more significant in this respect is the influence of Kierkegaard, from whom Bloch derived and adapted the notion of the self-encounter as that core of subjectivity where utopia confusedly lurks in the darkness of the moment.[21] Bloch's image of darkness, moreover, exhibits a kabbalistic provenance as it points to the self-encounter of the identity of God and the self in mystic union. For the young Bloch, "redemption" meant the irruption of the utopian into the sphere of subjectivity as an act of liberation, analogous to the gnosis that emancipated the soul from the prison of the body.[22] In this respect, *The Spirit of Utopia* joins Hölderlin's insistence that the "nearest" is the "most faraway," so that, in a dialectical reversal, absolute closeness opens subjectivity up to an intimation of the utterly other ("Near is / And difficult to grasp, the God."[23])

The darkness of the moment is also the foundation for another defining aspect of Bloch's thought: the philosophy of anticipatory consciousness and the "not-yet." Expecting, hoping, and waiting are for Bloch ontological acts inherent to being, which is open-ended and always in search of completion. In contrast to Heidegger's, Bloch's "being" is process, an intrinsically unfinished matter.[24] In the privileged moments of art, music and happiness, as well as in "days of expectancy," the not-yet manifests itself as a form of consciousness that transgresses the boundary dividing the present instant from the future. Hence, for Bloch, two simultaneous operations are performed within that time span we call the present: the already mentioned remembrance of the just lived moment; and a projection toward the unknown future of the not-yet. Both "obscurities" (what lies "too near" perception and what is "yet-to-come") merge in the darkness of the lived moment to constitute the "latency of the primordial secret" that moves within the now.[25]

One of the main differences between the 1923 second edition of *Spirit of Utopia* and the first edition from 1918 is the postulation of a link between the two categories of utopian anticipation: the darkness of the lived moment and not-yet-conscious knowledge. The rich conceptual plasticity of the instantaneity motif in Bloch's early work resides, precisely, in this identification of a two-way relationship between the temporality of individual awareness—the darkness of the lived moment—and that of utopian anticipation. The first dimension of this relationship is the insight that utopia—the objective dreams of a better future—is first intuited in the sphere of individual subjectivity. This insight would determine Bloch's overall approach to temporality and eventually ramify into other significant conceptual developments.

In Bloch's account, the future enriches the experience of time in the present.[26] His vision of temporality thus constitutes a sort of photographic negative of the Hegelian philosophy of becoming. The not-yet is the manifestation of the "positivity" of "nothingness," of something that has not yet become, but already exists in the here and now as anticipation. The darkness of the lived moment conveys a sense of incompletion that is also "a presentiment of our future freedom, an initial interference by the 'Kingdom.'" The not-yet, then, inevitably supposes the experience of a particular feeling—hope—as if it were integral to the very awareness of the now. In the feeling of hope, Bloch tells us, the obscurity of the present moment "brightens,"[27] because in it, by means of the presentiment of a coming freedom, the future becomes contemporary of the present.

The concept of the not-yet entails an image of time more complex than linear temporality. A "dark moment" pregnant with the possibilities of an unknown future implies a certain simultaneity of past, present, and future,[28] as well as an ensuing stratification of the now into several temporal layers: the now of the obscure and unmediated instant; the mediated present of the reminiscence of the just-lived moment; and the premonition of a future which has not become, but that is somehow already here by virtue of the not-yet. This multilayered reality of time is conveyed, for example, in what Bloch calls the *historical nonsynchronism* of music, that is, music's capacity to evoke the features of a future world that will be "the final expression of the Absolute."[29] In the 1930s, Bloch would develop the social and political dimension of the notion of noncontemporaneity and turn it into the central concept of *Heritage of Our Times*, his analysis of the historical nature of German society in the wake of Nazism's ascent to power.

The second dimension in the two-way relationship that establishes a link between the instant and utopia is the exploration of the *We-problem*, Bloch's term for the collective existence of community beyond the subjective and individual reality of the self-encounter. As previously discussed, the signs of utopia reside at the inner core of the darkness of the lived moment under the form of the not-yet. But, although these signs are first experienced individually, in the interior realm of personal subjectivity, they inevitably end up calling for their outer projection and realization into the exterior world. This realization demands the unity of all individual psyches into a certain common objectivity, which Bloch calls the external "world of the soul."[30]

Therefore, along with the We-problem, he addresses the significant question of political action. In "Karl Marx, Death, and the Apocalypse," *The Spirit of Utopia*'s final section, Bloch states that the task of any utopian politics is to devise a political program that could bring about the "practical" consequences of the connection between the darkness of the moment and the We-problem in a manner that transforms "everyday life's structural horizon." The final objective of this politics is the relocation of the utopian insight from "the inner sanctum onto a broader domain"—that is, from the visions of self-encounter to the shared space of a common political project. The creation of this space through a utopian praxis would represent the attainment of "real personal freedom."[31]

The discussion of the political implications of the not-yet concept brings up the issue of Bloch's Marxism and to what extent Marx was a defining influence on *The Spirit of Utopia*. In the late 1910s, Bloch was politically distant from orthodox Marxism. He defined his own political stance as "revolutionary democratic socialist" and was critical of Bolshevism's bureaucratic and authoritarian derivations. He found himself close to the positions of the USPD (Unabhängige Sozialdemokratische Partei Deutschlands), the Independent Social Democratic Party of Germany, which had been established in 1917 as the result of a scission within the Social Democratic Party (SPD) after left-wing groups that disagreed with SPD's position respect to the war formed their own organization.[32] Not surprisingly, this political distance was also an intellectual one. Many of *The Spirit of Utopia*'s most important ideas, such as the darkness of the moment and the concept of utopia itself, had in fact been formulated under the ascendancy of currents of thought different from Marxism, such as anticapitalist Romanticism, Jewish messianism, and some combination of both in a mystical anarchist position with an ethical dimension. Like Gustav Landauer, the Romantic anarchist thinker who participated in the Bavarian republic of councils of 1919, the young Bloch hoped for the establishment of a "mystical democratic community." In Bloch's version, the origins of this ideal can be traced back to the kabbalistic notion of *tikkun* (restoration), which is the conviction that the arrival of the Messiah will be accompanied by the total disruption of the world.[33] At the time, utopia mainly meant for Bloch the realization of a "fraternal community of equal men and women" who would organize themselves in cooperative structures to escape from capitalism's alienating conditions.[34]

Bloch's adoption of a Marxist political stance would not become explicit until the publication of *Thomas Münzer als Theologe der Revolution* in 1921.[35] Written right after the Russian Revolution and the outbreak of revolutionary events in Germany in the period of 1918–1919, *Thomas Münzer* reflects its author's recognition—under the influence of Lukács—that a vast historical transformation was imminent in Europe and that the ideas of Lenin and the Bolsheviks had merit.[36] The book is a sign of Bloch's decisive turn to Marxist ideas, especially his alignment with the theories of alienation and social revolution; however, it also represents a continuation of his interest in utopian and protorevolutionary forms of religious faith.[37] What results is an unorthodox "religious atheist" reading of emancipation opposed to more conventional, economistic interpretations of Marxism.[38] Bloch perceived a religious archetype of the revolutionary stance in the figure of Thomas Münzer, a sixteenth-century theologian and insurgent leader during the German Peasants' War, who wanted to establish a theocratic protocommunist society where private property and political authority were suppressed. He thought Münzer's sermons and activities of political agitation contained the seeds of a compelling "theology of revolution" as well as significant parallels with Marxism and the contemporary political situation. Bloch compared revolutionary Russia with the Germany of the Peasants' War, and saw the rebellious peasants led by Münzer as the forerunners of modern revolutionary groups, such as the Spartacists. By introducing a connection between earlier Christian utopias and contemporary social revolutions—in a gesture that anticipates Walter Benjamin's figure of *Eingedenken*, or "remembrance"—the *Thomas Münzer* book is Bloch's first application—"in reverse," as it were—of the not-yet principle to the question of historical heritage. This application entails a discontinuous, nonlinear vision of history that Bloch maintained throughout the evolution of his early philosophical thought. For Bloch, history is not in any sense identifiable with progress; it is, rather, "a hard and dangerous journey, a suffering, a pilgrimage, a stumbling, seeking the hidden homeland; full of a tragic confusion, in boiling, cracked by fissures, breaks, isolated promises, discontinuously charged with the consciousness of light."[39]

This closer approach to Marx's ideas explains best the differences between the 1918 and the 1923 editions of *The Spirit of Utopia*. Although the reference to Marx is already present in 1918, the 1923 edition is more systematic in its attempt to achieve a fusion with Marxism, perhaps as a result of Bloch's intention to align with more orthodox positions.[40] The end result of this fusion can alternately be construed as the introduction of a Marxist revolutionary dimension into the temporality of mysticism or as the insertion of a mystical formula into the Marxist dialectic. In any case, by virtue of the Blochian synthesis, the materialist philosophy of history received a utopian charge originating from unexpected religious sources.[41]

In 1924, a year after the publication of the book's second edition, Bloch would insist on the fundamental importance of the relationship between the notions of the instant and utopia in his review of Lukács' *History and Class Consciousness*. Contrary to Lukács, who sees actuality and utopia as opposites, Bloch asserts his conviction that "the now is in the end the only theme of utopia" and that utopia is the incognito presence in all actuality. What is hidden and unique within the now, Bloch continues, is precisely the driving force of utopia as anticipation.[42] Bloch's contribution to utopian thinking resides in this emphasis on temporality, which shifted the center of gravity of utopia from space to time. His utopianism puts aside the discussion of the abstract accounts of the ideal society and focuses instead on the concern with the present moment as the place where the presentiment of utopia dwells. As *Traces*—his book of philosophical and literary miniatures from 1930—will show, in Bloch's approach utopia can manifest itself even as an experience in the everyday,[43] especially in those instantaneous perceptions of an eschatological presence that confirm, in themselves, the coming of a better future.

It must be emphasized that Bloch, despite his repeated references to a "better future," was never a properly historicist thinker. As Klaus Vondung affirms, in periods of crisis, when expectations are destroyed, hope does not come from the future, but rather from "outside of history."[44] In Bloch's case, this "outside of history" was the instant's ahistorical present such that his idiosyncratic idea of the future was not the result of an immanent historical process or gradual unfolding. Since all moments are charged with the potentiality of utopia, the future for Bloch was, rather, a possibility latent at every instantaneous present. In Rabinbach's words, "Actuality and utopia do not constitute antinomies because the latter is always a potential within existence, an already present desire which, in attempting to transcend the given order of things, recurrently manifests itself."[45] Within instantaneism, it is the present—not the future (as in most versions of historicism) nor the past (as in traditionalism and certain variations of conservatism)—that claims a temporal priority, whether ethical, historical, or political. Feelings and emotions conventionally associated with the future, such as hope and waiting, have meaning only as dynamic forces in the present. In later stages of his intellectual development, Bloch would name this phenomenon "concrete utopia," which Arno Münster defines as "a praxis founded on the identification of the will of men and women to act with a view to the construction of a better world."[46]

In instantaneism, such primacy of the fleeting present is associated, in turn, with the historical dislocation of the linear sequence of past, present, and future. Bloch's *Thomas Münzer*, and Benjamin's theory of the dialectical image show that the logic of the not-yet concept is, in fact, reversible. The not-yet-conscious can, paradoxically, reside in a still-unfinished event of the past. This logic therefore postulates an antilinear temporality punctuated by moments of instantaneous ahistoricity—moments when the promises hidden in the fragments of the past are accomplished in the present.

Bloch's instantaneist utopianism belongs to what Rüdiger Graf has called the "temporal structures of expectation" of German culture after the end of the First World War.[47] Such temporal structures were founded on the already mentioned prewar assumption that Germany was going to enter a new era of transformation after the conclusion of the armed conflict. One of the main signs of their prevalence was the particular rhetorical strategy of the "locating the future in the present," manifest not only in Bloch's but also in Hans Freyer's and Karl Mannheim's images of utopia as "a mental force in the present that would usher in future change."[48] Bloch's utopianism was also symptomatic of another phenomenon identified by Graf: the correlation of crisis to the development of utopian schemes as a way out of pessimistic impasses. Since during times of crisis the present is perceived as turbulent, antihistoricist "visions of break and renewal" become more popular than "expectations of continuous development."[49] In these circumstances, such rhetorical figures that locate "the future as already existing in the present" become attractive.[50] In Bloch's case, this "place" of utopia in the present was connected, above all, with specific life forms and experiences.

The Search for "Traces"

In *Traces* (*Spuren*), his second major work from the interwar period, Bloch gave literary expression to some of the insights of *The Spirit of Utopia*. Written between 1910 and 1929 and published in 1930,[51] *Traces* explores those signs that, hidden in the midst of everyday life, provide the intimation of a utopian presence. Bloch's intention is to read these "traces"[52] of anticipatory consciousness as "units of interpretation"[53] in the process of universal becoming. The world of *Traces* is "an immense storehouse of figures," and the task of the philosopher is to interpret them as indications leading to a utopian condition.[54] Bloch's literary explorations took the form of the "thought-image" (*Denkbild*), which is a narrative form of reflection that, through the devising of "philosophical miniatures" and "textual snapshots," purports to find in apparently superficial phenomena the hidden meanings of political and cultural processes.[55]

As with *The Spirit of Utopia*, the sources for *Traces* go back to Jewish messianism and, particularly, to the mystical search for traces of lost meanings as a method of restoring an original state.[56] Nonetheless, there is a specifically modern aspect to this endeavor as well. What Bloch perceives as "ciphers of utopia" are always transitory, instantaneous aspects of the phenomenal universe—objects, details, and situations.[57] In the context of the Weimar Republic's urban modernity, this attention to the minute and the insignificant frequently transforms itself into, as Adorno calls it, an exercise in "naïve philosophy," a recovery of "sub-cultural elements" and the "openly trashy."[58] Bloch's appropriation of kitsch and the everyday situates him within the cultural debates typical of Germany during the interwar years, when, faced with the crisis of high culture after the collapse of Wilhelmine Germany, intellectuals attempted to find an alternative either in mass cultural production or the radical creations of the avant-garde.[59] Bloch's distinctly Baudelairean move is his recognition that the fleeting and the transitory—particularly in their manifestations in the setting of modern city life—constitute "the other half of art," that particular kind of beauty that perceives the eternal and which the French poet called *modernité*.

Inspired by the kabbalah and Baudelaire, Bloch created an original short prose form—a literary style as much as a thought process[60]—for exploring the mundane signs of utopian anticipation. These texts depict images of hope and waiting, premonitions of the unknown, and situations where the dream of a cause that "has not yet come" enters the world. They are pictures of the "half-ness" inherent in every now, such as the moment of parting, when the "Now that was stays with us" and "haunts us," or the sound of a knocking on the door, which reveals that being is a "being-in-half," susceptible to disruption by something that lies "beyond."[61] Other of Bloch's *Denkbilder* are supernatural allegorical stories of failed redemption in the midst of city life—the prostitute who was in fact an angel in disguise; the *passante* who, never reached, imposes on the observer the "idolatry of the unknown."[62] Some are redemptive, like the content of a greeting, the utopian but almost never noticed fact that "we simply assume it's going well."[63] These *Denkbilder* are prosaic experiences of wonder at simple things, at the most natural facts, such as existence itself; images, motifs, patterns, stories, that together form those "few symbols of arrival" with which the "homelessness of people on this earth goes on." All these experiences are part a larger, all-encompassing process, the dispersed signs that in the end will converge: "The traces of the so-called Ultimate, indeed even of a hospitable Becoming, are themselves just the imprints of a Going that must still be gone into the New. Only very far beyond will everything that one meets and notices be the Same."[64]

From all of these experiences of utopian anticipation in the details of the everyday, one stands out as particularly pregnant with the not-yet: the feelings, emotions and sensations related to the very experience of having an identity, of being oneself. The mystery of our nearness is grasped in some of those insignificant moments, when the now of identity takes place.

Sometimes that now is a pure negativity, an absence—an enormity that eludes us. When something utterly important we have to say slips our mind, that slippage is the true time of personal identity, the "hole we've fallen into." As the title of one of Bloch's *Denkbilder* asserts, one is always "incognito to oneself." The now of identity is dark precisely because we are in it: "Not only the Now where we always find ourselves is still dark. Instead it is dark above all because we, as the living, find ourselves in, quite properly are, this Now."[65]

Bloch's attempt in *Traces* to reconstruct a new form of experience among the ruins of the traditional patterns of cultural activity and sensory perception is in some ways analogous to Jünger's treatment of technological society. Bloch's search for meaningful, redemptive details in the waste products of mass culture and the commonplace situations of urban city life represents a counterpart, informed by Jewish mysticism, to Jünger's perception of the artificial environment as an opportunity for a specifically modern kind of experience. Another similarity between Jünger's and Bloch's treatments of instantaneity is their common identification of a blurring of the regular distinctions between ordinary and extraordinary experiences of time. In analogy to Jünger's postulating danger as the a priori of a "transformed thought," Bloch postulates the existence of a "messianic a priori" of perception: an intent toward the not-yet that touches on every aspect of human awareness. If for Jünger the ubiquity of accidents and political turmoil had turned risk into the new standard of perception, for Bloch the very configuration of everyday temporality is, in itself, a manifestation of the most exceptional, which by definition lies in a "no-place"—utopia.

Traces is also the work where Bloch's relationship with the avant-garde developed into a more explicit engagement. Ever since the publication of *The Spirit of Utopia*, Bloch had been one of the first thinkers to give a philosophical foundation to avant-garde art and literature.[66] In his first major work he had discussed expressionist art as the privileged repository, in both its formal structures and thematic contents, of an eschatological expectation. Expressionism, he believed, was indistinguishable from a "utopian orientation"; its products represented "the most immediate space before the dwelling of a coming *Parousia*."[67] In *Traces*, however, Bloch went a step further; he left behind the mere thematization of expressionism and turned the book into an avant-garde artwork in its own right. Bloch's use of the figure of the thought-image, for example, constitutes a persuasive literary equivalent of the montage technique. He was applying the principle of the image in surrealism—that the best images are the ones that connect the two most distant realities—not to poetry, but to philosophical prose, as in the passage where he describes the contradictory spectacle of a proletarian eating a lobster.[68]

Throughout the 1930s, this creative engagement would prove to be a lasting intellectual gesture, as montage became the centerpiece of an extensive debate between Bloch and Lukács on the political and cultural significance of the avant-garde. As will be discussed later in this chapter, Bloch presented a vehement defense of montage as the art form that best captured the fractures in subjectivity and dislocated historical experiences typical of modernity. For Bloch, montage also had the capacity to bring about anticipatory consciousness, as the juxtaposition of dissimilar materials created a space for the imagination of utopia and the integration of the unexpected into the artwork.[69]

In his discussion of the darkness of the lived moment Bloch had privileged nearness as the defining characteristic of instantaneity, but in his theoretical treatment and creative use of montage he privileged the sudden. In Bloch's next major work of the 1930s, suddenness would become, in turn, the critical framework for the understanding of the historical present.

Heritage of Our Times and the Theory of Noncontemporaneity

The publication in 1935 of *Heritage of Our Times* (*Erbschaft dieser Zeit*)[70] inaugurated a decidedly new stage in Bloch's thinking about temporality. The phases that had produced *The Spirit of Utopia* and *Traces* were concerned with utopian anticipation and the darkness of the lived moment, but this new one was preoccupied with the forms of historical consciousness and the kinds of political action that were to be derived from those forms. The context for Bloch's ideas was no longer the atmosphere of apocalyptic expectation brought about by military defeat in the war and the triumph of revolutionary politics in Russia, but a German society that, impoverished by economic crisis, felt trapped within the sensation of cultural breakdown that the Wilhelmine Empire's collapse engendered.

The question of historical continuity and discontinuity became a common problematic during these years, and it found expression as a cultural motif in the language of crisis and rupture favored by such authors as Jünger, Benjamin, and Bertolt Brecht. The perception prevailed that it was no longer possible to appeal to once unwavering points of reference, such as reason, language, or the self.[71] Moreover, the vertiginous political rise and arrival to power of National Socialism during the early 1930s did nothing but intensify this sense of cultural crisis and political discontinuity. In Germany, the new had taken the form of Nazism, which led to perplexity and confusion, especially among the ranks of socialists.

Heritage of Our Times was Bloch's response to this situation. He wanted to make sense of Nazism's sweeping cultural and political success, German socialism's setback, and the socio-cultural configuration that made both developments possible. Fundamental to Bloch's effort was a new framework for discussing the problem of "cultural heritage." This notion had to be transformed, so that it could make room for the specific forms of continuity and discontinuity that predominated in postwar German society. In particular, this enlarged version of the idea of heritage had to be able to integrate the products of what the general Marxist stance considered periods of "cultural decadence." Postwar Europe itself was deemed an interregnum era between the disintegration of classical bourgeois civilization and the coming, but yet uncertain, birth of a new socialist culture.

Bloch's reaction to the crisis in cultural continuity consisted in the formulation of a new concept that complicated the model of linear, one-dimensional historical time: *Ungleichzeitigkeit*—"nonsynchronism" or "noncontemporaneity."[72] He explains *Ungleichzeitigkeit* in "Noncontemporaneity and Obligation to Its Dialectic," the central essay of *Heritage of Our Times*. It presents a sociological and historical vision based on the temporality of the present moment: the now of noncontemporaneity. Bloch perceived that the patterns of German society in the 1920s and 1930s did not match the conventional interpretation of class struggle as a univocal conflict between two clearly identifiable groups—the proletariat and the bourgeoisie. He found something quite different: an "unfinished past" of social and economic relations typical of previous epochs, which coexisted with the industrial capitalist forms of production and exchange. The result was a social whole characterized by the presence of groups that were juxtaposed in space, but that existed, both subjectively and objectively, in different historical times. Bloch writes: "Not all people exist in the same Now. They do so only externally, through the fact that they can be seen today, but they are thereby not yet living at the same time with the others."[73] Social temporality was, therefore, not homogeneous, but qualitatively differentiated according to a number of factors, such as class belonging, geographical location or cultural mind-set. Bloch concludes that a reform in the regular understanding of the Marxist-Hegelian dialectic is necessary. A more accurate image of the convulsive German social reality would be that of a "multi-layered dialectic" in which different temporalities are superimposed on the same historical now. Decidedly antihistoricist, Bloch's theory of noncontemporaneity opposed the simple discourse on the "decadence" of bourgeois culture, which was embedded in the orthodox Marxism of his time. But it equally opposed the optimistic historicism of inevitable progress, of which Stalinism was an incarnation.

Heritage of Our Times shares with *The Spirit of Utopia* a preoccupation with "untimeliness" in modes of time-experience—from the not-yet of utopia and the obscure lived moment to the noncontemporaneity of the different groups that formed Weimar society. In fact, noncontemporaneity was already present in seed form in *The Spirit of Utopia*, where Bloch refers to the "historical nonsynchronism" of music. Furthermore, noncontemporaneity depends on a spatial representation of temporality that can be traced back to the young Bloch's early formulations on the darkness of experience. If "space is the form of a perceived coincidence of objects or events in time,"[74] then certain spatiality is at work in Bloch's concepts of simultaneity. In the darkness of the moment, for example, this spatiality accounts for the "contiguity" of the unmediated "blind spot" of instantaneous experience and the actual, post-fact awareness of that experience. In Bloch's characterization of noncontemporaneity, this same "spatial coincidence," whose graphical form is juxtaposition, is key to understanding his historical moment.[75]

Bloch sees Germany as "the classical land of noncontemporaneity"[76] because, until 1918, the country had not undergone an equivalent of the British or French bourgeois revolutions. In the concrete sociopolitical circumstances of Weimar Germany, this noncontemporaneity expressed itself in three main "trends" that "ran crosswise in the Now": youth and its longing for a leader; the peasantry and its rootedness in the soil; and the impoverished urban middle class and its willingness to be seduced by a blood-based gospel of the corporate state.[77] The core of the noncontemporaneous tendency was the "impoverished center," the petite bourgeoisie that had suffered the consequences of economic crisis and tried to compensate for its loss of status with the embrace of an ideology of home, soil, and nation, and an attachment to superstitious beliefs, such as "the ghostly Jew and the new Baldur."[78]

Communist militants were bewildered: why did the middle class, who had been objectively "proletarianized" by economic crisis, not follow the seemingly "rational" path of joining socialism, and instead support a movement, Nazism, that did not represent a real danger to capital? For Bloch, the answer to this question was to be found in fascism's ability to identify and exploit the noncontemporaneous elements of German society.[79] Nazism had devised an "intoxicating" ideology of "urban peasants" and "Saxons without forests" who succumbed to the "lure of an irrational drive"—an appeal to neopaganism, the archaic, the primitive—congenial to their own nonsynchronous features.[80] This ideology obscured the impoverished center's connections with the proletariat, nurtured the petite bourgeoisie's false consciousness, and mobilized noncontemporary contradictions in the service of capitalism.

However, the usability (*Verwendbarkeit*) of these nonsynchronous features—and this is one of Bloch's main points—was not an exclusive attribute of fascism. In fact, it was a problem of Marxist criticism and politics too. The irrational elements that appealed so much to nonsynchronous groups contained an objectively explosive social energy that could not be simply dismissed as "reactionary." As Rabinbach notes, Bloch was one of the few observers that realized that fascism "filled a void at the heart of Enlightenment rationality—a vacant space (*Hohlraum*)."[81] That Nazism had filled this void through an appropriation of these irrational elements did not mean that they could not be also exploited from a progressive perspective. The noncontemporaneous contradictions were inherently ambiguous and, as such, potentially recoverable for revolutionary intentions. There were elements in the heritage of previous times—for example, a powerful anticapitalist stance, and concepts such as life, soul, nation, and Reich—that could indeed be "occupied" and mobilized against the forces of reaction. With the proper "dialectical hook," many of these images could be "helped along" from a socialist perspective. In his call for the critical appropriation of the irrational and seemingly reactionary, Bloch establishes yet another connection to his earlier writings, in this case *Traces*' searching for lost meanings even among the "trash" that resulted from the disintegration of bourgeois culture.

Bloch's concept of noncontemporaneity was a cultural and political program for German socialism as much as it was the postulation of a new theoretical problem for Marxism. The cornerstone of this political program was the establishment of an alliance of social groups led by the proletariat. The proletariat, Bloch writes, bears a privileged relationship to the *present*. As a class, it assumes the truly *contemporaneous* contradiction to the capitalist *now* as well as to the *future*, for only its revolutionary action can activate the seeds of futurity dormant in the now.[82] The political counterpart to the theoretical problem of the "multi-layered dialectic" is the mastering of the noncontemporaneous elements of peasants and petite bourgeoisie by the proletariat. The solution to this problem implies a simultaneous operation of cultural criticism and political organization. That solution would be the achievement of a distinction between mere "stale modes of being" and those historical images and concepts that are "non-past" because they "never wholly became" and are therefore "lastingly subversive and utopian."[83]

In *Heritage of Our Times*, Bloch identifies a series of such historical images and concepts, which contain genuine revolutionary material, but which National Socialism hijacked and perverted into reactionary symbols. Such is the case of two figures that had historically stimulated revolutionary consciousness in late medieval and early modern Germany: the savior-liberator and the Third Reich.[84] These emblems of redemption emerged from the German Peasants' War as images of emancipation. Bloch had touched on that war in *Thomas Münzer*, where he had posited the existence of a dialectical relationship between past and future in which the nonfulfilled promises of the past could be used as sources of revolutionary energy in the present.[85] The misappropriation of traditional images of liberation by Nazism could only happen because German socialism had already neglected the radical inheritance of the Peasants' Wars, leaving the space clear for the Nazis to stream into these "vacated, originally Münzerian regions" of history and of the mind.[86]

Bloch derives a characteristic vision of history from the existence of these noncontemporaneous contradictions and their potential mobilization for progressive ends. According to this vision, "history is no entity advancing along a single line, in which capitalism, for instance, as the final stage, has resolved all the previous ones; but it is a *polyrhythmic and multi-spatial entity, with enough unmastered and as yet by no means revealed and resolved corners.*"[87] One can notice a parallel between Bloch's image of history—the acknowledgment of the persistence of previous, so-called backward historical formations in the present—and Sigmund Freud's image of the psyche as a multilevel object in which the events of the past keep operating on the present. The real affinity, however, is with Benjamin's theses on the philosophy of history, as Bloch shares with Benjamin a nonlinear and antihistoricist view of historical time—in which different epochs coexist simultaneously in a complex, multilayered present, the formations of the past are still actively alive, and the prefigurations of the future are intensely, if confusedly, at work.

Despite all their political differences, one even finds a certain similarity between Bloch's idea of history and Jünger's realization that in modern industrial societies the primeval powers of fate are operating through the moments of danger brought about by modern technology. This shared approach is the intuition that progress does not necessarily involve a cancellation of the past, as in an irreversible evolution, but that, rather, it represents an incongruous process, so that sometimes the newest machinery and equipment can paradoxically put us back into the precarious existential situation of primitive man. Beyond political divides, the Weimar consciousness of crisis seems to entail an awareness of its own temporal condition as defined by deep historical contradictions. This critical attitude toward linear, progressive visions of history and their inability to make sense of one's temporal experience ties Bloch, Benjamin, and Jünger (and, with him, the "conservative revolutionaries") together. For these authors, the true sense of the temporality of Weimar Germany was to be found in some form of simultaneity: the juxtaposition of fragments originating from dissimilar time frames, whether the persistence of the past, the new developments of the present, or the intuitions of the future. The classical landscape for this image of history was the modern metropolis, and the aesthetic metaphor for its inner logic was montage.

Bloch's theory of noncontemporaneity was also a response to a theory of time (the philosophy of history) that comprised all possible varieties of historical temporality: progress and decline, continuity and crisis, gradual transition and sudden birth, the permanence of tradition and the irruption of the new. Bloch's interpretation dissociates the experience of time from any particular temporal modality (past, present or future) and in fact encompasses all of them in a conflicting (yet coherent) montage-like image. In terms of the history of instantaneous temporality, Bloch's theory of nonsynchronism complexifies our understanding of the historical now through the realization that what we call the present is indeed a multifaceted compound of different temporalities, whose most distinguishing characteristic is *temporal dissimultaneity* in a setting of *spatial coexistence*. Just as in his earlier elaboration of the present as the darkness of the lived moment, in nonsynchronism the time of the present is always already a temporality of delay and anticipation, the mediated reverberation of a past occurrence and the intuition of something that is yet to come.

The Expressionism Debate

Heritage of Our Times was Bloch's response to the cultural and political success of National Socialism, but it was also Bloch's forceful declaration of his position on the historical significance of avant-garde art and literature as a cultural formation. Several years after its publication, this *prise de position* would become the conceptual basis for Bloch's intervention in one of the most significant aesthetic polemics of the interwar period in Europe: the Expressionism Debate (*Expressionismusdebatte*). Although a number of authors participated, the impassioned argument between Bloch and Georg Lukács, his friend and colleague from earlier years, took center stage.[88]

Given the multiple cultural connotations of the term *expressionism* and the importance of expressionist painters and writers in the German tradition, Bloch's discussion of it in *Heritage of Our Times* and in the debate concerns something more than painterly or literary style. Bloch's used the term *expressionism* to mean different things. Sometimes it refers to the style of the arts and literature of the painters and authors typically associated with the expressionist movement—such painters as August Macke and Franz Marc and such poets as Gottfried Benn and Georg Heym. But sometimes it has a broader sense and is interchangeable with the notion of avant-garde in general, or it emphasizes a particular aspect of the avant-garde aesthetic, such as montage and the practices of artistic juxtaposition typical of surrealist and Dadaist works. As Adorno put it, Bloch's conception of expressionism is related to the wide-ranging "idea of breaking through the encrusted surface of life."[89] What was at stake in the Expressionism Debate was then a "contest over the historical meaning of modernism in general,"[90] as well as a displaced dispute on fascism as a cultural form.[91] The debate entailed a deeper reflection on the relationship between art and politics and the place of aesthetic representation in the social whole. Just as happened with Baudelaire's musings on modernity a century earlier, the 1930s polemics on expressionism became a dispute over the nature of historical time, in general, and over the nature of German modernity, in particular. From the point of view of the images of temporality, the Debate was also an argument over the significance of instantaneity as a conceptual framework for the theorization of social and cultural mediation. Against Lukács' celebration of the uniform time of continuity in a coherent social whole, Bloch's position was the passionate defense of the avant-garde temporality of sudden rupture as the privileged repository of aesthetic value and historical content.

The Expressionism Debate was one manifestation of a much larger discussion over the role of artistic style in socialism. In the Soviet Union the debate found a dramatic analogue in the anti-Formalist campaign of 1936–1939, launched amid the show trials and intensified political repression of the Stalinist Great Purge. A wave of detentions ensued that imprisoned a number of artists and writers—including the German Ernst Ottwalt, an author of experimental novels who had been condemned in 1932 by Lukács himself for his "fetishization" of facts. The Party's official newspaper, *Pravda,* published repeated attacks on works bearing any association with an avant-garde aesthetics, most notably Dmitri Shostakovich's opera *The Lady Macbeth of Mtsensk.* As Katerina Clark has pointed out, the campaign against Formalism were part, along with the political purges and the birth of Stakhanovism as model for labor efficiency, of a broader shift in the "rhetorical strategies" of Soviet culture.[92] Although a Soviet affair, the anti-Formalist campaign had important international reverberations in the cultural debate over socialism and the avant-garde.

As Peter Zudeick has pointed out, Bloch's posture in the Expressionism Debate was representative of his main political contradiction in the 1930s. Whereas in his writings on art and aesthetics Bloch adopted a staunch anti-Stalinist stance against the cultural theses of official communism, in his journalistic work of the time he presented an enthusiastic defense of Stalinism as a general political outlook.[93] Although Bloch never became an official member of the German Communist Party, by the 1930s he had grown politically close to the party's pro-Soviet line. In 1917, Bloch still believed that a "true" revolution would originate in the West, but in the late 1930s, after the defeat of the Western left by fascism, he had given up all expectations on that possibility, and became convinced that, for the foreseeable future, the Soviet Union would remain the only point of reference in the international revolutionary process. Incompatible with his own humanistic, nondogmatic Marxism, Bloch's Stalinist position only makes sense in strategic geopolitical terms. He appeared to believe that criticizing the Soviet Union would weaken the fatherland of communism and its resistance against fascism.[94] Accordingly, in his articles from the period—published in the antifascist magazine *Die Neue Weltbühne*[95]—Bloch refuses to admit the real state of the Soviet Union at the time of the Stalinist purges and rather supports the official thesis of a Hitlerian-Trotskyist alliance used to condemn and persecute the opposition.[96] Bloch himself would later invoke a sour encounter with Adorno in New York after the latter had read his "Stalin essays."[97] In these texts, Bloch celebrates Stalin as a revolutionary leader[98] and actively supports the Moscow Trials from 1936 to 1937 as a legitimate form of defense of the Soviet state against the internal enemies who allegedly wanted to implant "German fascism in Moscow."[99] But Bloch's Stalinist commitment in the late 1930s was notably inconsistent with the importance given to the motif of instantaneous temporality in his works from the period. Stalinism represents a historical stance drastically opposed to instantaneism; it was, after all, a radical form of historicism expressed in the belief that the present moment does not hold any meaning of its own, but is entirely subordinated to an abstract goal residing in an unknown communist future.

The core of Bloch's outlook with respect to expressionism had been already expounded in "Poetry and Hollow Space," an essay from 1931 in which Bloch argues that reflection on contemporary cultural artifacts had to acknowledge that the disintegration of bourgeois culture had generated a world of fragments and unexpected juxtapositions: "How curious is this world: bourgeois decay did not only break up the contextual surface with a network of cracks, but at times it seems that, through those very breaks in what had been up to now the everyday surface of things, one might glimpse the union (as if in marriage) of the most separate, and the estrangement (demonic or utopian) of the most familiar."[100] Bloch calls for the devising of a "dialectical avant-garde" that would appropriate and "refunction" these fragments, subverting classic masterworks as much as the products of popular culture, such as pulp novels and fairy tales. This rebellious effort of reutilization, while working within the "hollow space" of a disenchanted world, can unleash utopian energies and anticipate the "dream of the actual," that is, the hidden utopian tendencies of the present. Bloch thus presents the structure of instantaneous temporality—with its rejection of harmonious transition in favor of conflict and shock—as defining the structure of the central aesthetic operation of the era.

In 1934 Lukács published his essay "Expressionism: Its Significance and Decline" in the Moscow-based journal *Internationale Literatur*. In the essay, Lukács presents expressionism as an irrationalist tendency typical of decaying bourgeois culture—a mere manifestation of decline. Expressionism, he writes, uses words only with an "expressive" purpose in mind, leaving aside their fundamental "referential" function. This movement features, then, a pure subjectivism that borders on solipsism, a "mental escape from reality" that is the accomplice to a disconnection between ideology and reality.[101] Therefore, expressionism not only thwarts the understanding of the social whole as a coherent totality—a requirement for adequate criticism and revolutionary transformation—but also nurtures the irrationalist tendencies that resulted in the cultural formation of fascism.[102]

"Marxism and Poetry," Bloch's intervention at the International Writers Congress for the Defense of Culture in Paris in 1935, was a preliminary reaction to some of the ideas stated in Lukács' expressionism essay. In his speech, Bloch disputes the alleged affinity of the conservative realist stance with the "official" aesthetic posture of Marxism because, from a Marxist perspective, reality is indeed coherent, but only as "mediated interruption." A truly Marxist-dialectic account would acknowledge the process-like nature of the world and the fact that reality is "still open, [and] therefore objectively fragmentary." This mediated understanding would necessarily lead to the historical truth of montage as the most accurate way of depicting the dislocated condition of the social world.[103]

Bloch's attempt to reconcile Marxism with interruption is reminiscent of early German Romanticism aesthetics of the fragmentary. As Friedrich Schlegel did a century before, Bloch identifies a connection between the process-like, open-ended nature of reality with the constant production of dislocated fragments, which create, in turn, the occasions for experiences of instantaneity. History is, as a result, always unfinished, "incomplete," composed entirely of fragments looking for its signification in the sudden encounter with other fragments. Benjamin's philosophy of history is another version of this theoretical use of the aesthetics of the fragmentary. From that perspective, "authentic" historical time is formed only at the moment of the sudden juxtaposition of a fragment of the present with a fragment of the past. The general proposition of Bloch's and Benjamin's visions of discontinuity would then be that instantaneity and the idea of history as a process are interrelated.

The question of the nature of the social whole—or, in Lukács' terminology, the *totality*—would become a principal aspect of the discrepancy between Bloch and Lukács over the historical meaning of expressionism. The discrepancy can be traced back as early as 1924, when Bloch published his review of Lukács' *History and Class Consciousness*. In the review, Bloch had already asserted his interpretation of totality as an essentially unfinished, open-ended reality.[104] The contest over the avant-garde added a new layer to their disagreement: the problem of "cultural tradition" in the phenomenon of fascism. According to Bloch, the perception of social reality as a coherent whole evaded the important fact that "cultural heritage" was the result of a complex dialectic of all sorts of materials, even those originating from periods of decline.[105]

This additional layer of disagreement between Bloch and Lukács would become explicit in the passages of *Heritage of Our Times* devoted to montage, which contain Bloch's chief exposition of his stance on the avant-garde. For Bloch, montage is an example of those products of bourgeois disintegration that include something more than mere decay. The creative techniques of montage—the breaking off in parts of a certain context; the combination

of these parts into new figures; the "process of interruption"[106]—had configured an "image-explosion" that counters the realist aesthetic of the "coher-
ences of the surface." By giving expression to "the irregular," montage also
contains a promising contradiction "composed of genuine Today, of both
Today and concrete Tomorrow." This method, then, is not only a precise
instrument for the comprehension of the historical now,[107] but also the
reserve of a vast surplus of utopian potential—"a kind of crystallization on
the chaos that has come, attempting to mirror in a bizarre way the coming
order."[108] All montage art dramatizes a caesura. By recreating the experience
of a sudden break, it provides a vantage point from which to reflect on the
larger experiences of collective historical rupture. Suddenness is then the
key to the recreation of these utopian insights—the light shining through
the cracks of an incomplete "totality."

In his essay "Expressionism, Seen Now" on the *Degenerate Art* exhibition
organized by the Nazis in Munich in 1937 (which had mainly featured works
by expressionist artists), Bloch further explains the nature of expressionism
with respect to the cultural heritage.[109] Expressionism had presented the problem of cultural inheritance anew, because it had achieved something that no
other art form had before: the integration of the archaic into the utopian, and
of the past into the "unknown obscurity" of the future. After expressionism,
the association of art with the past could no longer stay the same. The epi-
gonic copying and repetition of the objet d'art had been exhausted and would
simply no longer do. The montage technique constitutes the heart of this
new relationship of aesthetic creation with the art of previous eras, because it
refunctions past art forms as useful elements in present-day explorations of
the future. In montage, the past "explodes," as it were, into full relevance for
the actuality of the present. Expressionism had thus transformed the problem
of cultural inheritance into a problem of contemporaneity.[110] Bloch's ideas on
montage and expressionism constituted, indeed, an aesthetic counterpart to
his theory of noncontemporaneity; his whole approach represented a comprehensive intellectual alternative to Lukács' homogenizing totality of capitalist synchronicity (that is, the belief in the existence of a single, univocal
historical now) as articulated in *History and Class Consciousness* as well as in
his writings on the avant-garde.[111]

The Expressionism Debate proper began in 1937 in the pages of *Das
Wort*—a Moscow-based journal meant as a forum for antifascist writers in
exile. Under the pseudonym of Bernhard Ziegler, a disciple of Lukács, Alfred
Kurella, published an essay attacking expressionism. Largely inspired by

Lukács' 1934 piece, the essay sparked an intense debate on the connections between fascism and avant-garde art. Bloch's response to Kurella's piece, "Discussing Expressionism," appeared in *Das Wort* in 1938. There, Bloch addressed Lukács directly and defends the relevance of avant-garde experiments with fragmentation, interpolation, and montage. Since the world is not the closed reality that Lukács imagines, he argued, formal experiments are true to a world-picture already chopped to pieces, whose deeper nature is *interruption*.[112]

Lukács' reply, "Realism in the Balance," was published that same year and focused on Bloch's justification of the avant-garde as a poetics for a time of crisis. Crisis, Lukács wrote, is precisely the time when the unity of the whole is reaffirmed. "Subversive tendencies," such as expressionism, do not tackle anything but superficial matters and thus fail to perform the role of art and literature, which should be the representation of bourgeois society's objective whole. For Lukács, to argue for the value of expressionist artworks, as Bloch does, is a mistake, since it amounts to taking the subjective experience of disintegration typical of mental life in the "age of imperialism" for "the thing itself." Distorted perception is not an ultimate truth, but a mere moment that, if properly mediated, becomes subsumed in the totality. The task of such mediation is exactly what montage fails at. A photomontage, Lukács argued, is a superficially aesthetic artifact; it is alienated from the mediations of the objectively real and has in the end "the same sort of effect as a good joke."[113] The motif of suddenness, for Lukács, far from being a revelation of historical truth, was at best a secondary epiphenomenon whose only significance was to vanish as it assimilates back into the whole.

In 1940, Bloch would take up the question of mediation in times of crisis in the essay "The Problem of Expressionism Once Again."[114] In the midst of a crisis-ridden era, Bloch asserts, "reality" is not attainable by the "broad-calm" mediation of realist art and literature that Lukács defends. What is required is the "abrupt" mediation of montage, whose aesthetic and social effects go beyond the limits of formalism and subjectivism. Only montage is capable of finding the manifestations of the new in the gaps and holes—the "hollow spaces"—that have emerged as a result of capitalist crises and the collapse of the old society.[115] Or, in other words, nothing but the sensibility of sudden rupture would do for creating a form of art and consciousness truly attuned to the historical rhythm of the era.

With his vindication of montage in the Expressionism Debate, Bloch had adopted a number of significant intellectual positions. First, he was making the case for a mode of aesthetic representation that he deemed more multi-faceted and precise than the static notion of reality entailed by the conventional approach of realism. Second, he was asserting that suddenness and abrupt juxtaposition were the emblems of the age, signs that simultaneously provided a reflection on and an intervention in the era's structure of socio-historical temporality. In Bloch, as in Baudelaire, aesthetic forms are the avant-garde of social reality and thus prefigure political transformations to come. Third, he was providing a philosophical commentary on the nature of historical experience during the Weimar years and the beginning of the Nazi era. His characterization of this experience was as a series of unexpected juxtapositions of contrasting forms of social consciousness. The simultaneist aesthetics of the avant-garde was a subtler form of realism, a more sophisticated mimesis, precisely because the interwar years had turned out to be such an unending source of fragmentary material and striking associations.

Occasioned by the hectic succession of war, military defeat, economic collapse, political agitation, and the rise of Nazism to power, Bloch's plea for avant-garde art throughout the 1930s can indeed be construed as the author's response to the same "crisis of experience" identified by such Weimar contemporaries as Jünger and Benjamin. Like Jünger, Bloch did not equate this crisis with an "end" of experience as such; he interpreted it instead as the beginning of a *new* kind of experience. For Bloch, it was as if the years of the war and the Weimar era had represented a series of extreme conditions and exceptional situations that, by the sheer force of its radicalism, had ended up creating the patterns for new human experience based on the fragmented logic of montage-like perception.

This intuition is best expressed in "Montages of a February Evening," a piece from *Traces*, in which the distinctions between montage and human perception, as well as art and nature, become blurred. In the text, Bloch describes the atmosphere and landscape of an urban winter evening as if the formal features of montage were not characteristics of a man-made work of art, but qualities of the landscape itself, as well as mechanisms organically embedded in the structure of perception. In a February evening like that there is "no more transition"; reality seems to imitate art of a particular kind: avant-garde art and symbolist poetry. Bloch writes: "What was familiar, separates; a proclaimed landscape appears, the habitual juxtaposition drops out in the aforementioned night in Berlin 1932. Conversely, very distant elements reveal themselves in this stark outlook as assembled, as by the exquisitely strange syzygies of a poem by Rimbaud."[116] In this montage-like perception, nature reveals itself as a sort of experimental manifesto that proclaims the overcoming of old aesthetic standards:

> A transformed vision notices new ensembles in nature, and not only for vision is the city transported on such nights: Nature in person wanders out of the appointments of the Romantic century, even the mythological centuries. There remains beauty, but it upsets us; it has nothing clearly before it, then the collapse of the old spheres, the montage of once impenetrable zones behind it. . . . The dislocation of such an evening is montage, separating what is near, bringing together what is furthest, as intensified in paintings like Max Ernst's or de Chirico's.[117]

This dislocated perception had always been there, in the nature of things, but avant-garde poetry and art intuited it and the social transformations of modernity have now illuminated it: "This shattering in things is certainly objectively there, even if the more or less accurate sense for it has only awakened now, brought about by the social earthquake. As we said, artists and poets were the first to register direct connections between things so distant."[118] It is significant that this period of Bloch's work both began and concluded with an identification of the role of instantaneity in the patterns of human perception. From the "darkness of the lived moment" in *The Spirit of Utopia* to the montage-like experience alluded to throughout the debate on expressionism, Bloch presents the features of the instant, either its nearness or its suddenness, as essential for the accurate description of human consciousness in modernity.

Ernst Bloch's Instant

The scope of Bloch's thematization of instantaneous temporality reveals the notion's capacity to integrate a wide range of conceptual dimensions. From the subjective experience of the darkness of the moment to the historical element of utopia, and from the disjointed beauty of montage to the politics of messianic expectation, Bloch's instant presents itself as simultaneously individual and collective, political and aesthetic. Accordingly, the trajectory of the Blochian concept of instantaneity between 1918 and 1938 can be inserted in a number of traditions to illuminate different aspects of its intellectual role.

It is possible to read Bloch's engagement with the instant, for example, as an element in the larger project of making sense of the origins, contents, and fate of the socialist movement in the first decades of the twentieth century. For Bloch, the categories associated with the now presented themselves as the conceptual key to understanding crucial aspects of this history, such as the role of radical change and messianic time in the imagery of socialism or, later on, the demand to complicate the Hegelian dialectic with new layers of temporality.

It is also possible to interpret Bloch's involvement with instantaneity as an attempt to come to philosophical terms with the phenomenon of the avant-garde. Forms of sudden temporality, such as the ones featured in works of montage, proved to be for Bloch a fundamental tool for integrating the artistic production that resulted from the new experimentation into broader historical and philosophical frameworks. This is the case, for example, with the interpretation of the cultural "fragments" left behind by the disintegration of bourgeois culture as "traces" where an intuition of utopia could be perceived. Another instance is the understanding of noncontemporaneity as the extrapolation of the aesthetics of montage into the field of historical consciousness—a conceptual innovation that could justly be regarded as an avant-garde theory of history and the experience of historical time. The contribution to Marxism that this theory entailed had no precedents in the history of this current of thought. It brought about an integration of cultural heritage into the Marxist corpus, as well as a reform in the critique of ideology. It could no longer be conceived of as a mere "unmasking," but also had to be interpreted as the "uncovering and discovering" of the "unrealized dreams, lost possibilities, abortive hopes—that can be resurrected and enlivened and realized in our current situation."[119]

Above all, the repercussions of Bloch's foundational establishment of a connection between the lived moment and utopia would manifest themselves in a distinctive vision of history. Mark Lilla has pointed out that there is a certain critique of modernity that believes in an overcoming of the Enlightenment by means of a "leap out of history."[120] The original aspect of Bloch's vision is that, through the gestures of utopian anticipation and hope, he makes of this leap out of history a fundamental part of history itself. By devising a formula for the expression of messianic expectations, Bloch turned the leap into a constitutive aspect of historical awareness in general. For Bloch, every instant's temporal pattern replicates the larger structure of history and contains within its actuality the complete historical development of a utopian expectation. As in Jünger's writings on terror, the temporal structure of the present in Bloch's philosophy of utopia is a historically informed matter. But whereas Jünger's temporality of terror depends on the modern prevalence of danger in a totally mobilized society, Bloch's approach to temporal perception mobilizes revolutionary hope as one of the concerns of his age.

Bloch's approach to instantaneous temporality represents, for all the above reasons, an attempt to recognize some of the philosophical problems posed by early twentieth-century modernity in Europe. Bloch's thinking situates Baudelaire's "present moment"—the French poet's identification of the present as a historico-ontological condition—at the heart of the philosophical endeavor, for in Blochian thinking the question of the now becomes in a certain sense identical with the question of being itself. The philosophy of Bloch thus presents itself as a sort of post-Baudelairean thought in which *transitoriness*—or, in Bloch's terms, the temporal incompleteness implied by the not-yet—is postulated as a specific form of relationship to historical temporality. This logic of modernity—the incessant appearance of the new—bears the traces of a revelation of the ontology—the way of being—of reality as such.

To make sense of Bloch's temporality of the new, then, is to observe the essentially unfinished structure of reality. Every aspect of the social and historical world is "in process" and endures the mark of the not-yet. Every being is in a certain sense a fragment, and therefore involves a utopian content— that is, the promise of its complete realization in the future. And if reality is fragmentary, then all efforts at cognition and acts of perception are, in a certain way, montage. It remains Bloch's accomplishment to have formulated this understanding of historicity out of his intellectual elaboration of the series of turbulent events that took place in Germany between the end of a world war and the beginning of a second. Bloch's particular configuration of modern time and perception remains one of the era's most original accomplishments—an enduring expression of Weimar, not only as a time period but also as a distinct style of criticism and thought.

CHAPTER 5

Walter Benjamin and
the Now-Time of History

The work of German thinker and literary critic Walter Benjamin (1892–1940) is marked by his lifelong concern with the present as a category of philosophical analysis. From his early writings as a student concerning the historical situation of youth in the late Wilhelmine era to his last known manuscripts devoted to the impact of the rise of fascism on conventional understandings of history, the concepts associated with the instantaneous temporality of the now—such as suddenness, rupture, and shock—occupy a prominent place in the theoretical framework of Benjamin's intellectual production. His conceptualizations range from attempts at coming to terms with the experience of catastrophe in its military and political forms; to the philosophical elucidation of the consequences of the capitalist economy on culture; and the project of devising a new critical language for examining the effects that the extreme stimuli of urban life exerted on the human psyche. From among them arise three main areas where Benjamin focuses on the notion of the instant and its variants. The first is Benjamin's preoccupation with the fate of experience in the modern, technological world. He responded to this fate through a critical exploration of suddenness as a category of experience, an exploration that crystallized around the notion of *shock*. The second is Benjamin's project of developing a style of writing about historical events from the point of view of *discontinuity*, which was articulated in a series of concepts related to the simultaneity of historical correspondences, including the historical index, the now of recognizability, and the dialectical image. The third is Benjamin's intention to formulate a standpoint for thinking about history different from both historicism and progress, and which concretized itself in the sketch of an eventist philosophy of history based on the notion of the now-time (*Jetztzeit*).

By following this thematic rather than chronological presentation, I intend to give a sense of the conceptual nonlinearity of Benjamin's own "constellations," which resist assimilation into a strictly sequential or evolutionary schema.

Benjamin's intellectual itinerary, from his analysis on the new forms of shock-like experiences to his elaboration of an antihistoricist vision of historical events, represents the most accomplished expression of the instantaneist historicity regime during the Weimar era. Benjamin systematically crystallized the motif of sudden time into a coherent articulation of instantaneity as a figure of historical consciousness, on both the individual and collective levels. He presented a thorough formulation of instantaneous time consciousness as a theoretical response to a historical period marked by discontinuity. In his response, instantaneity provided a form of mediation between the personal realm of subjective perception and the space of political action, and his resulting vision of temporal experience presented a powerful alternative to historicism.

The Experience of Shock

The first instance of Benjamin's treatment of instantaneous temporality is framed within his larger preoccupation with the nature of experience and perception in the novel setting of technological, urban society. Like his contemporary political antagonist Ernst Jünger, Benjamin identified the years of the First World War and the birth of the Weimar Republic as an era of unprecedented rupture in historical continuity, which was closely mirrored in an analogous break in subjectivity represented by the irruption of multiple instances of sudden perception in the everyday. Mass mobilization and death on the battlefield, as well as urbanization, industrialization, and the use of new forms of transportation and communication in the civilian space imposed challenging demands on the human sensorium. As Georg Simmel had observed, the modern metropolis—with Berlin as one of its emblematic examples—became the scenario of a profound dislocation of individual mental life, brought about by a proliferation and intensification of abrupt stimuli.[1] This dislocation turned the first decades of the twentieth century into the "paradigmatic breeding ground" for experiences of the unexpected and the unknown.[2] Along with Simmel, Benjamin distinguished himself as one of the main theorists of this new variety of extreme experience, for which he turned to concepts related to sudden temporality, and, most prominently, to the figure of *shock*. Benjamin's appraisal of the transformation in the nature of experience under the aegis of instantaneous temporality, however, would remain highly ambivalent. He alternated, sometimes even within the same text, between, on the one hand, an insistence on the erosion of experience and the anaesthetizing of human perception brought about by modern technology and, on the other hand, on that same technology's emancipatory potential and ability to create the conditions for a new form of experience.[3]

"Experience and Poverty," from 1933, and "The Storyteller: Observations on the Works of Nikolai Leskov," from 1936, are two representative essays that contain Benjamin's first accounts of the "destruction of experience" by modern capitalism and technology. After the war, Benjamin writes in "Experience and Poverty": "Experience has fallen in value, amid a generation which from 1914 to 1918 had to experience some of the most monstrous events in the history of the world. . . . Wasn't it noticed at the time how many people returned from the front in silence? Not richer but poorer in communicable experience?"[4] Benjamin interprets the war as the most powerful expression of a larger modern trend, by which a "completely new poverty has descended on mankind": the denaturing of experience. The "new poverty" signals the end of traditional "long experience" (*Erfahrung*), the continuity in the collective transmission of common knowledge and wisdom from generation to generation. This atrophy in long experience was commensurate with a disquieting decline in the communicability of experience—the "ability to share experiences"[5]—epitomized in the obliteration of the art of storytelling. Experience and storytelling had "fallen in value" as the result of a process activated by the war, when soldiers returned from the battlefield in silence, unable to communicate their experience.[6]

Nevertheless, elsewhere, Benjamin himself provides the elements for a different, genuinely dialectical reading of this story of decline, which recovers the culturally productive elements of the crisis. To a great extent, Benjamin's interest (which Ernst Bloch notably shared) in fragmentation as an aesthetic motif capable of conveying the deeper historical significations of so-called eras of cultural decay provided the theoretical context for this dialectical interpretation. This interest in fragmentation had been informed by art historian Alois Riegl's notion that certain periods' "will to art" is expressed through works characterized, precisely, by their broken, unfinished nature. Benjamin identified one such period in the German Baroque, whose *Trauerspiel*, or "mourning play," was the subject of *The Origin of German Tragic Drama*, Benjamin's *habilitationsschrift*, published in 1928. There he established a revealing parallelism between the cultural products of the German Baroque and the fragmented works of expressionist and avant-garde montage.[7] Accordingly, because the cultural productions of the avant-garde, with its techniques of juxtaposition and montage, embodied the aesthetics of fragmentation, Benjamin interpreted his own time as another such period.[8] Avant-garde montage, Benjamin believed, incarnated the crisis in subjectivity. But, at the same time, it appropriated the elements of this crisis—the dislocation of perception and the ruptures in the continuity of experience—in order to produce a new kind of "modern beauty" and a new, restored form of experience.

Benjamin's interest in the cultural and historical possibilities of the aesthetics of juxtaposition can be traced back to his connection, in the early 1920s, to avant-garde circles and ideas. This encounter left a deep intellectual imprint on his work and, particularly, on his ideas about the search for a new experience mediated by technology. Benjamin's association with experimental art began in Berlin in 1922, when he became acquainted with a group of avant-garde artists and authors, who came mainly from the ranks of Dadaism and constructivism: László Moholy-Nagy, El Lissitzky, Hannah Höch, and Raoul Hausmann, among others.[9] The contents and compositional style of One-Way Street, Benjamin's "montage work" from 1928, embodied the productive tension that he believed characterized avant-garde montage.[10]

One-Way Street represents the vibrant literary manifestation of Benjamin's ambivalent attitude toward the fate of experience in the setting of modern urban metropolis. It is composed from the point of view of the aesthetics of juxtaposition, in which the central literary devices of instantaneity and suddenness expose both the discoveries and the shortcomings of the new formulas of modern perception. Like Bloch's Traces (1930), Benjamin's book is written as a series of "thought-images," or Denkbilder. They reveal the influence of the avant-garde, as well as a particularly surrealist sensibility for sudden encounters with disparate materials in an urban setting. One-Way Street, for example, presents reading and writing as activities analogous to walking down a street: the stroll of a literary flaneur. What results from this mental promenade is a montage of images and sensations, a mixture of street signs and childhood memories, aphorisms and advertisements that, according to Bloch, introduces the "revue form" in philosophy: a form of reflection based on the juxtaposition of contrasting images.[11]

One-Way Street announces, in line with Hungarian artist and photographer László Moholy-Nagy's reflections on the creation of a "new human sensorium," the possibility of a new form of collective experience mediated by

technology. In his 1922 essay, "Production-Reproduction," published in the
Dutch journal *De Stijl*, Moholy-Nagy argued that there would be progress in
humankind's "functional apparatuses" of perception only if these are "trained
to the limit of their capacity" by experimental art; after this experimentation,
art will be capable of producing "new, so far unknown relations."[12] This is the
spirit of *One-Way Street*'s concluding fragment, "To the Planetarium," where
Benjamin presents modern technology as the central element for a reconstitution of the ancient experience of collective union with the cosmos. Significantly, Benjamin frames the implications of this union with recourse to the
Blochian terminology of the "darkness of the lived moment," when he writes:
"It is in this experience alone that we gain certain knowledge of what is nearest to us and what is remotest from us, and never of one without the other."[13]

The possibility of this renewed union with the cosmos, Benjamin adds,
had been made "terribly clear" by the catastrophe of the First World War and
the revolutionary upheavals that followed it: "In the nights of annihilation of
the last war, the frame of mankind was shaken by a feeling that resembled the
bliss of the epileptic. And the revolts that followed it were the first attempt of
mankind to bring the new body under its control. The power of the proletariat is the measure of its convalescence."[14] There is a remarkable similarity
between Benjamin's reflections in "To the Planetarium" and Jünger's theses
on total mobilization as the process of the exhaustive and nonstop deployment of a society's resources for war purposes, which I discussed in Chapter 3. For both authors, the war represented an episode in the simultaneous
destruction and collective reorganization of society, after which the nature of
human interaction was utterly transformed. Whereas Jünger named this new
form of intercourse between humanity and the cosmos mediated by industrial technology total mobilization, Benjamin understood it as an attempt to
control humankind's new collective "body." But both authors coincide in the
appreciation of war, political upheaval and modern industrial technology as
the occasion for the unexpected return of primeval forces. In a tone strik-
ingly similar to Jünger's, Benjamin concludes his book referring to the new
historico-technological situation as a "state of continuous emergency" that
imposes "the sense of an imminent crisis requiring a decision."[15]

In his 1929 essay "Surrealism: The Last Snapshot of the European Intelligentsia," Benjamin further explores the notion of a collective body susceptible to undergoing a communal experience.[16] The essay also represents
Benjamin's first attempt at offering a theorization of the experience of shock

in modernity. The concept that fuses together both intellectual concerns is the foundational notion of *profane illumination*, identified by Benjamin in emblematic works of surrealism, such as Andre Breton's *Nadja* and Louis Aragon's *Paris Peasant*. A profane illumination is that kind of sudden epiphanic moment that, while preserving the revelatory aspects of traditional religious, and especially Catholic, mysticism, represents a fundamentally materialistic experience resulting from an "anthropological inspiration."[17] Examples of profane illuminations in surrealism are the experiences of love, dream, and—in a foreshadowing of the future Benjaminian formulation of an interaction between fashion and the dialectical image—"the outmoded."[18] Surrealism's innovation resides in its project of winning "the energies of intoxication for the revolution"—that is, of mobilizing the revolutionary potential of significant individual experiences for collective political purposes. Profane illuminations create that "image space" where subjectivity opens up to the experience of a "bodily collective innervation" brought about by the new technological organization of society.[19]

Some of Benjamin's most momentous writing from the 1930s constitutes a gradual unpacking of these ideas on the "innervation" of the collective by means of experimental art and modern technology.[20] This is certainly the case with "Little History of Photography" (1931) and "The Work of Art in the Age of Its Technological Reproducibility" (1935–1936), the two pieces in which Benjamin introduces the *optical unconscious*, a crucial concept associated with temporal instantaneity. The optical unconscious is that zone of obscurity hidden from regular perception, which is illuminated by the operation of the camera in film and photography. This is photography's revolutionary dimension. Its utmost precision allows it to capture, for the first time in history, the secret life of instantaneity, that "tiny spark of contingency, of the here and now" that lurks in the subjects of the camera. A sense of futurity inhabits the "inconspicuous spot" of immediacy registered in the picture, and is rediscovered in retrospect by the observer's gaze.[21] Just as psychoanalysis had discovered the contents of the instinctual unconscious, photography now exposes the hidden strata of the optical unconscious: those dimensions of reality that "lie outside the *normal* spectrum of sense impressions."[22] The "quite unknown aspects" that occur within the limits of the instantaneous present constitute the optical unconscious. "We have no idea at all what happens during the fraction of a second when a person actually takes a step," Benjamin writes, but photography, through the techniques of slow motion, enlargement, and close-up, "reveals the secret."[23] There is a clear affinity between Benjamin's ideas on the optical unconscious and Bloch's notion of the darkness of the lived moment. It is as if Benjamin were stating that the existential significance of photography resides in its ability to have us penetrate the "darkness of the moment" by the means of a "technical illumination" capable of exploding "this prison-world with the dynamite of the split second."[24] In Blochian terminology, Benjamin's optical unconscious represents the technological expression of the "not-yet-conscious," that zone of the mind pregnant with futurity.

In "The Work of Art in the Age of Its Technological Reproducibility," Benjamin continues to develop ideas on the creation of a new kind of experience. There he identifies the function of film as the training of the spectators in new forms of shock-like perception. By virtue of its narrative structure based on the constant variation of images (as opposed to the fixed image of painting), film presents itself as the art form that most closely corresponds to the changes in perception and intensive stimuli that every modern passerby undergoes in big-city traffic.[25] Film liberates the effect of physical shock and, in so doing, cultivates the human mind through the demands of extreme sensory stimulation.[26] Here another noticeable agreement between Benjamin and Jünger comes to the fore—namely, their shared conception of media as a training device for the human sensorium in a shock-ridden era. Benjamin's musings on film's political function with respect to shock closely parallel Jünger's interpretation of photography as the medium through which perception could habituate itself to the omnipresence of "danger."

Benjamin's theory of film constitutes the cornerstone of the German author's "technological utopianism"[27]—that is, his belief in technology's potential to reconstitute a modern, enlarged form of experience. In Benjamin's theory, film represents a new form of communicability that integrates within it the principle of interruption in order to create a transformed version of storytelling. That transformation is accomplished, however, through a new subject of experience that is no longer individual but collective,[28] such as the audience in the cinema or the crowd in city traffic. It is significant that in Benjamin's articulation of an altered notion of experience, the idea of instantaneous temporality—in the form of modernist, distorted perception—operates as the bridge between individual subjectivity and communal innervation. The aforesaid camera's entrance into the darkness of the moment constitutes a collective operation, realized through the body of spectators in the cinema and the act of shared simultaneous reception.

Integral to this operation was the destruction of the "aura" of the work of art, brought about by the "technological reproducibility" of film. The aura is that "strange tissue of space and time: the unique apparition of a distance, however near it may be,"[29] which establishes a privileged relationship between a unique object and the concentrated attention of a single spectator. The end of aura represented the end of works of art designed with individual perception in mind. Post-auratic forms of art, such as film, were to be received by the masses in an "instructive and critical" exercise of collective reception. This change in the function of art is what Benjamin understands by its "politicization."[30] In Benjamin's writing, the posing of a new collective subject of experience is inseparable from the posing of a subject of revolutionary praxis. The aim of revolutions is to accelerate the process of adaptation to technology already begun by cinema: "Revolutions are innervations of the collective— or, more precisely, efforts at innervation on the part of the new, historically unique collective which has its organs in the new technology."[31] This identification is revelatory of instantaneous temporality's capacity to fuse together the historical and the subjective, as well as the political and the aesthetic, in a unitary figure of experience.

Benjamin's preoccupation with sudden shock fits within a larger early twentieth-century intellectual tradition of thinkers who aimed to provide a new interpretation of the role of temporality in subjective experience, authors like Henri Bergson, Edmund Husserl, and Martin Heidegger.[32] As with these thinkers, the attempt to reexamine the philosophical implications of lived temporality led Benjamin to a detailed study of the present moment as an existential point of reference. For Benjamin, the main manifestation of the experience of the present was the perception of shock that characterized the life of the senses in the era of art's mechanical reproducibility. But, owing to two fundamental features, Benjamin's shock was qualitatively different from the modalities of the present analyzed by Bergson, Husserl, or Heidegger. These two features are shock's suddenness and its collective dimension. Benjamin's closest peers in the examination of the lived present are to be found, rather, in Jünger and Bloch, as the conceptual structure of shock in Benjamin's thought is analogous to that of Jünger's "terror" and Bloch's "darkness of the moment."

Benjamin presents a more systematic conceptual treatment of the idea of shock in one of his last published writings: the 1940 essay "On Some Motifs in Baudelaire." The essay belongs to the larger constellation of texts, notes, and drafts that revolved around the unfinished *Arcades Project*.[33] By the beginning

of the 1940s, the reflections on the shock experience—from Simmel's analyses of mental life in modern metropolises to surrealism's adoption of "convulsive beauty" as an aesthetic program—already constituted a sort of modern
tradition in its own right. Benjamin's examination of the shock concept in
"On Some Motifs" took the form of a reconsideration of that tradition's origin
in the work of Charles Baudelaire.

For Benjamin, shock is the "hidden figure" informing Baudelaire's lyric
poetry. The French poet's verses display an unprecedented "change in the
structure of experience,"[34] according to which the "isolated experience"
(*Erlebnis*) of exposure to shock has turned into a new norm of modern sensibility.[35] Shock thus displaces "long experience" (*Erfahrung*) as the conventional framework for human perception. Benjamin interprets the isolated
experience of shock as a sudden happening—a "gap in experience"[36]—filtered
by consciousness and different from the unmastered stimulus that passes
directly into the unconscious mind.[37] Shock, for Benjamin, is the everyday
form of extreme perception that cannot be integrated into any narrative or
cumulative notion of experience. In *Beyond the Pleasure Principle* (1921), Sigmund Freud had established the correlation between memory and consciousness, which is that only what escapes consciousness enters into the deeper
layers of the unconscious.[38] In Benjamin's reading of Freud, consciousness
represents a protection of the psyche against the extreme stimuli so prevalent in modern city life. The impressions worked out by the conscious mind
would, therefore, not penetrate into the space of long experience, but remain
as mere *Erlebnisse*, "isolated experiences."[39]

Baudelaire's poetry expresses this transformation in the patterns of experience by identifying a connection between the figure of shock and the coexistence with the urban masses. Baudelaire's poems do not explicitly refer to
the multitude in the modern metropolis but are nevertheless written as if
assuming that the reader's experience has been already determined by the
"standardized, denatured existence" of the city crowd.[40] One example of this
ghostly presence/absence of the masses in Baudelaire is the sonnet "À une
passante," from *Les Fleurs du mal*. It depicts the fleeting notice of an anony-
mous woman in the midst of a never mentioned, but implicitly active, roar-
ing urban crowd and the instantaneous love "at last sight" that it incites. This
scene is the archetypal deployment of the figure of shock. The city dweller
stands in complex, contradictory relationship with the masses. The multitude arouses feelings of "fear, revulsion, and horror"[41] in the observer, but
at the same time it contains fascinating elements, such as the mysterious

passerby. The interaction of the individual with big-city traffic is another prototypical representation of this conflicting but highly stimulating experience. In Benjamin's words: "Moving through this traffic involves the individual in a series of shocks and collisions. At dangerous intersections, nervous impulses flow through him in rapid succession, like the energy from a battery. Baudelaire speaks of a man who plunges into the crowd as into a reservoir of electric energy."[42] For Benjamin, the Baudelairean crowd thus constitutes a prefiguration of the public at the cinema. In the encounter with hectic traffic and tumultuous streets, the mid-nineteenth-century individual received a training in shock analogous to that of film's formal principle of interrupted perception.

According to Benjamin, the "sensation of modernity" par excellence for Baudelaire is, precisely, the experience of being "jostled by the crowd." But this sensation could only be had for a price, which is "the disintegration of the aura in immediate shock experience."[43] In other words, the crisis in perception implied in the shock experience—just as its counterpart, the crisis in representation entailed by the technical reproducibility of works of art—supposes, like the reproducibility of cinema, the breakdown of the "aura." The aura is the set of associations that "seek to cluster around an object of perception,"[44] and which implant this object into the space of memory and long experience. The coexistence with the crowd is the unmistakably post-auratic experience, resembling photographs in its sudden structure. By means of this operation of destruction, Baudelaire bestowed on isolated, immediate experience (*Erlebnis*) the weight of long experience (*Erfahrung*). In Giorgio Agamben's words, Baudelaire responded "to the expropriation of experience by converting this expropriation into a reason for surviving and making the inexperiencible its normal condition"; and in Benjamin's interpretation of Baudelaire, this "destruction" became the "commonplace" experience of modernity—it was turned into "man's new abode."[45] Being exposed to the isolated experience of shock "in all its nakedness"[46] is one aspect of what Baudelaire called *spleen*—a state determined by a sensibility for suddenness. According to Benjamin: "In spleen the perception of time is supernaturally keen. Every second finds consciousness ready to intercept its shock."[47]

Such is the temporal framework for the new kind of experience that Benjamin finds in the poetry of Baudelaire. Benjamin's theses on the French poet, again, closely resemble Jünger's musings on twentieth-century danger and horror as the phenomena that had devastated the traditional understandings of experience only to later institute themselves as the crucial figures of a new form of perception. This resemblance is another telling sign of the convergence between their accounts of modern technological society, despite their political differences and even antagonism, and it is a symptom of their shared belonging to a historicity regime based on instantaneity.

The Dialectical Image

Benjamin's reading of the shock figure in the poetry of Baudelaire was an integral part of a larger project: the fashioning of a style of historical thinking based on the temporality of sudden rupture, which would constitute an alternative to conventional historical visions, such as historicism and the "vulgar" Marxist and social democratic ideology of progress. This aim of developing a discontinuous view of history constitutes the second area of Benjamin's involvement with instantaneous temporality. The fashioning of this style is one of the most significant expressions of the instantaneist chronotope during the Weimar era because it involves, explicitly, the coinage of new language capable of expressing the new historical consciousness based on the instant.

Benjamin's search for a sudden style of historical writing is inseparable from the author's most ambitious intellectual endeavor, the *Arcades Project*, with its interest in the role of "the new" in modernity. Although the *Arcades* remained unfinished,[48] Benjamin left a series of notes, drafts, and essays— some of them published during his lifetime—that make it possible to discern the work's overall content and intention.[49] In the *Arcades*, Benjamin focuses on the Paris of the Second Empire in order to elaborate a far-reaching interpretation of the conditions of experience in capitalist urban modernity. Benjamin wants to show that the penetration of the commodity economy in all the realms of life in nineteenth-century France had devalued the human environment and incited a particular form of historical experience: the "eternal repetition" of massively produced and commodified reality.[50] In this world of eternal recurrence brought about by the commodity form, only the new could alter the "consciousness of time's empty passage."[51] But, at the same time, it was precisely the mass-produced artifact that eternally reappeared under the guise of "the newest."[52] This dialectic of the new and "the ever-same"—as expressed, for example, in fashion and its cycles—defines nineteenth-century capitalist modernity. According to Benjamin, this constellation of concepts, images, and experiences received a definitive historical expression in the poetry of Baudelaire, which, in turn, had found its "historical signature" in the idea of eternal return as articulated in the works of Friedrich Nietzsche and the French revolutionary Louis-Auguste Blanqui, author of *L'Éternité par les astres* (1872), a work that prefigures Nietzsche's doctrine of the eternal return.[53]

Benjamin conceived the original plan for the *Arcades* in the late 1920s, with Louis Aragon's *Paris Peasant* and its ideas on the existence of a "modern mythology" of urban city life as a major influence.[54] In the mid-1930s, after criticisms by Theodor W. Adorno and his encounter with Bertolt Brecht, Benjamin reframed his original surrealist inspiration within the coordinates of a more explicit materialist perspective that emphasized the project's historical and sociological dimensions. Benjamin now stressed that, whereas an author like Aragon persisted within "the realm of dream," in the *Arcades* he looked for a dialectical treatment of "dream images" in order to find the "constellation of awakening."[55] Every epoch, Benjamin writes, entertains a "dream image" of its successor. In this image, the latter epoch "appears wedded to elements of primal history—that is, to elements of a classless society."[56] The image of "awakening" designates the act of reentering the dream from the perspective of its realization, that is, a dialectical transcendence, or "sublation," of the opposition between dream and reality: "Dialectical thinking is the organ of historical awakening. Every epoch, in fact, not only dreams the one to follow but, in dreaming, precipitates its awakening."[57]

The origins of Benjamin's "informal espousal of Marxism" date back to 1924, when he met the Latvian communist theater director Asja Lacis and read Georg Lukács' *History and Class Consciousness*.[58] The reading of Lukács' book would prove highly influential on Benjamin's general outlook, as it provided the German critic with an "epistemological guarantee of wholeness,"[59] later evident in the *Arcades'* conceptual plan. Benjamin's linkage of the atrophy of experience with modern industry and commodity production, for example, shows that he had absorbed a Lukácsian interpretation of Marx. For a short period—between 1933 and 1936—Benjamin's political posture would even somewhat approach that of official Soviet Communism, a move that coincided with the German critic's search for a utopian and progressive vision of technology, exemplified by his "Work of Art" essay of 1935, and that can be explained in terms of the rise of Hitler in Germany and the perception of the Soviet Union as "the last bulwark against fascism."[60]

However, despite the prominent integration of a Marxist element, the core of Benjamin's politics remained, even during his later years, the same amalgamation of anarchism and Jewish messianism that he had embraced in his youth. This fusion located its "common foundation" in a Romantic anticapitalist stance—the concomitant critique of capitalist industry and nostalgia for forms of communal life prevalent in early twentieth-century German intellectual circles that had determined the stance toward modernity of thinkers such as Max Weber and Ernst Bloch.[61] In the cases of Bloch and Benjamin, the Romantic anticapitalist perspective adopted a particular orientation to the future that aimed to achieve radical changes in the present by looking to the past for potentially revolutionary materials.[62] This stance, however, remained political only in an indirect way. Benjamin began to endorse "communist action" after 1924, not so much out of a strictly political intention, but out of a moral concern. At the time, communism for Benjamin seemed to be the most appropriate moral standpoint to adopt within the context of international class struggle. As Sándor Radnoti states, politics for Benjamin "is important not as politics, but as the adequate form of morally and philosophically decisive action."[63]

The Benjaminian theory of the "dreaming collective" required a new epistemology of history that could make sense of the dialectics of awakening as the model for historical cognition.[64] In turn, this new epistemology required a radical transformation in the perspective of historical investigation: a shift in methodological focus from *the past* to *the present moment*. What resulted from this shift, which Benjamin compared to a "Copernican revolution in historical perception," was a disruption of the concept of *historical event*. For Benjamin, the "what has been" of a historical event could no longer be considered a fixed moment in time; one should consider it, rather, as an open field, unsealed by its vibrant association with the present. This incomplete, open vision of the past involved the creation of a way of thinking and writing about historical events with an instantaneous logic. Benjamin looked to a radically antilinear and antihistoricist temporality, characterized by the abrupt discontinuity of "the flash of awakened consciousness," which made explicit the nature of the relationship between past and present events.

Benjamin's concerns with a historical vision that adopted the point of view of the present are discernible in his early writings. In "Metaphysics of Youth" (written in 1913–1914), Benjamin formulated a notion of the present as the dialectical site of an encounter between past and future. In this encounter—a prefiguration of the dialectical image—the past illuminates the present just as the dream illuminates awakened life.[65] The importance of a philosophical discernment of the present was also the subject of "The Life of Students," published in 1915 in *Der neue Merkur*. In this essay, Benjamin countered the progressive view of history with a historical vision that responds to the "demands of the present" and that concentrates its attention on "a single focal point." Suggestively, "The Life of Students" also provides the first expression of Benjamin's methodological concern with the value of the marginal. In the essay, he writes that "elements of the ultimate condition" appear "in the form of the most endangered, excoriated, and ridiculed ideas and products." The "historical task" is to disclose those elements and make them visible.[66] With its reentry into the deep strata of the past, or its historical "rubble," the *Arcades*' program of precipitation of awakening continues this intuition. Its concern with the materiality of the past parallels Bloch's undertaking in *Traces*, from 1930. As Benjamin wrote in a letter to Gershom Scholem, the *Arcades* was an "attempt to retain the image of history in the most inconspicuous corners of existence—the detritus of history, as it were."[67]

The *Arcades*' epistemology of history was an expression of Benjamin's enduring involvement with the ideas of Nietzsche, and, in particular, his critique of historicism and his position that the present is the central category of historical interpretation.[68] Nietzsche's most complete elaboration of this critique is "On the Utility and Liability of History for Life"—one of his *Unfashionable Observations*—in which he states: "Only from the highest power of the present can you interpret the past."[69] Echoing Nietzsche's dictum, Benjamin advocates a methodology in which the historian is expected to do justice not only to the *historical situation* of the studied object, but also to the *present interest* taken in that object, which is always preformed in the historical object itself. With respect to historical objects, Benjamin writes, "One could speak of the increasing concentration (integration) of reality, such that everything past (in its time) can acquire a higher grade of actuality than it had in the moment of existing."[70] For Benjamin, the present is, as it were, an *actualization* of the past. The "now being" of a previous historical object—that is, its present existence under the historian's gaze—is a "higher concretion" of the object itself. Historical objects, then, realize themselves through a sort of fragmentary projection into the future.[71] From this perspective, then, there is a moment of the past that anticipates the present moment; conversely, that same present is, in its turn, the anticipation of a moment of the future. The way in which these different moments relate to each other is not continuity, tradition, causality, or organic evolution, but the "flash of awakening" of their sudden juxtaposition in a constellation.

The key concepts in Benjamin's dialectical materialist method are the *historical index*, the *now of recognizability*, and the *dialectical image*. The historical index refers to the idea that images and events do not belong in an exclusive manner to a certain historical period, but that they stand in a relation of synchronicity with a moment of the present. That moment is their now of recognizability—the time when that event of the past becomes "legible" in that present.[72] The dialectical image is that space where that past and that present conjoin in a now of recognizability, where "what has been comes together in a flash with the now to form a constellation." This dialectical space—the now-being, or actualization, of the past—represents the dissolving of the "phantasmagoria" of the "eternal return of the same" and constitutes the moment of historical awakening.[73] Benjamin's epistemology of history thus represents a second, deeper level of the discourse on the new in the *Arcades*. The practice of this method conjures and dispels the reified vision of newness entailed in the commodity form, and, as a result, it creates the conditions for the identification of the authentically new in history.

Benjamin's method radically transforms the understanding of history. One can no longer perceive history as the mere continuity of past and present. Rather, it becomes the place of an abrupt "dialectical presentation,"[74] in which particular epochs of the past are blasted "out of [a] reified 'historical continuity'"[75] in order to be associated with a moment in the present. The "founding concept" of this view of history is the sudden actualization[76] of the past in the present—an act that "explodes the continuum of history."[77] In Benjamin's definition, this image incarnates "the dialectic at a standstill";[78] it is the "picture" of a becoming or, as Adorno calls it, "the photographic snapping of an instant."[79] At first sight, Benjamin's dialectical image could be interpreted as the fusion of two contradictory conceptual universes: on the one hand, Hegelian becoming—associated with linear, accumulative time; and, on the other, the Nietzschean and Kierkegaardian instant—a principle of discontinuous sudden temporality. However, after a more detailed examination, one realizes that in Benjamin the term *dialectic* stresses not so much the sequential nature of the stages of a historical unfolding, but, on the contrary, the simultaneity of those stages in a synthetic moment. Moreover, each of those dialectical stages or moments is not conceived as comprehensives totalities, but, precisely, as incomplete historical fragments. In fact, Benjamin's methodological emphasis on abrupt discontinuity and fragmentariness constitutes, like Bloch's theory of noncontemporaneity, a transposition of the avant-garde principle of montage into history,[80] or the relocation of "the formal structure of the caesura from art to time."[81] This application of the compositional logic of juxtaposition to history led Benjamin to the discovery of new dimensions of historical writing,

such as the possibility of the noncausal association between distant phenomena. Benjamin's practice of montage-like citation also became a sort of textual
shock-experience that shattered the historical continuum by putting the fragments of past and present events in a "relation of simultaneity."[82]

The dialectical image disrupts the notion of linear history and posits an
original conception in which the synchronic dimension of time is as important as the diachronic one, and perhaps even more so. This disruption results
in the establishment of a distinction between two forms of temporality: the
chronological time where the conventional, continuous relation of the present
to the past takes place; and the *figural* (*bildlich*) time where the dialectical
relation between what has been and the now occurs. The latter constitutes
for Benjamin the only authentically historical time, which is characterized by
the introduction of graphic, spatial categories that account for the primacy of
instantaneous simultaneity over sequential continuity. Just as in his theory of
shock, Benjamin's distinction between two forms of temporality fits within a
larger modern tradition of differentiations between a regular and an extraordinary—or a false and a genuine—time. This tradition includes Kierkegaard's
opposition between mechanical and substantive temporality; Bergson's contrast between time as a mere reflection of space and time as duration; and
Heidegger's articulation of two understandings of time, one "vulgar" and the
other "authentic."[83] Benjamin outlines a vision in which the source of historical meaning lies neither in the past (as it does for tradition) nor in the future
(as it does for progress), but in the *present instant*, insofar as the instant orga-
nizes a temporal force field where the contents of the past, the present, and
the future (what has not-yet been, the new) coincide to form a truly historical
image. History is then not only the consciousness of what has been, but also
an awareness of what is to come: a "remembrance" of the past in the present,
and a simultaneous understanding of the future as contained in the present
under the form of historical possibility.

Benjamin's conviction that the future was a source of energy latent in the
heart of the present points to a subject that deserves special attention: the
influence of Bloch on the *Arcades Project*. The relationship between Bloch and
Benjamin, which began in 1919 while both were in exile in Switzerland, was
rich and complex. At the time, Benjamin considered Bloch the decisive influence for the birth of his interest in political theory, and he even wrote a long
review, now lost, of Bloch's *The Spirit of Utopia*.[84] Bloch would later remember
their "shared sense for the particular and for the so often overlooked meaning
of the peripheral," and evoke with enthusiasm a period of "true symbiosis"

between him and Benjamin during their stay in Paris in 1926.[85] The friendship, however, was not without moments of tension, as when Benjamin's
repeatedly complained that Bloch plagiarized his ideas, most notably in *Heritage of Our Times*.[86] With respect to Bloch's influence, Adorno talks about
Benjamin's alliance with Bloch's "theoretical messianism" as expressed in "the
intention to interpret inner-worldly experience as a cipher for transcendental experience."[87] This alliance becomes explicit in the *Arcades*, whose model
was, as Rolf Tiedemann points out, Bloch's *The Spirit of Utopia*.[88] It can indeed
be argued, for example, that Benjamin's theory of the dialectical image represents an explicit relocation of the Blochian darkness of the lived moment
to the realm of the historical and the political. For Benjamin, "historical phenomena remain opaque, unilluminated for the dreaming collective," just as,
in Bloch's perspective, immediate perception remains obscure for the individual subject.[89] A central point of convergence between Bloch and Benjamin's philosophy is the fact that both thinkers suggest that "the point at which
experience touches us—at which we experience—is a blind spot."[90]

Similarly, in Benjamin, as in Bloch, the "darkness" of experience also
constitutes the starting point of a path directed toward the communal imagination of utopia. Thus, Benjamin's presentation of the "dream image" emphasizes the connection to a utopian future, or not-yet, implicit in that image.[91]
Moreover, when considered through Blochian terminology, a new dimension
of the Benjaminian collective subject of experience becomes apparent; that
is, its relation to the contents of the past as the not-yet of historical experience. In this dimension, the present's deep historical signification resides
elsewhere, perhaps hidden in a historical event of long ago. The realization
of this mystery of the historical nearness between two events far apart in
time constitutes the awakening of a collectivity. In the early sketches of the
Arcades, Benjamin explicitly resorts to the Blochian terminology of the not-
yet when he identifies the task of the historian with the "rescuing" of the
past. This task entails the investigation of the not-yet-conscious, which has
the structure of a dream. The "knowledge" of this not-yet-conscious—its
becoming "aware"—constitutes the awakening from the dream.[92] In Benjamin's language, "awakening" stands for the entrance into the "darkness of the
moment," its deciphering.[93] Benjamin thus projects Bloch's dimension of the
not-yet-conscious onto the past itself.

Despite its references to utopia, Benjamin's instantaneism does not state any
precedence of the future over the present or the past. Reversible and antilinear,
the logic of the not-yet entails, rather, the preeminence of the present as the plane

of temporality when events, images, or fragments collide in a dialectical image. The present is, then, the time of the simultaneity of these disparate fragments, the privileged temporal perspective in which the past "actualizes" or in which the future is realized in an act of anticipation. This aspect also accounts for the special place of the new in instantaneism. In the thought of Benjamin, as in that of Bloch, the new does not stand in an exclusive relation to the future. Rather, it is a concept in which the relation of the present to the past is just as fundamental for the creation of historical meaning and authentic newness.

Benjamin's "Copernican turn" in historical thinking entails not only a shift of focus from the past to the present, but also a change of emphasis from history to politics, by which the theory of awakening is converted into a model for political praxis.[94] By dispelling capitalism's "phantasmagoria" of eternal repetition, the historical materialist method opens up the doors of historical possibility to "authentic political experience," whose function is becoming the means for the irruption of the absolutely new in history. Benjamin identifies this radical political newness, however, with an entirely indeterminate future. For him, the other face of the new is, just as for Baudelaire, the absolutely *unknown*.

This aspect of Benjamin's political thought in the *Arcades* represents an explicit return, after his embrace of certain Marxist elements, to the anarcho-nihilist stance of his youth. The main characteristics of this stance were a critique of state institutions, such as parliament or the police, the rejection of organized political action, and a celebration of the pure violence of the "deed."[95] Its origins can be traced back to Benjamin's first intellectual reflections on politics, encouraged by his encounter with Bloch in Switzerland in 1919, and framed within his confrontation with the catastrophic aftermath of military defeat and the failed German Revolution of 1918.[96] A fusion of libertarian and messianic motifs, Benjamin's early politics received the imprint of anarchist or anarcho-syndicalist thinkers such as Leo Tolstoy, Gustav Landauer, and Georges Sorel, and featured a "utopian-restorative structure" and a "revolutionary/catastrophist perspective of history."[97] Michael Löwy even argues that Benjamin's approach to Soviet communism between 1925 and 1935 was probably connected to the "apocalyptic" nature of the Comintern's official doctrine during those years that world revolution was imminent, which mirrored the basic tenets of Benjamin's anarcho-messianic creed.[98]

The most complete expression of Benjamin's anarchism is found in "Critique of Violence," published in 1921 in the *Archiv für Sozialwissenschaft und*

Sozialpolitik. The essay embraces a radically nihilistic vision of politics in the form of "revolutionary violence"—that is, the violence of pure negativity that contests the more conventional forms of violence that either create (law-making) or preserve (law-preserving) a legal order. For Benjamin, the most characteristic contemporary expression of revolutionary violence was the notion of the "general strike" as expounded by the anarcho-syndicalist political theorist Georges Sorel in his work *Reflections on Violence* (1908).[99] Benjamin follows Sorel's distinction between the merely *political* strike, whose end is the strengthening of state power, and the genuinely proletarian *general strike*, whose single purpose is the destruction of that power.[100] The context for Benjamin's reflections was the failed Kapp Putsch from 1920. The Social Democratic government had successfully used the general strike as a "law-preserving" device to counter the destabilizing forces.[101] For Sorel, the "drama of the general strike,"[102] envisioned as a sort of apocalyptic event, condensed the whole question of socialism. One important influence over Sorel, and especially over his tendency to give preeminence to action over reflection, was Bergson's idea of intuition as a leading faculty, superior to analytical knowledge. In Sorel's analogy, the general strike would be the event "by which workers would intuit socialism as a whole, instantaneously."[103] Sorel's maximalist logic featured no compromise with reformism. His was a decisionist posture that advocated the radicalization of social tensions until the friend-enemy distinction of the class war became so unbearable that an apocalyptic general strike—that perfect "picture of complete catastrophe"—came about.[104] Following Sorel, Benjamin privileges a notion of violence as a noninstrumental, expressive act—a "politics of pure means."[105] Benjamin's political philosophy can thus be described as based on a nihilistic interpretation of revolution as "simple revolt," lacking a revolutionary program and having no image of the shape of society after the insurrection. In the words of Howard Eiland and Michael W. Jennings, "Walter Benjamin liked to think of the conventional world order going 'pop'—being suddenly suspended."[106]

As Löwy has argued, there exists a telling "elective affinity" between Benjamin's anarcho-nihilist posture and his engagement with Jewish messianism. This affinity is particularly evident in Benjamin's "Theological-Political Fragment." [107] Written either in 1920–1921 or 1936–1937, the fragment states that the regular dynamics of politics—what Benjamin calls the "order of the profane"—can participate, even if in an indirect way, in the realization of transcendent ends (e.g., the "coming of the Messianic Kingdom"). Transcendent ends are always realized under the form of an "interruption." As a result, a form of mediation is possible between the "profane" struggles for emancipation, such as communism, and the actual realization of the messianic promises of "restitution," a notion taken from Bloch's *The Spirit of Utopia* that alludes to "the eschatological return of all things to their original perfection."[108] Throughout his life, Benjamin remained convinced that the authentically significant goals were not political, but rather "messianic ends." Any kind of political action, including revolutionary communism, would prove relevant only insofar it provided a method for achieving those ends.[109]

Messianism, Interruption, and the Now-Time

Until his very last writings, Benjamin intensively examined the link between the historical and the political. Nowhere did this examination take a more concentrated form than in his series of theses on the philosophy of history known as "On the Concept of History." Written in the first months of 1940, just before Benjamin's failed attempt to escape Vichy France and his ensuing suicide on the French-Spanish border, the manuscript remained unpublished during his lifetime, even though the author had shared it with some close colleagues and friends, including Gretel Adorno and Hannah Arendt. In the manuscript, the motif of suddenness that characterized the *Arcades Project*'s historical materialist method is further explored and transformed into an unambiguous embrace of instantaneous interruption as the central category of meaningful historical cognition and political action.

A direct response to the turbulent experiences of the first decades of the twentieth century in Europe, Benjamin's theses revise the traditional concept of history that informed the social democratic movement's understanding of progress as inevitable and universal. They also addressed the historicist German school, or *Historismus*, which, in its attempt to represent the past "as it actually happened" (*wie es eigentlich gewesen*),[110] cast historical events as everlastingly static. From the war experience of total destruction to the Weimar Republic's perplexing political and economic instability, it had proved impossible to reconcile the historical events of the era with these schools' conventional image of history as a form of rational accumulation.[111]

A particular "constellation of dangers" provided Benjamin with the immediate political context for the writing of the theses: the rise of fascism in Europe, and the European left's collapse in the face of this apparently unstoppable ascent.[112] With the signing in 1939 of the Molotov-Ribbentrop Pact between the Soviet Union and Nazi Germany, communism had joined forces with fascism, which epitomized the "tradition of oppression." For Benjamin, the intellectual background to this collapse was the left's enduring adherence to the aforesaid view of history as the automatic path of inexorable progress. The core of "On the Concept of History," then, is a piercing critique of progress and the formulation of an alternative vision entirely divorced from inevitability and open to the irruption of the unexpected: an eventist philosophy of history grounded on the notion of now-time (*Jetztzeit*).[113]

In terms of politics, "On the Concept of History" announces Benjamin's final break with official communism after the signature of the Molotov-Ribbentrop Pact. This break had been preceded by his earlier disaffection with the Soviet Union after the 1936 Moscow Trials and by his renewed interest in Leon Trotsky's critique of Stalinism.[114] With this break came a new intellectual stance. With a new critical attitude toward modern technology, he broke with his previous technological utopianism, which the "Work of Art" essay epitomized. Benjamin's critique of technology was a return to the core of his earlier anticapitalist Romantic position, but it was now charged with a Marxist revolutionary dimension. In Benjamin's theory of history, Marxism provided the necessary vocabulary with which to replace progress—a concept that, having been taken over by the bourgeoisie, was no longer endowed with a critical function—with the notion of *actualization*.[115]

The central image of thought behind Benjamin's reconstitution of historical temporality around the now-time is abrupt interruption.[116] Like Bloch's reflections on utopian anticipation, Benjamin's image of interruption derives from the author's involvement with the intellectual universe of Jewish messianism[117]—a religious perspective whose prominence in "On the Concept of History" cannot be overstated. Indeed, it operates as a "kind of methodology of historical research."[118] The presence of a messianic element represents the resurgence of the author's early involvement with mystical Judaism in his years as a student in Munich and at the beginning of his friendship with Scholem (who of course later became a major scholar of Jewish mysticism). Benjamin's association with messianism was, just as Bloch's and Scholem's was, part of the renewed significance of Judaism's mystical teachings among much of the Central European Jewish intelligentsia, who, in the first decades of the twentieth century, found in it the basis for an alternative to the nineteenth-century model of assimilation into liberal humanist German culture.

Benjamin's interruption motif represents, in this sense, the preservation and critical expansion of one of the key aspects of the messianic sensibility. It conceived of redemption as a radical caesura that entails "a decisive and total break," not only with the past but also with historical immanence as such.[119] Benjamin wrote in his "Theological-Political Fragment" that the sudden occurrence of redemption—the irruption of the messianic age or the "Kingdom of God"—does not represent the accomplishment of history, but rather its interruption or termination.[120] Benjamin's concept of messianic redemption does not coincide, then, with any telos proper of a historical dynamic. Redemption is not "the goal" but "the end."[121]

This distinction forms a fundamental aspect of Benjamin's outlook. It reveals the profound difference between a *historicist* and a properly *instantaneist* vision of crisis. Despite its reference to rupture, the concept of crisis usually entails strong historicist connotations. This is the case, for example, when it is understood as a generator of progress, as the "crossing of an epochal threshold," or as the marker of an adjustment within a future-oriented process.[122] In this sense, crisis implies the *acceleration* of progress and does represent a certain *culmination* of history: the final crisis at the end of a process. In contrast, the instantaneist crisis is a secularization of the temporality of the messianic. This crisis is brought about by a sudden irruption—the arrival of the Messiah—that takes place, not when a goal is accomplished, but potentially *at any time*. Accordingly, there can be no prefigured form of history as an all-encompassing process, for it remains unfinished and open-ended. While historicist crises—no matter how radical their consequences—remain within the realm of historical immanence, instantaneist crises originate from "outside of history," pointing to forms of ahistorical time consciousness.

The notion of messianic interruption appears in "On the Concept of History" in the figure of the now-time, the conception of the present that results from the dialectical image.[123] The now-time constitutes the category specific to the heterogeneous, substantive, qualitative time where truly historical images take place. Half avant-garde "profane illumination" and half "mystical union" with the Messiah, the now-time signals the instant when history is brought to a stop "as if by a surrealistically produced shock."[124] As such, it is radically different from the ordinary abstract now of the "homogeneous, empty time"[125] (*homogene und leere Zeit*) typical of progressive views of history.

The now-time constitutes a genuine interruption in the flow of regular time, because it breaks with the understanding of the present as a mere moment of transition; it proposes instead the existence of an instantaneous present in which "time takes a stand [*einsteht*] and has come to a standstill."[126] The standstill of history in the now-time finds its formal expression in the

montage of historical images or the "constructive principle." In the notes for
the *Arcades*, Benjamin drew upon the principle of montage to characterize
the formal logic behind the dialectical image. In "On the Concept of History,"
however, he develops this principle further and installs it as the basic formal
structure of a new philosophy of history. The new philosophy features the
simultaneity of images as a new form of historical narration, which could represent a tangible alternative to the already disrupted conventional narrative
character of the "communicability of tradition."[127]

    In the "standstill" passage, Benjamin is presumably linking, as Werner
Hamacher has argued, the term *Einstand* (of infrequent use in German) to
the French *instant*.[128] The now-time would represent the equivalent in historical time of the instant in individual subjectivity, sharing all of its conceptual features, such as the "photographic" arrest of historical movement.[129] The
now-time's sudden stop is a model of messianic time, because, as in the Jewish
mystical figure of *tikkun olam*, or restitution of the world, it "comprises the
entire history of mankind in a tremendous abbreviation."[130] Benjamin characterizes this crystallization of historical thinking as a "monad." He is turning
here to Gottfried Wilhelm Leibniz's concept from his 1714 work *Monadology*.
The monad refers to those individual substances that contain within themselves the trace of all their past properties, as well as the potential of all their
possible attributes in the future. In each monad, the whole universe is, as it
were, "folded up," waiting to unroll its infinite complexity.[131] Every constellation of past and present assembled by remembrance constitutes a monad—
that is, the "brief instant of complete possession of history prefiguring the
whole, the saved totality, the universal history of liberated humanity."[132]

    The monadic structure is a trope that evokes historical materialism's intu-
ition that what we call history is nothing but the diachronic perception of a
synchronic reality. The "angel of history" is the image that evokes the unmediated perception of that reality in its actual simultaneity. Benjamin sees "one
single catastrophe" where we see nothing but a "chain of events."[133] This is the
"shape of time" for Benjamin. Every instant contains the total sum of temporality and represents a recapitulation of all of history.[134] In the work of Benjamin—as in that of Bloch—there seems to be, in fact, a correlation between
the notions of the instant and history as structures of temporality. The Benjaminian instant presents itself as a miniature model of history's shape. This
parallel constitutes the monadic structure of instantaneous temporality. In
historicism the standpoint for the contemplation of the totality of history is
its completion in the future, and, as a consequence, the meaning of history

is to be found in its organic development toward that goal. In Benjamin and Bloch, however, that standpoint is nothing but the sudden irruption of the instantaneous in the present.

As in the case of Benjamin's theory of awakening, the implications of the now-time's temporality of suddenness are not limited to the realm of historical thinking. One of the underlying assumptions in "On the Concept of History" is the existence of an analogical relation between the now-time's "standstill" and revolutionary interruption.[135] Revolutionary France provides a historical example of this analogy's consequences: "What characterizes revolutionary classes at their moment [*Augenblick*] of action is the awareness that they are about to make the continuum of history explode. The Great Revolution introduced a new calendar. The initial day of a calendar presents history in time-lapse [*Zeitraffer*] mode. And basically it is this same day that keeps recurring in the guise of holidays, which are days of remembrance [*Tage des Eingedenkens*]."[136] The new revolutionary calendar is a new historical temporality born out of an episode of radical foundation. When its first day "presents history in time-lapse mode," that amounts to a political enacting of the monadic structure of messianic time. The time-lapse is, precisely, the photographic technique that most closely resembles this monadic structure. Its visual effect consists in condensing, into a brief time, processes, such as the movement of the sun, whose normal development is not discernible to the normal human eye. Just as slow-motion film techniques allowed human perception to penetrate into the "darkness of the lived moment" in the "optical unconscious," the time-lapse photographic procedure implied in the time-consciousness of the revolutionary calendar makes possible a critical exploration of messianic time.

Another important consequence of Benjamin's linking of the temporality of interruption and political action is a transformation of the notion of the "revolutionary situation." To the idea of the revolution as the "goal" of progress, Benjamin opposes a vision of revolution as an instantaneous disruption in historical time, a "leap out of history" into classless society.[137] And to the understanding of the revolutionary situation as something that one should wait for "with more or less equanimity"[138] in the anteroom of "empty, homogeneous time," Benjamin counters with the messianic certainty that "every historical moment" offers its own "peculiar revolutionary chance."[139] For Benjamin, every moment of history can turn into the moment of revolution, if comprehended in the specificity of its situation. The conviction that transformation is only possible under the form of "changing all, all at once," and that this change can take place at any given moment of time, forms the core of what Hent de Vries has called Benjamin's "apocalyptic epistemology."[140] One of the central tenets of this epistemology is the opposition between *infinity* and *suddenness* as two mutually exclusive principles of action and thought. In Benjamin's "On the Concept of History," the disruptive *nowness* of the revolutionary instant is the exact opposite of the *infinite task* of socialism in its social democratic version. Benjamin's old nihilist "politics of the deed" is at play here, as his revolutionary voluntarism of abrupt interruption features a putschist version of anarchism. To this extent, Benjamin's thought is representative of the role of instantaneity in the modern history of sudden political change. His "politics of interruption" is both a revolutionary reinterpretation of the decisive-moment motif—so dear to Benjamin's conservative contemporaries, Heidegger, Jünger, and Schmitt—and an introduction of subjective, "epiphanic" visions of temporality into politics.

For Benjamin, the revolutionary instant is fundamentally "the retroactive redemption of past failed acts."[141] This means that the revolutionary potential inherent to every moment of historical time is dependent on this moment's "messianic" relation to the past—that is, dependent on the present instant's ability to identify itself as the "now of legibility" of an unfinished past in search of completion. In Benjamin's conception of revolution, the future is no longer the central category. The revolutionary moment's content is, rather, an actualization of a fragment of the past that can potentially take place at any moment of the present. This is what Benjamin refers to when he says that each present generation has been endowed with a "*weak* messianic power,"[142] which resides in the possibility of fulfilling the expectations of previous generations.[143] This power is weak, because nothing guarantees that it will be actually exerted. Its precondition is an instantaneous vision of historical coincidence, "an image that flashes up at the moment [*Augenblick*] of its recognizability, and is never seen again."[144] The act of performing this legibility is the moment of insurrection. Benjamin's interpretation of historical legibility is the counterpart to the idea—introduced in "Paris, the Capital of the Nineteenth Century," the 1935 exposé of the *Arcades*—that each society dreams of its successor as having utopian elements. In "On the Concept of History," it is the society of today (the present generation) that, in an act of "remembrance" (*Eingedenken*) becomes aware of the former society's dream of a better future. Benjamin's image that every second can be "the small gateway in time through which the Messiah might enter,"[145] accounts for this latency of revolution in each moment. Benjamin's Messiah is not, of course, a concrete religious figure, but the structure of historical time itself. Each historical moment can potentially be interpreted as messianic, which means to be structured by an act of historical remembrance that incites an opening up of historical possibility.[146]

One image that characterizes the interactions between historical remembrance and political action in "On the Concept of History" is that of *fashion*, which can play a role in the constitution of a now-time by means of enacting a dialectical image. Benjamin explains fashion's role with the example of French revolutionaries "citing" ancient Rome as a model for its own republican endeavors: "To Robespierre ancient Rome was a past charged with now-time, a past which he blasted out of the continuum of history. The French Revolution saw itself as Rome reincarnate. It cited ancient Rome exactly the way fashion cites a bygone model of dress. Fashion has a nose for the topical [*das Aktuelle*], no matter where it stirs in the thickets of long ago; it is the tiger's leap into the past."[147] Benjamin identifies ancient Rome as the historical index of revolutionary France, and, conversely, the French Revolution as the now of recognizability of the Roman Republic. In this constellation, the phenomenon of fashion features a paradoxical capacity for interruption through the act of citation, owing precisely to its power to establish repetitions between the styles of the present and the past.[148] Benjamin suggests a parallelism between the cycles of fashion and the revolutionary moment: "The same leap in the open air of history is the dialectical leap Marx understood as revolution."[149] His suggestion should be read in the context of his observation, in the notes for the *Arcades*, were he says that fashion is the authentic figure of that "increasing integration" which "serves to ignite the explosive materials that are latent in what has been."[150] He implies that the return of the "ever-same" typical of fashion can also participate in the kind of repetition inherent in the historical materialist method. If fashion is the authentic expression of what has been, then perhaps fashion can transcend its tendency toward reification and allow a space for ruptures and sudden breaks within historical phenomena.

With his insistence on interruption in the "On the Concept of History," Benjamin aims to break away from historicism's notion of tradition as reified historical reception (or as another face of the phantasmagoria of historical time). He considers this version of tradition to be a "catastrophe" because it consists of a large chain of moments in which the opportunity of radical change was missed, and therefore represents the unbroken continuity of the status quo. Characterized by a continual empathy with the victors and agents of class oppression, this tradition represents a permanent "state of emergency." The task of genuine historical consciousness—both in the space of historical writing and in the realm of political action—is "to bring about a real state of emergency"[151]—that is, an authentic "state of exception" that would incite a disruption in the tradition of the victors. It would be a truly exceptional event, a limit-historical experience, such as the secular arrival of the Messiah in the coming of the classless society.[152]

Benjamin's formulation is an explicit reply to Carl Schmitt's definition of political sovereignty in *Political Theology* (1922): "Sovereign is he who decides on the exception."[153] These authors' political allegiances diverged. Benjamin's politics was anarcho-revolutionary, and Schmitt's was authoritarian conservatism (with a subsequent engagement with Nazism in the 1930s). But, despite this, both Schmitt and Benjamin converged in the affirmation of the intellectual significance of "the exception" as a rupture in the continuity of regular time. In his politicization of the exceptional and in his postulation of the caesura in ordinary time as the premise for a completely original idea of politics and history, Benjamin was to a certain extent following Schmitt's steps.[154] In the thought of Benjamin, the caesura in time became the foundation for a critique of the idea of tradition. This critique was grounded on the perception of revolutionary upheavals as historical exceptions that interrupt the rule of a constant, inexorable system of domination.

Benjamin's critique of tradition is accompanied by a concurrent redefinition of the idea of progress. Progress is no longer related to the evolution or accumulation of certain historical facts along a predetermined goal, but to their sudden interruption. "Progress," Benjamin writes in one of the notes for the *Arcades*, "is not based in the continuity of elapsing time but in its interferences: where the truly new makes itself felt for the first time with the sobriety of dawn."[155] But the truly new—the authentic face of progress—only emerges when "the first revolutionary measure [is] taken."[156] Benjamin's idiosyncratic identification of genuine progress with episodes of revolutionary interruption contains a trace of the Jewish mystical association of catastrophe with the utopian contents of realized messianism. In Benjamin's restructured theory of progress, as in the Jewish mystical vision, the "transition from every historical present to the Messianic future"[157] exhibits the traits of a cataclysmic event.

The now-time's effect on conventional ways of thinking about history is a fundamental negation of historical reason's basic presuppositions—continuity, causality, and progress. Benjamin philosophy of history dismisses any version of historical coherence or teleological purpose in favor of the disruptive singularity of the event. The cornerstone of this eventist philosophy, Stéphane Mosès has argued, is the concept of instantaneous time: the idea that the completion of history is not the end result of a process, but something that can only be accomplished in the actuality of the now. For Benjamin, history is not a succession of moments following a certain axis of orientation in an irreversible development, but a juxtaposition of unique occurrences, qualitatively distinct from each other, in which historical time operates as a "permanent creation" in the "ceaseless emergence of the new."[158] To a great extent, the conceptual innovation of Benjamin's now-time, Mosès notes, resides in its nature as a transposition of the contents and characteristics of the notion of *lived time* from the domain of personal subjectivity to the sphere of historical temporality. What Benjamin accomplished in the realm of historical time would be analogous to what Saint Augustine and Henri Bergson had achieved in the space of physical time. Benjamin substituted the notion of an objective, homogeneous, linear temporality for "the subjective experience of a qualitative time in which every instant is lived in its incomparable singularity."[159] Hence, the affinity between the experience of shock in individual perception and the dialectical image, which "can be defined as the involuntary memory of redeemed humanity."[160]

Benjamin's concept of the messianic arrest of time is indeed a key term for thinking the historical experience of rupture.[161] In the "On the Concept of History," interruption is refigured as the "standpoint of redemption," thus completing a "dialectical redemption of the destruction of tradition by the new."[162] The category of the now-time is a continuation of Benjamin's enduring pursuit of a new form of experience—an extrapolation of his earlier preoccupations with the fate of experience in modernity from subjectivity to the collective dimension of history. There is certainly an analogy between what Benjamin discerns about the perception of shock in "On Some Motifs in Baudelaire" and what he exposes with respect to historical experience in "On the Concept of History." The now-time of the dialectical image is that isolated, immediate historical experience (*Erlebnis*) that has now been endowed with the weight of "long experience" to form a new collective, shock-like *Erfahrung* of history.

For Benjamin there is an inseparable association between instantaneous temporality and the very possibility of historical time. Time can be articulated historically only in the single moment (*Augenblick*) of the dialectical image, in the moment when one recognizes the encounter of the present and the past in a constellation. In one of the notes for "On the Concept of History," Benjamin even states: "Historical knowledge is possible only within the historical moment [*Augenblick*]."[163] The historical is, then, the awareness of this appropriation in the present of a flashing memory of the past. It is an awareness that wins back the kairotic element of opportunity buried in that past in order to actualize that historical possibility in the present. In this way, Benjamin not only indicates the major incompatibility—noted by Karl Heinz Bohrer—between, on the one hand, suddenness and, on the other, the coherence of historical meaning in a progressive concept of history,[164] but he also formulates a new image of history that rehabilitates hope by means of a transformed figure of redemption. For Benjamin, as for Bloch, this hope is the latent possibility of utopia at each instant of time.[165] As a result, Benjamin effectuates a resolution of the two divergent tendencies of the messianic idea that Scholem identified: the return to a past condition *and* a utopian vision of the future.[166] In the now-time, the return and the vision coincide in the present instant, because, in the temporality of interruption, tradition is rediscovered as illuminated by a revolutionary future.[167]

The now-time is Benjamin's version of the philosophical notion of actuality—that is, the enacting of the present. The now-time is also Benjamin's reinterpretation and politicization of what Nietzsche called the "suprahistorical outlook": the standpoint where one "does not seek salvation in a process, but . . . instead the world is complete and has arrived at its culmination in every individual moment."[168] The suprahistorical is also the temporality of the eternal return, as it revealed in Zarathustra's words: "Everything breaks, everything is joined anew; the same house of being builds itself eternally. . . . In every Instant being begins."[169] Benjamin's philosophy of history represents the explosive encounter of a Nietzschean temporality with a vision of history punctuated by sudden interruptions. In this encounter, the now-time is the actualization of the eternal return—the flashing glimpse of the inner connection between present and past that opens up history. This encounter is the same that accounts for the paradoxical nature of instantaneity. Authentic historical action is possible only in interruption, outside of the conventional vision of history, as in the French revolutionary calendar.

Benjamin's version of actuality has the form of a "construction" or an avant-garde montage. It is the assemblage of an image of the present with an image of the past, which disrupts the flow of regular temporality. If for Bloch the techniques of juxtaposition were charged with a utopian potential, for Benjamin the montage-like nature of historical constructions is the repository of messianic powers. For both authors, it is the sudden temporality of montage that reveals a qualitatively rich and differentiated form of time. Perhaps Benjamin's establishment of the image of montage-like interruption as the cornerstone of a new vision of history was how he came to terms with the tensions between the two poles of his concern with historical temporality: the writing of history and the will to revolutionary change. This polarity can be interpreted, in turn, as the reappearance—in a dialectical image of sorts, internal to Benjamin's own work—of the young Benjamin's dilemma, expressed in "Critique of Violence," about finding a "point of continuity" between the demands of actual political activism and the Jewish messianic notion of a redemption in and through language.[170] Drawing from a collection of dissimilar influences—from mysticism and the Nietzschean eternal return to materialism, anarchic nihilism, and the avant-garde—Benjamin discovered in the temporality of the now-time a general category for genuine historical awareness, where political action and work with language could take place in a common space shot through with the "splinters of messianic time."[171]

CONCLUSION

Instantaneism as a Regime of Historicity

Between 1914 and 1940, Ernst Jünger, Ernst Bloch, and Walter Benjamin produced a series of conceptualizations of instantaneous temporality that, transcending the ideological divides of the period, contributed to the formation of a regime of historicity based on the notion of the sudden present. Grounded on the figure of interruption, the instant presented itself as a privileged category of analysis during this era of German history, which was characterized by experiences of rupture and crisis in the space of historical consciousness and the realm of subjective perception. These authors' conceptual endeavors draw upon two genealogies of reflection on suddenness. One spans from Goethe and the French Revolution to Nietzsche; the other originates in Baudelaire and continues, in the early twentieth century, with the historical avant-gardes. Building on the rich history of suddenness as a figure of thought, Jünger, Bloch, and Benjamin transformed the "formula of instantaneity" into an influential trope for the depiction and interpretation of war, revolution, and crisis.

The existence of these traditions of reflection on suddenness suggests that ideas can also have a "long duration"[1] that demands to be identified and traced. How do we make sense of the fact that a notion, such as the instant, with antecedents as far back as antiquity, constituted a central element in new forms of time consciousness based, precisely, on rupture and crisis? To answer this question, I begin by distinguishing among three different manifestations of the notion of instantaneity in intellectual history: (1) its incarnation as a philosophical *concept* from Plato to Nietzsche; (2) its manifestation as a systematic *discourse of temporal consciousness*, as expressed in the aesthetics of early German Romanticism, the political self-fashioning of the French revolutionaries, Baudelaire's theory of modernity, and the avant-garde methods of juxtaposition and montage; and (3) its embodiment as a *regime of historicity*, which is to say, a general mode for the experience of time that is representative of an entire historical era, such as the period between 1914 and 1940 in Germany.

There are, naturally, intersections and overlaps among these three different manifestations of the idea of the instant. An instantaneist regime of historicity depends, for example, on previous discourses on the instant as a form of temporal consciousness—either in philosophy, politics, or aesthetics. At the same time, however, the outline of such discourses is not comparable to the formation of an instantaneist chronotope. In a similar way, the mere reference to the concept of the instant in a philosophical or political text is not equivalent, by itself, to the actual sketching of a discourse on temporal consciousness. Despite the variances in their conceptual range and levels of integration, all these manifestations of the instant constitute different dimensions, in diverse intellectual settings and historical circumstances, of the rhetoric of instantaneity. One must also note that, while the history of the instant as a concept predates modern times, the history of its embodiments as a discourse and as regime is exclusive to modernity. But, as I have argued throughout this book, instantaneism constitutes a chronotope of its own and is to be clearly distinguished from the specifically *modern* regime of historicity: *historicism*.

The historicist chronotope coincides with what Reinhart Koselleck has defined as the forms of historical consciousness typical of modernity, or *Neuzeit*. Koselleck points out that modernity—insofar as it entails the introduction of new factors of historical change, such as the expansion of industrial technology and capitalism—transforms the future into the unknown territory of a complete historical "otherness." Ever since the introduction of these factors, modernity has been synonymous with the experience of an unforeseeable "newness."[2] What we call modernity, then, is characterized by the increasing disconnection between the "space of experience" and the "horizon of expectation," as action is shaped less by actual past experiences and more by the abstract outlook of future-loaded, utopian concepts. Ideal visions of society become predetermined historical goals toward which all historical events are expected to gradually progress.[3] The gap between *experience* and *expectation* is, then, "temporalized," by which Koselleck means that it is mediated by forms of *duration* in time, such as progress, transition, evolution, reform, or even some versions of revolution. The task of political and social action is to bridge this gap through a "process of fulfillment," the effects of which can be anticipated in prognoses or planning.[4] Koselleck labeled the period from 1750 to 1850 *Sattelzeit* (time of transition), because it was during this time that these fundamental historicist concepts formed.

In their musings on instantaneous temporality, Jünger, Bloch, and Benjamin address a process analogous to the *Sattelzeit*, but taking place during the first decades of the twentieth century in Europe. What happened at this time was not a reduction of the space of experience or an enlargement of the horizon of expectation but a *breakdown* of the traditional understanding of experience and a concurrent intensification of the present as interruption. This interruption then transformed into a new form of experience in itself. In this alternative model of instantaneous historical experience, the space of experience survives not as continuity, tradition, or accumulation, but as a *fragment* that finds its meaning only in the present moment. The horizon of expectation—in the form of "fate" and "total mobilization" (Jünger); "utopia" (Bloch); or "primal history" and the "classless society" (Benjamin)—is no longer deferred indefinitely to some unknown point of the future, but rather becomes another fragment, which is *juxtaposed* to yet another in the perception of instantaneity in the present. Together, the writings of Jünger, Benjamin, and Bloch formulate instantaneous rupture as a field of experience in itself. It involves a disjointed vision of temporality without teleological orientation, governed only by the sudden irruption of the unexpected, or the juxtaposition of disparate fragments. Its subsequent effects are incoherence, violent discontinuity, and shock.

Historicist formulations of the present as the time of modernity should be distinguished, then, from instantaneity as such. The instantaneist perception of "the new," for example, is different from the historicist experience of modern temporality, described by Koselleck as the encounter with an "unknown future."[5] In the former, no sense of continuous history is possible, because the advent of a historical event is accepted in its contingent and sudden nature. Moreover, in instantaneism the perception of "newness" does not stand in a special or privileged relation respect to the future. What the appearance of the new reveals is the juxtaposition of fragments of the future, the present, and the past (as in Bloch or Benjamin) or the irruption of primaeval fate in the conditions of modernity (as in Jünger). Therefore, instantaneist references to newness are not elements of a progressive vision, but rather a sort of vitalist affirmation of the event for the event's sake, something that by its very nature is not part of a plan.

Instantaneism should also be distinguished from *presentism*—the regime of historicity that, according to observers such as François Hartog and Hans Ulrich Gumbrecht, has replaced historicism as the prevalent form of time consciousness in the contemporary age. In both presentism and instantaneism, the past and the future become, in a sense, "presentized." But while in presentism this process takes place as a result of social acceleration, the expiration of optimistic visions of the future, and the breakdown of the category of historical time altogether, in instantaneism time is presentized as a result of the affirmation of the *sudden quality* of the present. Additionally, instantaneism, out of a sense of radical rupture, tends toward vital activism and decisive action, while presentism features a passive sense of the present and a feeling of historical stagnation.[6] In opposition to presentism's "broad present," the present of instantaneity is commonly a "moment of vision" or "decision" that, far from abolishing historical time, generates, by virtue of the irruption of ahistorical "now-times," the very possibility of history. Neither goal-driven narratives nor their expiration can give closure to instantaneism's sense of historical time, which remains arbitrary and open-ended.

The first discourses on instantaneity appeared as "splinters" of ahistoricity within a larger historicist era. During the period of the *Sattelzeit*, these splinters included the early German Romantic aesthetics of suddenness and, most notably, the "instantaneist moment" of 1789, which, given its temporal features, can be isolated from the broader historicist interpretations of the French Revolution. These discourses, however, did not give way at the time to the formation of a more general instantaneist chronotope. It was not until the period of 1914–1940 in Germany that a systematic form of ahistorical consciousness emerged, when the instantaneist regime of historicity proper expressed itself in an antihistoricist vision of the instant as the manifestation of the extraordinary in the everyday.

The years between 1914 and 1940 were a second "time of transition," or *Sattelzeit*, in which new concepts of temporality, such as instantaneity, responded to such new experiences of time as the crisis of progress and the collapse of the visions of history as coherent process. In this period of recurring crises, Benjamin, Jünger, and Bloch tried to make sense of these breaks and ruptures not by subsuming them within a higher teleology, but by interpreting them in their own historical terms. The great novelty of the instantaneist regime expressed in their work was the appearance of forms of *ahistorical time consciousness* that replicated themselves in individual perception and left behind historicism's linear temporality of progress. One decisive implication was, accordingly, a resignification of the notion of *crisis*, which became, in itself, a form of historical consciousness. As such, crisis incarnated instantaneism's understanding of temporality, which was different from the historicist perception of crises as transitional phases or steps in the path to progress—moments within a larger process of unfolding or development—and thus still internal to the "modern philosophy of history."[7]

Features of the Instantaneist Chronotope

The instantaneist chronotope formed in response to the crises in historical consciousness and individual perception brought about by war, revolution, and the rise of fascism in Europe. It provided the framework for the intellectual representation of an era defined by historical discontinuity and an analogous break in subjectivity and everyday experience. Between 1914 and 1940, the proliferation of episodes of rupture was accompanied by an experience of time as disjointed, incomplete, fragmented, and thus susceptible of being suddenly juxtaposed with other such fragments. Instantaneism represents the conceptual articulation of these singular kinds of experiences of temporality. As a chronotope, it has four distinct features.

The first feature is *the affirmation of ahistoricity as a form of historical consciousness*. Ahistoricity is the affirmation of a moment "outside of time" that obliterates both the past and the future in the name of an absolute present. In instantaneity's *collective dimension*, the figure of ahistoricity represents the paradoxical site of genuine historical consciousness and authentic historical action. This seeming aporia—the fact that the awareness of historical time originates in its negation—finds an effective formulation in instantaneism's antihistoricist perspective and eventist understanding of history, as well as in the idea of historical experience as a perceptual fragment. If the sudden present—in revolution, battle, accident, or catastrophe—is the primordial form of involvement with history, and this involvement, by virtue of its abruptness, is not assimilable to progress or any other notion of continuity or accumulation, it follows that the nature of this experience is fragmentary and expressed, for example, in the simultaneity or juxtaposition of disparate historical times.

The affirmation of an absolute instant entirely dissociated from a coherent historical process—whether the continuous past of tradition or the future of teleological goals—had appeared as a concept or discourse in the French revolutionaries' form of historical and political self-awareness, as well as in Baudelaire's definition of the historical condition of *modernité*. It also lurked in Kierkegaard's notion of contemporaneity and in Nietzsche's defense of the ahistorical and suprahistorical stances. But it turned into a general framework for the interpretation of historical and personal experience only in the works of Benjamin, Jünger, and Bloch. Despite their significant political differences, all these authors regarded the experiences of the First World War and the interwar period as the backdrop for the irruption of fragmentary temporal experiences. Their work was a genuine assault on historicism, both in its particular incarnation as "progress" and, in general, as a perspective that attributes a decisive causality to the historical process as a whole.

The work of these Weimar authors asserts that the ahistorical instant, once deployed as an analytical concept in the interpretation of a concrete historical situation, results in images of temporality that negate or complicate the conventional notion of historical time as linear and of modern time as progress. Instantaneity is thus at the base of their discontinuous readings of history and visions of radical foundation. It is also undergirds their ideas on the sudden return of elements of the past (as "fate" under the guise of "danger" for Jünger); the unpredicted contemporaneity of past events as anticipations of a utopian future (as in Benjamin's "dialectical image"); or the coexistence, against the expectations of progress, of so-called "surpassed" and somehow "premonitory" social formations (as in Bloch's notion of noncontemporaneity). Instantaneity is, accordingly, also foundational to these authors' ideas on newness, a category which is no longer future-oriented, but whose connection to the past is just as important as its relation to the future.

Their writings stage an interaction between a certain idea of history and a certain idea of the *atemporal present*. For example, Bloch and Benjamin understand the instant as a critique of the existing social and political reality. For both, the experience of the instant anticipates—and, in a certain way, realizes—the coming of a different, liberated world. Utopia is envisioned as an "alterity" of history that can be intimated in the actuality of the instantaneous present. The instant constitutes then the actualization of utopia, either in the prefiguration of a future completion (as in Bloch) or in the realization of the unfulfilled emancipatory promises of the past (as in Benjamin). Bloch's and Benjamin's accounts represent, in this sense, the politico-historical version of Nietzsche's and Kierkegaard's nineteenth-century model of the ahistorical present as the point of encounter between time and eternity. In their version, the instant is still the moment when time touches its "other"—an other that is no longer situated in "eternity"—but in the "no-time" of utopia.

Within instantaneism resides an important correlation between an antihistoricist consciousness and the vision of the instant as a form of exceptional perception in the everyday. The second main feature of the chronotope pertains, thus, to its *subjective dimension*, and is *the vanishing of the distinction between "ordinary" and "extraordinary" experience*. In the writings of the Weimar triad of Jünger, Benjamin, and Bloch, the conventional contrast between "everyday" and "limit" experience is transcended. For these authors, the conditions of the modern world—urban, industrial, and in constant exposure to the risks of revolution and war—have transformed exceptional occurrences and situations, such as trauma, accident, astonishment or shock, into the new standards of quotidian perception. In their accounts, the suddenness of instantaneity—either in the "profane illumination" of surrealism or the now-time of revolutionary interruption—has become the structure of a new common form of temporal consciousness that concerns the aesthetic as much as the political, and it has done so without losing its bewildering effects on the human psyche. Born from the discontinuity and interruptions of life in early twentieth-century metropolises, this new experience manifests itself, especially, in the fragmentation of sensory perception, a phenomenon that finds a formal framework in the avant-garde practices of visual and literary montage.

A consequence of this fragmentation is the acknowledgement of a conceptual distinction between *the instant and the present*. As a result of its abrupt nature, the actual moment of instantaneity is not accessible to regular observation; it is thus inseparable from a certain degree of obscurity or concealment. "The instant" denotes that obscure moment of sudden, unmediated experience—that *what happens but of which one is not aware*—in contrast to "the present," a form of perception that is always already mediated, and which designates the space of awareness that comes *before* or *after* the event. For Bloch the instant is the "darkness of the lived moment" or the "blind spot" that stands "too near" the subject such that it can be held "only immediately" after it actually happens."[8] For Jünger, the instant is the moment of "horror" or the space "that extends between the recognition of the downfall and the downfall itself."[9] For Benjamin, it is the "shock" of modern city life or the "isolated experience" parried only by conscious awareness.

The third characteristic of the instantaneist regime of historicity—really another facet of the second—is *the formulation of a new concept of individual perception*. Instantaneous temporality is essential to the attempts by Jünger, Bloch, and Benjamin to articulate a new form of experience in place of the conventional interpretation of experience as "accumulated knowledge."[10] The crisis around this concept in the late nineteenth and early twentieth centuries presented the possibility for the creation of other forms of personal experience, characterized by their immediate, spontaneous quality, entirely dissociated from the premises of continuity, and adapted to the conditions brought about by the involvement with technology, the urban masses, and experimental art. In their writings, Jünger, Bloch, and Benjamin register a typology of the actual sensations of suddenness that the individual subject can experience under the new conditions. Jünger's "danger," Bloch's "darkness of the moment," and Benjamin's "shock" constitute diverse responses to this crisis and an effort to interpret it not only in negative terms, as a catastrophe, but as the starting point for the identification of new forms of subjectivity predicated on instantaneity.

This formulation of novel concepts is coupled, moreover, with a transformation of the role of "religious experience" in modernity. In each of these authors, the encounter with the ephemeral creates the space for a certain "revelation"—of Jünger's reappearance of primeval pagan "fate"; of Bloch's "materialist gnosis" in search of the "traces" of utopia; and of Benjamin's "messianic time" and "profane illumination." In all of these instances, the ephemeral bears the traits of a form of transcendence. The instant, itself born as a kind of secular epiphany in its early modern formulations (such as in the poetry of Goethe), bears an ambiguous relation to the persistence of the sacred in modernity, because even the secularized, materialist deployments of the concepts call for the application of a religious language. Instantaneity belongs, in this sense, to the narratives on the *reenchantment* of modern temporality.[11]

The fourth and final characteristic of the instantaneist chronotope is the *articulation of a linkage between the collective and individual dimensions of experience*. The new concepts of instantaneous perception devised by Jünger, Benjamin, and Bloch depend on the formulation of an internal connection between the subjective awareness of personal time and the common time consciousness of politics and history. By simultaneously positing these two main dimensions of time, they couple them together into a single framework and invoke suddenness as a unifying category of experience. Jünger elaborates on the experience of suddenness on the battlefield and analyzes the prevalence of danger and terror in civilian life as a result of "total mobilization." Bloch responds to the experience of apocalyptic destruction entailed by the First World War with a temporalization of utopia as a "not-yet" reality hidden in the darkness of the lived moment. He also coins noncontemporaneity as a concept for understanding the juxtaposition of different historical times in the same now. Benjamin presents the dialectical image and the now-time as the categories necessary for a view of history based on interruption as an alternative to the commonplace historical temporality of progress.

Moreover, an essential aspect of these authors' articulation of the historical and the subjective is the establishing of a connection between sudden temporality and the positing of a *collective subject of experience*. Benjamin's "shock" is attached to the "innervation" of the collectivity, just as Jünger's "terror" is to the total mobilization of society, and Bloch's "darkness" to the We-problem of the external realization of utopia.

In the works of Jünger, Bloch, and Benjamin, then, instantaneity, a concept that originated in the realm of individual perception, becomes the reference point for the understanding of collective historical experience. But once configured, this new type of historical consciousness transforms, in turn, the conceptualization of subjective temporality itself. During the years of the First World War, the Weimar Republic, and the rise of Nazism, the idea of the instant effectuated a series of migrations from the space of individual subjectivity to the realm of history and politics and back, with the effect of creating new political, philosophical, or aesthetic meanings of the term.[12] The instant thus constitutes a representative example of the "transposition of concepts into new contexts."[13]

Instantaneism Beyond Weimar?

It is challenging to find, given the specific characteristics of instantaneism, other examples of this chronotope beyond the 1914–1940 period in Germany. More typically, as the example of the French Revolution indicates, forms of instantaneity have found themselves subsumed within historicist frameworks. Vladimir I. Lenin's theses on revolutionary action constitute a notable twentieth-century example of this phenomenon. In opposition to all orthodox Marxist prescriptions, which advised against initiating a socialist revolution in a backward, mostly peasant, poorly industrialized nation such as Russia, Lenin advocated in 1917 for an instantaneous "seizing of the moment" of the exceptional political juncture that had been opened up by that year's events. Lenin's position, however, was only concerned with the moment of the revolutionary taking of power, leaving untouched communism's basic historicist concept: the prescription of a program of social and economic evolution toward a predetermined goal. The Russian Revolution's own "instantaneist moment" coexisted, then, with the historicist interpretation of revolution as the gradual unfolding of a historical reason. And soon, it was entirely conflated with it. There are other instances of revolutionary upheaval, such as the Paris Commune of 1871

or the Soviet Republics of Bavaria and Hungary of 1919 that could be interpreted as embodiments of an instantaneist time consciousness. But while an
instantaneist political logic was certainly present in the historical self-image
of the protagonists of these events, these upheavals remained isolated revolutionary "moments" that did not give way to the formation of a far-reaching
instantaneist regime of historicity.

The instantaneist chronotope is not useful, moreover, for analyzing the
history of Germany itself after the end of the period between 1914 and 1940.
Even though postwar German history begins, after a disastrous military defeat
and the first prospects of reconstruction, with a discourse on the *Stunde Null*
moment of 1945, the idea of radical sudden change lost its appeal during
the second half of the twentieth century and became marginal to German
intellectual life. With only a few exceptions, most of the significant thinkers
of the period either adopted a pessimistic tone of "cultural despair" incompatible with radicalism or aligned themselves with the politically moderate
spirit of the reconstruction that aimed to leave behind the era of political
extremism, a moderate spirit that Germany shared with the rest of Europe
and in particular with the design of the new European communitarian institutions. All of the major postwar German theorists of modernity—Martin
Heidegger, Max Horkheimer, Theodor W. Adorno, Hans Blumenberg, Jürgen
Habermas, or Reinhart Koselleck himself—developed intellectual discourses
on contemporary society that left out or explicitly rejected the consideration
of instantaneist forms of political consciousness or action. Some of the intellectual productions that circulated around the student radicalism of the late
1960s and early 1970s, such as the ideas of Herbert Marcuse or Jacob Taubes,
possibly represent a revision of this antiradical tendency, but they remained
an exception within what can be considered a robust intellectual consensus
against political radicalisms of any ideological sign.

The instantaneist regime, however, can still be applicable to the interpretation of recent historical junctures or political genealogies in other
countries. For example, while most of the other Western—and even East-
ern—European nations shared Germany's antiradical consensus during the
postwar era, the French intellectual tradition, in certain of its aspects, took
Germany's place as the center of the reflections on instantaneous temporality.
Since the years of German occupation and up to the students' and workers'
revolts of 1968 and their cultural aftermath, French intellectuals have produced an important number of philosophical, aesthetic, and political formulations of the instant. One can mention, among many examples, Emmanuel

Lévinas' instant of self-positing, Henri Cartier-Bresson's reflections on the photographic moment, Georges Bataille's and Maurice Blanchot's explorations of inner and limit experience, Henri Lefebvre's theory of moments, Guy Debord's construction of situations, and Michel Foucault's epistemic breaks.

More specifically, the series of theoretical and political reflections that called for, or subsequently elaborated on, the practice of radical political action around the year 1968—and that derived from a number of different ideologies, from anarcho-syndicalism and Trotskyism to Maoism and situationism—constituted another, albeit short-lived and less theoretically developed, incarnation of a properly instantaneist regime of historicity. What united these dissimilar tendencies was a convergent intellectual interpretation of the student and worker mobilizations—the street protests, the general strikes, the occupations of factories and universities, and their corresponding echoes in personal subjectivity and individual mores—as new incarnations of instantaneism, both as the horizon of political action and the condition of historical consciousness. May 1968 in France was perhaps the last moment in Western European history when a conjuncture of the experience of abrupt political rupture and the formulation of new concepts turned instantaneism into an influential modality for the perception of personal and historical time.

Since 1968, other notable deployments of the motif of instantaneity have occurred, not as full-fledged incarnations of the chronotope, but as more localized forms of aesthetic or political consciousness. One example of these recent deployments is the series of aesthetic discourses and styles that during the 1980s were grouped together under the label of *postmodernism*.[14] With its emphasis on the fragmentary and collage-like nature of the processes of artistic creativity and reception, and on the manipulation of previous art through parody, reappropriation, and pastiche, postmodernism reiterated some of the basic tenets of the avant-garde aesthetics of juxtaposition. One might even say that postmodernism represents the most recent iteration of a series of associations between specific aesthetic movements and periods of historical rupture. Examples of these links would be German Romanticism's response to the French Revolution, as well as the dialogue of the historical avant-gardes with the aftermath of the Russian Revolution and the First World War. A similar linkage exists between postmodernist aesthetics and the crises of late industrial capitalism of the 1970s and 1980s. In all these instances, the aesthetic movements involved have privileged fragmentary genres and styles.

In the last decades, a more philosophical—and political—version of the instantaneist consciousness has arisen around the discourse of the "return of the event," in the work of such authors as Alain Badiou, Giorgio Agamben, and Slavoj Žižek.[15] An *event* is the unexpected irruption of a unique and singular occurrence that introduces a radical discontinuity in history and marks a before and after in the flow of time. One can neither foresee an event, François Dosse writes, nor give it some comprehensive post facto meaning, because it remains ungraspable.[16] The event incarnates, in this sense, some of the main features of instantaneity when it is displayed in the dimensions of history and historical knowledge. An event, like an instant, emerges "out of nothing"; it is, in Žižek's words, an "autonomous, abysmal act, founded on itself,"[17] the irruption of the entirely new and unknown that cannot be derived from any preexisting condition. The notion of the event thus affirms the present as a self-sufficient form of temporality, independent from both the future and the past. Given this autonomy, it escapes from any mechanical view of history, as well as from any teleology—hence, its association with the notions of *historical possibility* and an *open future*. In different ways, for Agamben, Badiou, and Žižek, the event constitutes a significant framework for the understanding of social, aesthetic, and political experience. These authors' writings are symptomatic of the current use of instantaneity as a valid notion for the interpretation of the contemporary age's relationship to temporality.

NOTES

Introduction

1. François Hartog, *Regimes of Historicity: Presentism and the Experiences of Time*, trans. Saskia Brown (New York: Columbia University Press, 2015), 9.

2. Although my research deals specifically with works written and published between 1914 (such as Ernst Jünger's war diaries, the basis for his 1920 memoir *Storm of Steel*) and 1938 (the ending year of the "Expressionism Debate" between Georg Lukács and Ernst Bloch and the year of the publication of the second edition of Jünger's *The Adventurous Heart*), I have extended the time span of my research to 1940 in order to include the key texts that Walter Benjamin produced in that year, such as "On Some Motifs in Baudelaire" and the theses of "On the Concept of History."

3. In my analysis, I follow Michael Löwy's interpretation of the notion of elective affinity as a "convergence, a mutual attraction, an active confluence" that "develops between two social or cultural configurations." Michael Löwy, *Redemption and Utopia: Jewish Libertarian Thought in Central Europe. A Study in Elective Affinity*, trans. Hope Heaney (London: Verso, 2017), 6.

4. Oswald Spengler, *Der Untergang des Abendlandes: Umrisse einer Morphologie der Weltgeschichte* [The Decline of the West], vol. 1 (Munich: C. H. Beck, 1918), 176, quoted in Stephen Kern, *The Culture of Time and Space: 1880–1918* (Cambridge, MA: Harvard University Press, 1983), 258.

5. Karl Heinz Bohrer, *Die Ästhetik des Schreckens: Die pessimistische Romantik und Ernst Jüngers Frühwerk* (Munich: Carl Hanser Verlag, 1978); Karl Heinz Bohrer, *Suddenness: On the Moment of Aesthetic Appearance*, trans. Ruth Crowley (New York: Columbia University Press, 1994); Anson Rabinbach, *In the Shadow of Catastrophe: German Intellectuals Between Apocalypse and Enlightenment* (Berkeley: University of California Press, 1997); Löwy, *Redemption and Utopia*.

6. Kern, *The Culture of Time and Space*; Modris Eksteins, *Rites of Spring: The Great War and the Birth of the Modern Age* (Boston: Houghton Mifflin, 1989).

7. I will follow Martin Jay's definition of experience as "a potential learning process produced by an encounter with something new, an obstacle or a challenge that moves the subject beyond where it began." Martin Jay, *Songs of Experience: Modern American and European Variations on a Universal Theme* (Berkeley: University of California Press, 2006), 403.

8. Heidrun Friese, introduction to *The Moment: Time and Rupture in Modern Though*, ed. Heidrun Friese (Liverpool: Liverpool University Press, 2001), 2.

9. Henry George Liddell and Robert Scott, comps., *A Greek-English Lexicon* (Oxford: Clarendon Press, 1968).

10. François Dosse, *Renaissance de l'événement: Un défi pour l'historien: entre sphinx et phénix* (Paris: Presses Universitaires de France, 2010), 2, 5; Alain Badiou, with Fabien Tarby, *Philosophy and the Event*, trans. Louise Burchill (Cambridge: Polity, 2013), 8; Slavoj Žižek, *The Event: Philosophy in Transit* (London: Penguin, 2014), 2.

11. Bohrer, *Suddenness*, vii; Robin Durie, "The Strange Nature of the Instant," in *Time and the Instant: Essays in the Physics and Philosophy of Time*, ed. Robin Durie (Manchester: Clinamen Press, 2000), 9.

12. See Augustine, *Confessions*, trans. Henry Chadwick (Oxford: Oxford University Press, 1998); Maurice Blanchot, *The Infinite Conversation*, trans. Susan Hanson (Minneapolis: University of Minnesota Press, 1993), 202–229; Hannah Arendt, "What Is Freedom?," in *Between Past and Future* (New York: Penguin Books, 1977), 142–69.

13. Rüdiger Safranski, *Martin Heidegger: Between Good and Evil*, trans. Ewald Osers (Cambridge, MA: Harvard University Press, 1999), 173.

14. "For the instant [*exaiphnes*] seems to signify something such that changes proceed from it into either state. There is no change from the rest while resting, nor from the motion while moving; but this instant, a strange nature [*physis atopos*], is something inserted between motion and rest, and it is no time at all [*en chrono oudeni ousa*]; but into it and from it what is moved changes to being at rest, and what is at rest to being moved." Plato, *Parmenides*, trans. H. N. Fowler (Cambridge, MA: Harvard University Press, 1939), 156d–e.

15. Durie, "Strange Nature of the Instant," 2.

16. Aristotle, *Physics*, trans. P. H. Wicksteed and F. M. Cornford (Cambridge, MA: Harvard University Press, 1957), bk. 4, chaps. 10–14.

17. "Behold, now is the favorable time; behold, now is the day of salvation." 2 Cor. 6:2 (English Standard Version).

18. 1 Cor. 15:52 (ESV).

19. Augustine, *Confessions*, bk. 11.

20. Gaston Bachelard, *L'Intuition de l'instant* (Paris: Édition Stock, 2006), 13, 15.

21. Bohrer, *Suddenness*, vii.

22. Timothy Bahti and Jenny C. Mann, "Trope," in *The Princeton Encyclopedia of Poetry and Poetics*, ed. Roland Green, Stephen Cushman, Clare Cavanagh, Jahan Ramazani, and Paul Rouzer, 4th ed. (Princeton, NJ: Princeton University Press, 2012), 1463–1464; Daniel Weidner, "The Rhetoric of Secularization," *New German Critique* 41, no. 1 (2014): 11.

23. Anne Marie Guglielmo, "Motif," in Green et al., *Princeton Encyclopedia*, 900–901.

24. Darrin M. McMahon, "The Return of the History of Ideas?," in *Rethinking Modern Intellectual History*, ed. Darrin M. McMahon and Samuel Moyn (Oxford: Oxford University Press, 2014), 21.

25. Peter E. Gordon, *Continental Divide: Heidegger, Cassirer, Davos* (Cambridge, MA: Harvard University Press, 2010), 4.

26. Peter R. Gordon and John P. McCormick, introduction to *Weimar Thought: A Contested Legacy*, ed. Peter R. Gordon and John P. McCormick (Princeton, NJ: Princeton University Press, 2013), 2.

27. The term *chronotope* was originally coined by the Russian literary critic Mikhail Bakhtin to mean the configuration of time and space specific to each literary genre or form of writing. See Mikhail Bakhtin, "Forms of Time and of the Chronotope in the Novel," in *The Dialogic Imagination* (Austin: University of Texas Press, 1981), 84–258.

28. Hans Ulrich Gumbrecht, *Our Broad Present: Time and Contemporary Culture* (New York: Columbia University Press, 2014), xii; Hans Ulrich Gumbrecht, "Nuestro amplio presente:

sobre el surgimiento de una nueva construcción del tiempo y sus consecuencias para la disciplina de la historia," in *Historia/Fin de siglo*, ed. Guillermo Zermeño Padilla (Mexico City: El Colegio de México, 2016), 126.

29. Hartog, *Regimes of Historicity*, 106.

30. Hartog, 9.

31. Hartog, xvi.

32. Alexandre Escudier, "'Temporalization' and Political Modernity: A Tentative Systematization of the Work of Reinhart Koselleck," in *Political Concepts and Time: New Approaches to Conceptual History*, ed. Javier Fernández Sebastián (Santander: Cantabria University Press and McGraw-Hill Interamericana de España, 2011), 144.

33. Reinhart Koselleck, "Introduction and Prefaces to the *Geschichtliche Grundbegriffe*," trans. Michaela Richter, *Contributions to the History of Concepts* 6, no. 1 (2011): 21.

34. Gumbrecht, "Nuestro amplio presente," 126.

35. Hartog, *Regimes of Historicity*, xv, xviii; Hans Ulrich Gumbrecht, *Production of Presence: What Meaning Cannot Convey* (Stanford, CA: Stanford University Press, 2004), ix, 128.

36. Gumbrecht, "Nuestro amplio presente," 128. Translations mine.

37. Hans Blumenberg, *The Legitimacy of the Modern Age*, trans. Robert M. Wallace (Cambridge, MA: MIT Press, 1999), 30.

Chapter 1

1. Andreas Anglet, *Der "ewige" Augenblick: Studien zur Struktur und Funktion eines Denkbildes bei Goethe* (Cologne: Böhlau Verlag, 1991), 1. Translation mine.

2. M. H. Abrams, *Natural Supernaturalism: Tradition and Revolution in Romantic Literature* (New York: W. W. Norton and Company, 1971), 387.

3. Karl Löwith, *Von Hegel zu Nietzsche: Der revolutionäre Bruch im Denken des neunzehnten Jahrhunderts* (Stuttgart: S. Fischer, 1964), 32.

4. Löwith, in fact, identifies Goethe's fundamental time concept as the notion of "eternity as perpetual present." Löwith, *Von Hegel zu Nietzsche*, 229.

5. As M. H. Abrams has suggested, Augustine's *Confessions* (bk. 11) provide the theological prototype for this experience, which Rousseau would later naturalize in his *Rêveries du promeneur solitaire*; Abrams, *Natural Supernaturalism*, 385.

6. Goethe quoted in Nicholas Boyle, *Goethe: The Poet and the Age, Volume I: The Poetry of Desire (1749–1790)* (Oxford: Clarendon Press, 1991), 503.

7. David E. Wellbery, *The Specular Moment: Goethe's Early Lyric and the Beginnings of Romanticism* (Stanford, CA: Stanford University Press, 1996), 14, 15.

8. "Werd'ich zum Augenblicke sagen: / Verweile doch! Du bist so schön / . . . / Dann will ich gern zu Grunde gehn! / . . . / Es sei die Zeit für mich vorbei!" Johann Wolfgang von Goethe, *Faust*, trans. Walter Kaufmann (New York: Anchor Books, 1963), 1699–1700, 1702, 1706; prose translation by Boyle, *Goethe: The Poet and the Age*, 767. According to Jane K. Brown, Goethe may have borrowed the expression "Linger on, you are so beautiful" from Rousseau's *Rêveries du promeneur solitaire*: "In our most vivid joys there is scarcely an instant at which our hearts could truly say: Would that moment might last forever." Jane K. Brown, *Faust: The Theater of the World* (New York: Twayne Publishers, 1992), 49.

9. Goethe, *Faust*, 11589.

10. Boyle, *Goethe: The Poet and the Age*, 767.

11. Nicholas Rennie, *Speculating on the Moment: The Poetics of Time and Recurrence in Goethe, Leopardi, and Nietzsche* (Göttingen: Wallstein Verlag, 2005), 61.

12. Mona Ozouf, *Festivals and the French Revolution*, trans. Alan Sheridan (Cambridge, MA: Harvard University Press, 1988), 10.

13. Miraculous in Carl Schmitt's secularized sense of an ex nihilo creation, unexplainable by the laws of causality. Schmitt, *Political Theology: Four Chapters on the Concept of Sovereignty*, trans. George Schwab (Chicago: University of Chicago Press, 2005), 36–37.

14. Matthew Shaw, *Time and the French Revolution: The Republican Calendar, 1789–Year XIV* (New York: Royal Historical Society and Boydell Press, 2011), 35.

15. Reinhart Koselleck, *The Practice of Conceptual History: Timing History, Spacing Concepts*, trans. Todd Samuel Presner, Kerstin Behnke, and Jobst Welge (Stanford, CA: Stanford University Press, 2002), 150.

16. Sanja Perovic, *The Calendar in Revolutionary France: Perceptions of Time in Literature, Culture, Politics* (Cambridge: Cambridge University Press, 2012), 1.

17. Shaw, *Time and the French Revolution*, 1, 34.

18. Perovic, *Calendar in Revolutionary France*, 1.

19. Walter Benjamin, "On the Concept of History," trans. Harry Zohn, in *Selected Writings, Volume 4: 1938–1940*, ed. Michael W. Jennings and Howard Eiland (Cambridge, MA: Belknap Press of Harvard University Press, 2003), 395.

20. Michael Löwy, *Fire Alarm: Reading Walter Benjamin's "On the Concept of History"*, trans. Chris Turner (London: Verso, 2005), 94.

21. Benjamin, "On the Concept of History," 395.

22. Reinhart Koselleck, *Futures Past: On the Semantics of Historical Time* (New York: Columbia University Press, 2004), 263.

23. Ozouf, *Festivals and the French Revolution*, 10.

24. Lynn Hunt, *Politics, Culture, and Class in the French Revolution* (Berkeley: University of California Press, 1984), 27.

25. Rebecca Comay, *Mourning Sickness: Hegel and the French Revolution* (Stanford, CA: Stanford University Press, 2010), 107. It is significant that even Hegel somewhat replicated the Jacobins' belief in the French Revolution's primordially *sudden* nature. The German philosopher interpreted the Revolution as a "glorious mental dawn," an apocalyptic "moment" that stood for the liberation of humanity from the bondages of servitude; quoted in Steven B. Smith, "Hegel and the French Revolution: An Epitaph for Republicanism," in *The French Revolution and the Birth of Modernity*, ed. Ferenc Fehér (Berkeley: University of California Press, 1990), 224.

26. Ferenc Fehér, introduction to Fehér, *French Revolution*, 5.

27. Alexis de Tocqueville's *L'Ancien Régime et la Révolution*, published in 1856, remains the classical refutation of the French Revolution's self-interpretation as a radical historical beginning. See Alexis de Tocqueville, *Tocqueville: The Ancien Régime and the French Revolution*, ed. Jon Elster, trans. Arthur Goldhammer, Cambridge Texts in the History of Political Thought (Cambridge: Cambridge University Press, 2011).

28. François Furet, *Interpreting the French Revolution*, trans. Elborg Forster (Cambridge: Cambridge University Press, 1981), 27.

29. Perovic, *Calendar in Revolutionary France*, 5.

30. François Hartog, *Regimes of Historicity: Presentism and the Experiences of Time*, trans. Saskia Brown (New York: Columbia University Press, 2015), 73.

31. For an analysis of the notion of secularization as reoccupation, see Hans Blumenberg, *The Legitimacy of the Modern Age*, trans. Robert M. Wallace (Cambridge, MA: MIT Press, 1999), 64.

32. Abrams, *Natural Supernaturalism*, 385.

33. Friedrich Schleiermacher, *On Religion: Speeches to Its Cultured Despisers*, trans. Richard Crouter (Cambridge: Cambridge University Press, 1996), 23.

34. Schleiermacher, 31.

35. Schleiermacher, 39.

36. Plato, *Parmenides*, in *Sämtliche Werke 4: Phaidros, Parmenides, Theaitetos, Sophistes*, trans. Friedrich Schleiermacher (Hamburg: Rowohlt, 1958), 156d–e. For the influence of Schleiermacher's translation on Kierkegaard, see William McNeill, *The Glance of the Eye: Aristotle, Heidegger, and the Ends of Theory* (Albany: State University of New York Press, 1999), 116.

37. Karl Heinz Bohrer, *Suddenness: On the Moment of Aesthetic Appearance*, trans. Ruth Crowley (New York: Columbia University Press, 1994), 74; Karl Heinz Bohrer, *Le Présent absolu: du temps et du mal comme catégories esthétiques*, trans. Oliver Mannoni (Paris: Editions de la Maison des sciences de l'homme, 2000), 7.

38. Since the nineteenth century, a significant current of interpretation, represented by figures such as Heinrich Heine and Karl Marx, has seen the German Romantics' intellectual enthusiasm for the French Revolution as a depoliticizing "idealization" of the Revolution's more disruptive content. See Adrian del Caro, "The Hermeneutics of Idealism: Nietzsche Versus the French Revolution," *Nietzsche-Studien* 22, no. 1 (1993): 158. The attitude of key German Romantic authors, such as Schlegel and J. B. Fichte, toward the Revolution shifted from an initial endorsement to a critical distance. This shift occurred once the first news on the radical phase of the Revolution, the Terror, had arrived in Germany and, significantly, after a German translation of Edmund Burke's *Reflections on the Revolution in France* became available in 1793; Ethel Matala de Mazza, "Romantic Politics and Society," in *The Cambridge Companion to German Romanticism*, ed. Nicholas Saul (Cambridge: Cambridge University Press, 2009), 191–196. Goethe himself never shared his German contemporaries' enthusiasm for the Revolution, an event which he believed had "crushed the natural order of things" and could offer nothing but chaos; W. Daniel Wilson, "Goethe and the Political World," in *The Cambridge Companion to Goethe*, ed. Lesley Sharpe (Cambridge: Cambridge University Press, 2002), 213.

39. Friedrich Schlegel, "Ideas," in *The Early Political Writings of the German Romantics*, ed. Frederick C. Beiser (Cambridge: Cambridge University Press, 1996), 130.

40. Friedrich Schlegel, *Athenaeum Fragments*, in *Friedrich Schlegel's "Lucinde" and the Fragments*, trans. Peter Firchow (Minneapolis: University of Minnesota Press, 1971), 233. Schlegel also characterizes the historical significance of this rupture in terms of the secular continuation of a religious undertaking; that is, the coming into being of "the revolutionary desire to realize the kingdom of God on earth" (192).

41. From Schlegel's Athenaeum Fragment 116, as quoted in Robert J. Richards, *The Romantic Conception of Life: Science and Philosophy in the Age of Goethe* (Chicago: University of Chicago Press, 2002), 22.

42. Friedrich Schlegel, "On Incomprehensibility," in *Schlegel's "Lucinde" and the Fragments*, 268.

43. Schlegel, *Athenaeum Fragments*, 164.

44. Rebecca Comay, *Mourning Sickness: Hegel and the French Revolution* (Stanford, CA: Stanford University Press, 2010), 107, 108.

45. Heinrich von Kleist, "On the Gradual Production of Thoughts Whilst Speaking," in *Selected Writings*, ed. and trans. David Constantine (London: J. M. Dent, 1997), 406.

46. Michael Hamburger, *Reason and Energy: Studies in German Literature* (London: Weidenfeld and Nicolson, 1970), 16.

47. Friedrich Hölderlin, *Poems and Fragments*, trans. Michael Hamburger (London: Anvil Press Poetry, 1994), 395.

48. Richard Unger, *Hölderlin's Major Poetry: The Dialectics of Unity* (Bloomington: Indiana University Press, 1975), 83.

49. Hölderlin, *Poems and Fragments*, 483.

50. According to Pierre Bertaux, Hölderlin's entire work can be considered a metaphor for the French Revolution. Pierre Bertaux, *Hölderlin und die Französische Revolution* (Berlin: Aufbau-Verlag, 1990), 12.

51. Hölderlin, *Poems and Fragments*, 395.

52. Richard Unger, *Friedrich Hölderlin* (Boston: Twayne Publishers, 1984), 82.

53. Theodor W. Adorno, "Parataxis: On Hölderlin's Late Poetry," in *Notes to Literature*, vol. 2 (New York: Columbia University Press, 1992), 130, 131.

54. Bohrer, *Le Présent absolu*, 28–29.

55. Paul de Man, "Temporality in Hölderlin's 'Wie wenn am Feiertage . . . ,'" in *Romanticism and Contemporary Criticism*, ed. E. S. Burst, Kevin Newmark, and Andrzej Warminski (Baltimore: Johns Hopkins University Press, 1993), 55.

56. Martin Heidegger, *Hölderlin's Hymn "The Ister"*, trans. Willian McNeill and Julia Davis (Bloomington: Indiana University Press, 1996), 9.

57. Martin Heidegger, *Elucidations of Hölderlin's Poetry*, trans. Keith Hoeller (New York: Humanity Books, 2000), 164–165.

58. Heidegger, *Elucidations of Hölderlin's Poetry*, 64–65.

59. Friedrich Hölderlin, *Essays and Letters on Theory*, trans. Thomas Pfau (Albany: State University of New York Press, 1988), 102, 108.

60. Jean-Luc Nancy talks about the motif of nearness in Hölderlin's poetry as the "hint" that points to the "non-place" where the divine gives itself. Nancy's position is discussed in Hent de Vries, "Theotopographies: Nancy, Hölderlin, Heidegger," *MLN* 109, no. 3 (1994): 474.

61. Giorgio Agamben, "What Is the Contemporary?," in *What Is an Apparatus and Other Essays*, trans. David Kishik and Stephan Pedatella (Stanford, CA: Stanford University Press, 1999), 44.

62. "The French Revolution, Fichte's philosophy, and Goethe's *Meister* are the greatest tendencies of the age." Schlegel, *Athenaeum Fragments*, 268.

63. Søren Kierkegaard, *Philosophical Fragments and Johannes Climacus*, trans. Howard V. Hong and Edna H. Hong (Princeton, NJ: Princeton University Press, 1985).

64. Søren Kierkegaard, *The Concept of Anxiety*, trans. Reidar Thomte in collaboration with Albert B. Anderson (Princeton, NJ: Princeton University Press, 1980).

65. Martin Heidegger, *The Fundamental Concepts of Metaphysics: World, Finitude, Solitude*, trans. William McNeill and Nicholas Walker (Bloomington: Indiana University Press, 1995), 150.

66. Jacques Colette, *Kierkegaard. La difficulté d'être chrétien* (Paris: Les Éditions du Cerf, 1963), 58.

67. See Galatians 4:4 (English Standard Version). "But when the fullness of time (*kairos*) had come, God sent forth his Son, born of woman, born under the law."

68. The analogy between Christian eschatology and existential events in the life of an individual would reappear in Heidegger's ontology as expressed in his 1920–1921 lectures on religion, which were published under the title *The Phenomenology of Religious Life*. According to Hent de Vries, the eschatological structure of kairos confirms that "a certain undecidability and restlessness form the necessary condition for wakefulness, for conversion, and finally for

resoluteness, all of which contribute to the enigma of faith as well as, *by analogy*, to that of factical life experience as such—that is to say, of human existence in its proper meaning." Hent de Vries, *Philosophy and the Turn to Religion* (Baltimore: Johns Hopkins University Press, 1999), 196.

69. Nelly Viallaneix, *Kierkegaard. El único ante Dios*, trans. Juan Llopis (Barcelona: Herder, 1977), 69.

70. Kierkegaard, *Philosophical Fragments*, 61. As in Hölderlin's poetry, the issue of contemporaneity in the philosophy of Kierkegaard can be understood as the mysterious nearness of the presence or absence of the divine in time.

71. M. Jamie Ferreira, "Faith and the Kierkegaardian Leap," in *The Cambridge Companion to Kierkegaard*, ed. Alastair Hannay and Gordon D. Marino (Cambridge: Cambridge University Press, 1998), 216; James Giles, "Kierkegaard's Leap: Anxiety and Freedom," in *Kierkegaard and Freedom*, ed. James Giles (New York: Palgrave, 2000), 71.

72. Kierkegaard, *Concept of Anxiety*, 61.

73. Kierkegaard, *Philosophical Fragments*, 111, 58.

74. Søren Kierkegaard, *Fear and Trembling*, trans. Alastair Hannay (London: Penguin Books, 2003), 66.

75. In Hent de Vries' words, "Abraham shows that in every genuine decision the ethical must be sacrificed. Morality ought to be suspended 'in the name of' an ab-solute duty or obligation that is always 'singular' and for which the name—the proper and most proper name—would be 'God.'" Hent de Vries, *Religion and Violence: Philosophical Perspectives from Kant to Derrida* (Baltimore: Johns Hopkins University Press, 2002), 158.

76. Kierkegaard, *Fear and Trembling*, 5.

77. See Bartholomew Ryan, "Carl Schmitt: Zones of Exception and Appropriation," in *Kierkegaard's Influence on Social-Political Thought*, ed. Jon Stewart (Farnham, UK: Ashgate, 2011), 178.

78. Again, *øjeblik* in Danish, which, like *Augenblick* in German, means "the blink of an eye." Kierkegaard's choice of the term was in fact determined by Schleiermacher's rendition of Plato's *exaiphnes* as *Augenblick* in his translation of the *Parmenides*; McNeill, *Glance of the Eye*, 116.

79. Kierkegaard, *Concept of Anxiety*, 87.

80. 1 Cor. 15:52 (ESV).

81. Kierkegaard, *Concept of Anxiety*, 88.

82. In the *Physics*, Aristotle introduces the classical rendition of the now as an abstract "boundary" that both divides and unites the past with the future. This simultaneous effect of dividing and uniting—whose spatial equivalent is a point on a line—determines the continuity of time; Aristotle, *Physics*, trans. P. H. Wicksteed and F. M. Cornford (Cambridge, MA: Harvard University Press, 1957), bk. 4, chaps. 10–14.

83. Kierkegaard, *Concept of Anxiety*, 89.

84. Karl Löwith, *Meaning in History: The Theological Implications of the Philosophy of History* (Chicago: University of Chicago Press, 1949), 185–186.

85. Søren Kierkegaard, *"The Moment" and Late Writings*, ed. and trans. Howard V. Hong and Edna H. Hong (Princeton, NJ: Princeton University Press, 1998), 91–92.

86. Although *moment* is the word used in the standard translation of this work by Kierkegaard, the original Danish term is *øjeblik*, "instant."

87. Kierkegaard, *"The Moment"*, 338.

88. Kierkegaard, 339.

89. Kierkegaard's definition also prefigures Alain Badiou's understanding of "the event." See Alain Badiou, with Fabien Tarby, *Philosophy and the Event*, trans. Louise Burchill (Cambridge: Polity, 2013), 9.

90. In David Kangas words, the instant is the moment of rupture that "gives or qualifies the present." David Kangas, *Kierkegaard's Instant: On Beginnings* (Bloomington: Indiana University Press, 2007), 172.

91. Friedrich Nietzsche, "On the Utility and Liability of History for Life," in *The Complete Works of Friedrich Nietzsche 2: Unfashionable Observations*, trans. Richard Gray (Stanford, CA: Stanford University Press, 1995), 83–168.

92. Nietzsche, 89, 94, 163.

93. Friedrich Nietzsche, *The Gay Science*, trans. Walter Kaufmann (New York: Vintage Books, 1974), 273.

94. Nietzsche, 273–274.

95. Nietzsche, 274.

96. Friedrich Nietzsche, *Thus Spoke Zarathustra*, trans. Adrian del Caro (Cambridge: Cambridge University Press, 2006), 125–126.

97. Friedrich Nietzsche, *The Will to Power*, trans. Walter Kaufmann and R. J. Hollingdale (New York: Vintage Books, 1968), 532–533.

98. Gilles Deleuze, *Nietzsche and Philosophy*, trans. Hugh Tomlinson (London: Continuum University Press, 2002), 72.

99. Michael Haar, "Nietzsche and Metaphysical Language," in *The New Nietzsche: Contemporary Styles of Interpretation*, ed. David B. Allison (Cambridge, MA: MIT Press, 1985), 31.

100. Stanley Rosen, *The Mask of Enlightenment: Nietzsche's Zarathustra* (New Haven, CT: Yale University Press, 2004), 178.

101. Deleuze, *Nietzsche and Philosophy*, 68.

102. Alexander Nehamas, *Nietzsche: Life as Literature* (Cambridge, MA: Harvard University Press, 1985), 150.

103. Martin Heidegger, *Nietzsche, Volume 2: The Eternal Recurrence of the Same*, trans. David Farrell Krell (New York: Harper and Collins, 1984), 154.

104. Nietzsche, *Thus Spoke Zarathustra*, 153.

105. Karl Löwith, *Nietzsche's Philosophy of the Eternal Recurrence of the Same*, trans. J. Harvey Lomax (Berkeley: University of California Press, 1997), 104.

106. Nietzsche, "On the Utility," 94.

107. Nietzsche, *Thus Spoke Zarathustra*, 175.

108. Philip Turetzky, *Time* (London: Routledge, 2000), 110–115.

109. Joan Stambaugh, *Nietzsche's Thought of Eternal Return* (Baltimore: Johns Hopkins University Press, 1972), 114.

110. One important difference between Kierkegaard and Nietzsche is that Nietzsche locates the instant's existential weight on every instant's significance in and for itself, not on its implications for eternal redemption or damnation. For this reason, Kierkegaard's understanding of the instant—in which the content of the present moment is defined in terms of a supernatural afterlife—would have struck Nietzsche as fundamentally nihilistic.

111. Haar, "Nietzsche and Metaphysical Language," 30.

112. Heidegger, *Nietzsche*, 182.

113. Heidegger, 207.

114. Nietzsche, "On the Utility," 92.

115. François Dosse, *Renaissance de l'événement: Un défi pour l'historien, entre sphinx et phénix* (Paris: Presses Universitaires de France, 2010), 31–33.

116. Nietzsche, "On the Utility," 93.

117. This same attitude can be found in Nietzsche's posture of disrespect to the French Revolution itself. Nietzsche considered the Revolution a "gruesome farce which, considered closely, was quite superfluous." Due to its active role in promoting Christian values, such as equality, the Revolution represented the beginning of the "last great slave rebellion." In the end, he found the Revolution's only justification not in its historical eventness, but in its having made possible an individual like Napoleon. Friedrich Nietzsche, *Beyond Good and Evil*, in *Basic Writings of Nietzsche*, trans. Walter Kaufmann (New York: Modern Library, 1992), 239, 251; del Caro, "Hermeneutics of Idealism," 159.

118. Nietzsche, *Thus Spoke Zarathustra*, 104.

119. Friedrich Nietzsche, *Twilight of the Idols and The Anti-Christ*, trans. R. J. Hollingdale (London: Penguin, 1968), 51.

120. Heidegger, *Nietzsche*, 139.

121. Friedrich Nietzsche, *Ecce Homo: How to Become What You Are*, trans. Duncan Large (Oxford: Oxford University Press, 2007), 68.

122. Nietzsche, *Thus Spoke Zarathustra*, 263.

Chapter 2

1. Jürgen Habermas, "Modernity versus Postmodernity," trans. Seyla Ben-Habib, *New German Critique* 22 (Winter 1981): 4–5.

2. Karl Heinz Bohrer, *Suddenness: On the Moment of Aesthetic Appearance*, trans. Ruth Crowley (New York: Columbia University Press, 1994), 27.

3. David Cunningham, "A Question of Tomorrow: Blanchot, Surrealism and the Time of the Fragment," *Papers of Surrealism* 1 (Winter 2003): 14, https://www.research.manchester.ac.uk/portal/files/63517385/surrealism_issue_1.pdf.

4. According to Maurice Blanchot, "Narration is not the account of an event but the event itself, its imminence, the site where it will occur." The temporal logic of the avant-garde subverts Blanchot's terms for the relationship between narration and the event. Whereas for Blanchot experience is only realized after the fact in the account of experience, the anticipation of experience is itself the event for the avant-garde. Maurice Blanchot, *The Sirens' Song: Selected Essays by Maurice Blanchot*, trans. Sacha Rabinovitch, ed. Gabriel Josipovici (New York: Harvester Press, 1982), 62.

5. The term *avant-garde* derives from the milieu of political radicalism. In mid-nineteenth century France, this military metaphor denoted an encounter between art and politics, and in particular, that art was indeed a precursor of radical political stances. Since that time, the reference to an avant-garde in art has been associated with a belief in aesthetics as capable of advancing social change. Renato Poggioli, *The Theory of the Avant-Garde*, trans. Gerald Fitzgerald (Cambridge, MA: Belknap Press of Harvard University Press, 1968), 9.

6. Tristan Tzara, "Dada Manifesto 1918," in *Seven Dada Manifestos and Lampisteries*, trans. Barbara Wright (Surrey, UK: Alma Classics, 2016), 12.

7. Filippo Tommaso Marinetti, "Electrical War," in *Futurism: An Anthology*, ed. Lawrence Rainey, Christine Poggi, and Laura Wittman (New Haven, CT: Yale University Press, 2009), 98.

8. Filippo Tommaso Marinetti, "The Founding and Manifesto of Futurism," in Rainey et al., *Futurism*, 51–52.

9. Alain Badiou, with Fabien Tarby, *Philosophy and the Event*, trans. Louise Burchill, (Cambridge: Polity, 2013), 76, 9.

10. Umberto Boccioni, Carlo Carrà, Luigi Russolo, Giacomo Balla, and Gino Severini, "Manifesto of the Futurist Painters," in Rainey et al., *Futurism*, 62.

11. Marinetti, "Founding and Manifesto of Futurism," 51.

12. Poggioli, *Theory of the Avant-Garde*, 69. For a study of the futurist moment as an aspect of avant-garde movements in general, see Marjorie Perloff, *The Futurist Moment: Avant-Garde, Avant Guerre, and the Language of Rupture* (Chicago: University of Chicago Press, 1986).

13. François Dosse, *Renaissance de l'événement: Un défi pour l'historien, entre sphinx et phénix* (Paris: Presses Universitaires de France, 2010), 6.

14. Arthur Rimbaud, *Rimbaud Complete, Volume I: Poetry and Prose*, trans. Wyatt Mason (New York: Modern Library, 2003), 366.

15. François Hartog, *Regimes of Historicity: Presentism and the Experiences of Time*, trans. Saskia Brown (New York: Columbia University Press, 2015), 108.

16. For an exploration of the connections between the avant-garde and the idea of progress, see Matei Calinescu, *Five Faces of Modernity* (Durham, NC: Duke University Press, 1987), 95. Renato Poggioli further studies the relations between the avant-garde and Romanticism in Poggioli, *Theory of the Avant-Garde*, 73.

17. Habermas, "Modernity versus Postmodernity," 4–5.

18. Charles Baudelaire, *Critique d'art*, ed. Claude Pichois (Paris: Gallimard, 1992), 153.

19. Charles Baudelaire, *The Flowers of Evil*, trans. by Robert Lowell (Norfolk, CT: New Directions, 1962), 185.

20. According to Adorno, Baudelaire, in establishing this association, articulated for the first time the centrality of the category of the new in the rise of "high capitalism" in mid-nineteenth-century Europe. This poetic statement was symptomatic of the origins of the new as a bourgeois category: innovation in the arts only replicated the logic of capitalist commodity production and its rejection of tradition. Theodor W. Adorno, *Aesthetic Theory*, ed. Gretel Adorno and Rolf Tiedemann, trans. Robert Hullot-Kentor (Minneapolis: University of Minnesota Press, 1997), 20–21. For a commentary on Adorno's analysis of the new, see Peter Bürger, *Theory of the Avant-Garde*, trans. Michael Shaw (Minneapolis: University of Minnesota Press, 1984), 59–60.

21. Charles Baudelaire, *The Painter of Modern Life and Other Essays*, trans. Jonathan Mayne (New York: Phaidon Press, 1965), 1, 13, 3.

22. Baudelaire, *Painter of Modern Life*, 4, 12.

23. Jürgen Habermas, *The Philosophical Discourse of Modernity: Twelve Lectures*, trans. Frederick Lawrence (Cambridge, MA: MIT Press, 2000), 9.

24. Baudelaire, *Critique d'art*, 241.

25. Calinescu, *Five Faces of Modernity*, 38, 49, 50, 52.

26. Significantly, Baudelaire's aporia of modernity echoes the classical aporias of time identified by Sextus Empiricus in the second century BC. But while for Sextus Empiricus these aporias were the ground for a skeptical attitude toward the existence of time, Baudelaire's aporia is the foundation for a staunch *affirmation* of modernity. In the *Confessions*, Augustine elucidated these aporias through their immersion in a new category and point of view: the understanding of time as concrete subjective experience.

27. Roger Shattuck, *The Banquet Years: The Origins of the Avant-Garde in France* (New York: Vintage Books, 1968), 332.

28. Shattuck, *Banquet Years, 332.*

29. Maud Lavin, *Cut with the Kitchen Knife: The Weimar Photomontages of Hannah Höch* (New Haven, CT: Yale University Press, 1993), 9.

30. Bürger, *Theory of the Avant-Garde*, 70, 54.

31. Adorno, *Aesthetic Theory*, 57, 155.

32. Charles Baudelaire, *Fussés, Mon coeur mis à nu, La Belgique déshabillée*, ed. André Guyaux (Paris: Gallimard, 1986), 72.

33. Charles Baudelaire, *The Flowers of Evil*, trans. William Aggeler (Fresno, CA: Academy Library Guild, 1954), 311.

34. Charles Baudelaire, *Le Spleen de Paris: Petits poèmes en prose*, ed. Robert Kopp (Paris: Gallimard, 2006), 104, 214; Charles Baudelaire, *Paris Spleen and La Fanfarlo*, trans. Raymond N. Mackenzie (Indianapolis, IN: Hackett Publishing Company, 2008), 3, 4.

35. Walter Benjamin, "On Some Motifs in Baudelaire," trans. Harry Zohn, in *Selected Writings, Volume 4: 1938–1940*, ed. Michael W. Jennings and Howard Eiland (Cambridge, MA: Belknap Press of Harvard University Press, 2003), 313–355.

36. Briony Fer, "Surrealism, Myth and Psychoanalysis," in *Realism, Rationalism, Surrealism: Art Between the Wars*, ed. Briony Fer, David Batchelor, and Paul Wood (New Haven, CT: Yale University Press, 1993), 187.

37. Georg Simmel, "The Metropolis and Mental Life," in *On Individuality and Social Forms: Selected Writings*, ed. Donald N. Levine (Chicago: University of Chicago Press, 1971), 325.

38. Dorothée Brill, *Shock and the Senseless in Dada and Fluxus* (Lebanon, NH: Dartmouth College Press, 2010), 18–19.

39. Lavin, *Cut with the Kitchen Knife*, 47.

40. Richard Huelsenbeck, "First German Dada Manifesto (Collective Dada Manifesto)," in *Art in Theory, 1900–2000: An Anthology of Changing Ideas*, ed. Charles Harrison and Paul Wood (Oxford: Blackwell, 1992), 257.

41. Lavin, *Cut with the Kitchen Knife*, 29–30.

42. Adorno, *Aesthetic Theory*, 14, 145.

43. Guillaume Apollinaire, "The New Spirit and the Poets," in *Selected Writings of Guillaume Apollinaire*, ed. Roger Shattuck (New York: New Directions Books, 1950), 233 (emphasis mine).

44. Apollinaire, 234, 237.

45. Umberto Boccioni, "The Italian Futurist Painters and Sculptors: Initiators of the Futurist Art," in Ester Coen, *Umberto Boccioni* (New York: The Metropolitan Museum of Art, 1988), 251.

46. Shattuck, *Banquet Years*, 345.

47. Blaise Cendrars, "Contrastes," in *Complete Poems*, trans. Ron Padgett (Berkeley: University of California Press, 1992), 58.

48. Alfred Döblin, *Berlin Alexanderplatz: The Story of Franz Biberkopf*, trans. Eugene Jolas (London: Continuum, 2004).

49. Theodore Ziolkowski, *Dimensions of the Modern Novel: German Texts and European Contexts* (Princeton, NJ: Princeton University Press, 1969), 208.

50. "Il est beau comme . . . la rencontre fortuite sur une table de dissection d'une machine à coudre et d'un parapluie." Comte de Lautréamont [Isidore Ducasse], *Oevres complètes, Les Chants de Maldoror, Lettres, Poésies I et II* (Paris: Gallimard, 1973), 233–234. Translation mine.

51. Charles Taylor, *Sources of the Self* (Cambridge, MA: Harvard University Press, 1989), 465. Adorno points out in this respect that "construction" and "expression" are "polar opposites"; Adorno, *Aesthetic Theory*, 100.

52. Henri Bergson, *Time and Free Will: An Essay on the Immediate Data of Consciousness*, trans. F. L. Pogson (Mineola, NY: Dover, 2001). For a discussion of the role of temporality in European modernist literature, see Ziolkowski, *Dimensions of the Modern Novel*, 191.

53. Adorno, *Aesthetic Theory*, 56; Theodor W. Adorno, "Looking Back on Surrealism," trans. Shierry Weber Nicholsen, in *Notes to Literature*, vol. 1 (New York: Columbia University Press, 1991), 87.

54. André Breton, *Manifestes du surréalisme* (Paris: Folio Essais, 1985), 31.

55. Breton, *Manifestes du surréalisme*, 33–36.

56. André Breton and Philippe Soupault, *Les champs magnétiques, suiviz de Vous m'oublierez et de S'il vous plait* (Paris: Gallimard, 1967).

57. Mark Polizzotti, *Revolution of the Mind: The Life of André Breton* (Boston: Black Widow Press, 2009), 96.

58. Breton and Soupault, *Les champs magnétiques*, 82. Translation mine.

59. Breton, *Manifestes du surréalisme*, 74; Polizzotti, *Revolution of the Mind*, 21.

60. André Breton, *Nadja*, trans. Richard Howard (New York: Grove Press, 1960), 19.

61. Karl Heinz Bohrer, "Instants of Diminishing Representation: The Problem of Temporal Modalities," trans. James McFarland, in *The Moment: Time and Rupture in Modern Thought*, ed. Heidrun Friese (Liverpool: Liverpool University Press, 2001), 113.

62. Breton, *Nadja*, 160.

63. Breton, *Manifestes du surréalisme*, 74.

64. Maurice Blanchot, *The Infinite Conversation*, trans. Susan Hanson (Minneapolis: University of Minnesota Press, 1993), 413–414, 10.

65. André Breton, *Communicating Vessels*, trans. Mary Ann Caws and Geoffrey T. Harris (Lincoln: University of Nebraska Press, 1990), 86. Breton attributes to Friedrich Engels the following quote: "Causality cannot be understood except as it is linked with the category of objective chance, a form of the manifestation of necessity" (91–92).

66. André Breton, *Mad Love (L'amour fou)*, trans. Mary Ann Caws (Lincoln: University of Nebraska Press, 1987), 14–15, 40.

67. Hal Foster, *Compulsive Beauty* (Cambridge, MA: MIT Press, 1995), 19–21.

68. For the role of the Hegelian-Marxist dialectic in surrealism and Breton's *Second Manifesto* in particular, see Michael Löwy, *Morning Star: Surrealism, Marxism, Anarchism, Situationism, Utopia* (Austin: University of Texas Press, 2009), 5. For the role of the dialectic in the writing of *Communicating Vessels*, see Gérard Durozoi, *History of the Surrealist Movement*, trans. Alison Anderson (Chicago, IL: University of Chicago Press, 2002), 189–190. For the Hegelian inspiration behind Breton's *Nadja* and Louis Aragon's *Paris Peasant*, see Anna Balakian, *Surrealism: The Road to the Absolute* (New York: E. P. Dutton, 1970), 138–139.

69. Adorno, *Aesthetic Theory*, 155.

70. Maurice Blanchot, *The Work of Fire*, trans. Charlotte Mandell (Stanford, CA: Stanford University Press, 1995), 92.

71. Blanchot, *Infinite Conversation*, 210.

72. Søren Kierkegaard, *Fear and Trembling*, trans. Alastair Hannay (London: Penguin Books, 2003), 5.

73. Albert Camus, *L'homme revolté* (Paris: Gallimard, 1951), 129.

74. Walter Benjamin, "Surrealism: The Last Snapshot of the European Intelligentsia," trans. Edmund Jephcott, in *Selected Writings, Volume 2: 1927–1934*, ed. Michael W. Jennings, Howard Eiland, and Gary Smith (Cambridge, MA: Belknap Press of Harvard University Press, 1999), 209.

75. Louis Aragon, *Paris Peasant*, trans. Simon Watson Taylor (Boston: Exact Change, 1994), 10.

76. Aragon, *Paris Peasant*, 10.

77. Löwy, *Morning Star*, 4.

78. Aragon, *Paris Peasant*, 12–13.

79. Philip Nord, *The Politics of Resentment: Shopkeeper Protest in Nineteenth-Century Paris* (New Brunswick, NJ: Transaction Publishers, 2005), 90.

80. Nord, *Politics of Resentment*, 141.

81. Aragon, *Paris Peasant*, 12–13, 14.

82. Aragon, 65, 114.

83. Aragon, 116.

84. Aragon also echoes Schlegel's early Romantic project for the creation of a new mythology. For a discussion of Schlegel's "Discourse on Mythology" in relation to surrealism, see Löwy, *Morning Star*, 14.

Chapter 3

1. Ernst Jünger, *Strahlungen I, Sämtliche Werke II* (Stuttgart: Klett-Cotta, 1979), 13.

2. Detlev J. K. Peukert, *The Weimar Republic: The Crisis of Classical Modernity*, trans. Richard Deveson (New York: Hill and Wang, 1993), 23–24.

3. Modris Eksteins, *Rites of Spring: The Great War and the Birth of the Modern Age* (Boston: Houghton Mifflin, 1989), 80, 64.

4. Norbert Bolz, *Auszug aus der entzauberten Welt: philosophischer Extremismus zwischen den Weltkriegen* (Munich: Wilhelm Fink Verlag, 1989), 11.

5. Peukert, *Weimar Republic*, 275; Peter Gay, *Weimar Culture: The Outsider as Insider* (New York: W. W. Norton, 2001), 11.

6. Peter R. Gordon and John P. McCormick, introduction to *Weimar Thought: A Contested Legacy*, ed. Peter R. Gordon and John P. McCormick (Princeton, NJ: Princeton University Press, 2013), 5.

7. Martin Jay, *Songs of Experience: Modern American and European Variations on a Universal Theme* (Berkeley: University of California Press, 2005), 314; Charles Bambach, "Weimar Philosophy and the Crisis of Historical Thinking," in Gordon and McCormick, *Weimar Thought*, 133.

8. Reinhart Koselleck, "Crisis," trans. Michaela Richter, *Journal of the History of Ideas* 67, no. 2 (2006): 397.

9. Rüdiger Graf and Moritz Föllmer, "The Culture of 'Crisis' in the Weimar Republic," *Thesis Eleven* 111, no. 1 (2012): 43; Rüdiger Graf, "Either-Or: The Narrative of 'Crisis' in Weimar Germany and in Historiography," *Central European History* 43, no. 4 (2010): 592.

10. Koselleck, "Crisis," 398.

11. Graf, "Either-Or," 604.

12. Michael Makropoulos, "Crisis and Contingency: Two Categories of the Discourse of Classical Modernity," *Thesis Eleven* 111, no. 1 (2012): 10.

13. Makropoulos, "Crisis and Contingency," 10–12.

14. For a study of the concept of decision in the thought of Jünger, Heidegger, and Schmitt, see Christian Graf von Krockow, *Die Entscheidung: Eine Untersuchung über Ernst Jünger, Carl Schmitt, Martin Heidegger* (Stuttgart: Ferdinand Enke Verlag, 1958).

15. Graf, "Either-Or," 614, 607.

16. Walter Benjamin, "Experience and Poverty," trans. Rodney Livingston, in *Selected Writings, Volume 2: 1927–1934*, ed. Michael W. Jennings, Howard Eiland, and Gary Smith (Cambridge, MA: Belknap Press of Harvard University Press, 1999), 731–732.

17. Dorothée Brill, *Shock and the Senseless in Dada and Fluxus* (Lebanon, NH: Dartmouth College Press, 2010), 45.

18. Stephen Kern, *The Culture of Time and Space: 1880–1918* (Cambridge, MA: Harvard University Press, 1983), 293–294.

19. Ernst Jünger, *Storm of Steel*, trans. Michael Hofmann (New York: Penguin Books, 2004), 5.

20. Jünger, *Storm of Steel*, 8.

21. Ernst Jünger, *Copse 125: A Chronicle from the Trench Warfare of 1918*, trans. Basil Craighton (New York: Howard Fertig, 1988), viii.

22. Anton Kaes, "The Cold Gaze: Notes on Mobilization and Modernity," *New German Critique* 59 (Spring–Summer 1993): 106.

23. Jünger, *Copse 125*, 149.

24. Jünger, *Storm of Steel*, 33, 211, 281.

25. Jünger, *Copse 125*, 50.

26. Benjamin, "Experience and Poverty," 731–732.

27. Thomas Nevin, *Ernst Jünger and Germany: Into the Abyss, 1914–1945* (Durham, NC: Duke University Press, 1996), 121.

28. Julien Hervier, *Ernst Jünger: Dans les tempêtes du siècle* (Paris: Fayard, 2014), 146.

29. Martin Jay, "Experience Without a Subject," in *Cultural Semantics: Keywords of Our Time* (Amherst: University of Massachusetts Press, 1998), 48.

30. Ernst Jünger, *Der Kampf als inneres Erlebnis*, in *Sämtliche Werke, Essays I. Betrachtungen zur Zeit* (Stuttgart: Klett-Cotta, 1978), 54; Nevin, *Ernst Jünger and Germany*, 59, 64.

31. Robert Wohl, *The Generation of 1914* (Cambridge, MA: Harvard University Press, 1979), 48, 54.

32. Anson Rabinbach, *In the Shadow of Catastrophe: German Intellectuals Between Apocalypse and Enlightenment* (Berkeley: University of California Press, 1997), 5.

33. Eric D. Weitz, *Weimar Germany: Promise and Tragedy* (Princeton, NJ: Princeton University Press, 2007), 3.

34. The application of the label "conservative revolution" to this group of right-wing German authors became widespread only after the publication, in 1949, of Armin Mohler's *Die Konservative Revolution in Deutschland 1918–1932: Ein Handbuch* (Graz: Ares Verlag, 2005).

35. Louis Dupeux, "Présentation Générale," in *La Révolution conservatrice allemande sous la République de Weimar*, ed. Louis Dupeux (Paris: Édition Kimé, 1992), 7, 10.

36. Dupeux, 11.

37. Gay, *Weimar Culture*, 81, 96; Daniel Morat, *Von der Tat zur Gelassenheit: Konservatives Denken bei Martin Heidegger, Ernst Jünger und Friedrich Georg Jünger 1920–1960* (Stuttgart: Wallstein Verlag, 2007), 35, 42–43.

38. Richard Wolin, introduction to Ernst Jünger, "Total Mobilization," in *The Heidegger Controversy: A Critical Reader*, ed. Richard Wolin (Cambridge, MA: MIT Press, 1992), 119; Richard Wolin, "Carl Schmitt: The Conservative Revolution and the Aesthetics of Terror," in *Labyrinths: Explorations in the Critical History of Ideas* (Amherst: University of Massachusetts Press, 1995), 103–122.

39. Jünger, *Der Kampf als inneres Erlebnis*, 74.

40. Hervier, *Ernst Jünger*, 147.

41. Ernst Jünger, "Fire," in *The Weimar Republic Sourcebook*, ed. Anton Kaes, Martin Jay, Edward Dimendberg (Berkeley: University of California Press, 1995), 20.

42. Ernst Jünger, *Copse 125*, x.

43. For example, he "internalizes" (*verinnerlichen*) the world in a visionary act in order to later reveal its fundamental essence. Jünger, *Der Kampf als inneres Erlebnis*, 75–77. For a commentary on Jünger's expressionist literary style, see Helmuth Kiesel, *Ernst Jünger. Die Biographie* (Munich: Siedler Verlag, 2009), 230–231.

44. First edition of 1929: Ernst Jünger, *Das abenteuerliche Herz. Erste Fassung: Aufzeichnungen bei Tag und Nacht*, in *Sämtliche Werke, Essays III. Das abenteuerliche Herz* (Stuttgart: Klett-Cotta, 1979); second edition of 1938: Ernst Jünger, *The Adventurous Heart: Figures and Capriccios*, trans. Thomas Friese (Candor, NY: Telos Press, 2012).

45. Karl Heinz Bohrer, *Die Ästhetik des Schreckens: Die pessimistische Romantik und Ernst Jüngers Frühwerk* (Munich: Carl Hanser Verlag, 1978), 187.

46. Plato, *Parmenides*, trans. H. N. Fowler (Cambridge, MA: Harvard University Press, 1939), 156d–e.

47. Jünger, *Adventurous Heart: Figures and Capriccios*, 158–159, 160.

48. "At one moment it is there, in the next moment it is gone, and no sooner is it gone than it is there again, wholly and completely. It cannot be incorporated or worked into any continuity, but whatever expresses itself in this manner is precisely the sudden." Søren Kierkegaard, *The Concept of Anxiety*, trans. Reidar Thomte in collaboration with Albert B. Anderson (Princeton, NJ: Princeton University Press, 1980), 130.

49. Jünger, *Adventurous Heart: Figures and Capriccios*, 64–65.

50. Kierkegaard, *Concept of Anxiety*, 42, 61.

51. Jünger, *Adventurous Heart: Figures and Capriccios*, 7.

52. Jünger, *Das abenteuerliche Herz*, 122.

53. Jünger, 123.

54. Jünger, *Adventurous Heart: Figures and Capriccios*, 62–63.

55. Jünger, 63.

56. Jünger, 61–62

57. Jünger, 49.

58. Jünger, 66.

59. Bohrer, *Die Ästhetik des Schreckens*, 325.

60. Bohrer, 186.

61. Bohrer, 187.

62. Bohrer, 161.

63. Karl Heinz Bohrer, *Suddenness: On the Moment of Aesthetic Appearance*, trans. Ruth Crowley (New York: Columbia University Press, 1994), 39.

64. Bohrer, *Suddenness*, 62, 110. Bohrer's thesis of an association between the early Jünger and avant-garde aesthetics, and the ensuing classification of the author among the ranks of literary modernism, has been actively contested. For Marcus Paul Bullock, it is difficult to talk about any kind of "aesthetic autonomy" in Jünger's literary writings from the period. What is found in them is rather a thematic content and a literary style greatly borrowed from right-wing ideology and politics; Marcus Paul Bullock, *The Violent Eye: Ernst Jünger's Visions and Revisions of the European Right* (Detroit, MI: Wayne State University Press, 1992), 104. Andreas Huyssen writes that Jünger can hardly be regarded as a modernist—a radical innovator in literary form—given the

fact that his works are nothing but the writing and rewriting of the same war experiences under different guises. The result is unvaried material—Jünger's memories from the front—"seamlessly coded and frozen in rhetorical armor," and thus shielded from what should be the essential avant-gardist intention: to put established forms into question through literary experimentation; Andreas Huyssen, "Fortifying the Heart—Totally: Ernst Jünger's Armored Texts," *New German Critique* 59 (Spring–Summer 1993): 4. Like Bullock, Huyssen rejects the thesis that Jünger's category of terror was dissociated from politics and history and asserts that this category was in fact devised as a direct response to the war and the right-wing political agitation of the Weimar years; Huyssen, "Fortifying the Heart," 12. But, perhaps Jünger can be regarded as a "modernist writer" if Modris Eksteins' conception of modernism is considered. For Eksteins, the idea of modernism subsumes both the notion of an aesthetic avant-garde *and* the general impulse for moral, social, and political "liberation." Eksteins thus argues that, because of its zealous embracing of the fusion of art and life as an ideal, expressed in the aestheticization of the war experience, early twentieth-century Germany constituted the "modernist nation *par excellence*"; Eksteins, *Rites of Spring*, xv, xvi. From this perspective, Jünger, as a representative author of that aestheticization, could indeed be considered as belonging in an expanded understanding of literary "modernism."

65. Charles Taylor, *Sources of the Self: The Making of the Modern Identity* (Cambridge, MA: Harvard University Press, 1989), 288.

66. Martin Heidegger, *Being and Time*, trans. John MacQuarrie and Edward Robinson (New York: Harper Perennial, 2008), 387–388, 394–401.

67. Karl Jaspers, *Psychologie der Weltanschauungen* (Berlin: Springer Verlag, 1960), 111. English translation in Daniel H. Magilow, *The Photography of Crisis: The Photo Essays of Weimar Germany* (University Park: Pennsylvania State University Press, 2012), 120.

68. Karl Jaspers, *Philosophy*, in *Basic Philosophical Writings: Selections*, ed. and trans. Edith Ehrlich, Leonard H. Ehrlich, and George B. Pepper (Athens: Ohio University Press, 1986), 97.

69. Karl Jaspers, *Reason and Existenz*, in *Basic Philosophical Writings*, 50–51.

70. Bohrer, *Suddenness*, 50.

71. Carl Schmitt, *Political Theology: Four Chapters on the Concept of Sovereignty*, trans. George Schwab (Chicago: University of Chicago Press, 2005), 15.

72. Jünger, *Copse 125*, 150.

73. Wolin, "Carl Schmitt," 119.

74. Jünger's Weimar political journalism is collected in Ernst Jünger, *Politische Publizistik, 1919 bis 1933*, ed. Sven Olaf Berggötz (Stuttgart: Klett-Cotta, 2001).

75. Hervier, *Ernst Jünger*, 167.

76. Hervier, 168.

77. Kiesel, *Ernst Jünger. Die Biographie*, 307.

78. Kiesel, 298.

79. Kiesel, 284.

80. Kiesel, 304.

81. Julien Hervier, "Ernst Jünger et la question de la modernité," in *La Révolution conservatrice allemande sous la République de Weimar*, ed. Louis Dupeux (Paris: Édition Kimé, 1992), 64.

82. Ernst Jünger, "Total Mobilization," in Wolin, *The Heidegger Controversy*, 119–139.

83. Kiesel, *Ernst Jünger. Die Biographie*, 373.

84. Jünger, "Total Mobilization," 127.

85. Kiesel, *Ernst Jünger. Die Biographie*, 377.

86. Kiesel, 378.

87. Ernst Jünger, "On Danger," in *The Weimar Republic Sourcebook*, ed. Anton Kaes, Martin Jay, and Edward Dimendberg (Berkeley: University of California Press, 1995), 369–372. Original German version: "Über die Gefahr," in *Der gefährliche Augenblick. Eine Sammlung von Bildern und Berichten*, ed. Ferdinand Bucholtz (Berlin: Junker und Dünnhaupt Verlag, 1931).

88. Jünger, "On Danger," 370.

89. Hervier, *Ernst Jünger*, 203.

90. Hervier, 224.

91. Ernst Jünger, *Der Arbeiter* (Stuttgart: Klett-Cotta, 1982), 48–52.

92. Bullock, *Violent Eye*, 140.

93. David C. Durst, *Weimar Modernism: Philosophy, Politics, and Culture in Germany 1918–1933* (New York: Lexington Books, 2004), 137.

94. Jeffrey Herf, *Reactionary Modernism: Technology, Culture, and Politics in Weimar and the Third Reich* (Cambridge: Cambridge University Press, 1984), 1–3.

95. Jünger, *Der Arbeiter*, 59.

96. Brigitte Werneburg, "Ernst Jünger and the Transformed World," *October* 62 (Autumn 1992): 52.

97. Bolz, *Auszug aus der entzauberten Welt*, 164. Translation mine.

98. Jünger, *Der Arbeiter*, 57. Translation mine.

99. Thomas Trezise has pointed out that for Sigmund Freud "the foremost example of a traumatic stressor was the railway disaster." To Freud, it represented the quintessential "single, sudden, and unforeseen accident." Thomas Trezise, *Witnessing Witnessing: On the Reception of Holocaust Survivor Testimony* (New York: Fordham University Press, 2013), 50.

100. Herf, *Reactionary Modernism*, 97.

101. Kaes, "Cold Gaze," 107.

102. Michel Foucault, *Remarks on Marx: Conversations with Duccio Trombadori*, trans. R. James Goldstein and James Cascaito (New York: Semiotext(e), 1991), 30–31.

103. Martin Jay, "The Limits of Limit-Experience: Bataille and Foucault," in *Cultural Semantics*, 66.

104. Alexander Irwin, *Saints of the Impossible: Bataille, Weil, and the Politics of the Sacred* (Minneapolis: University of Minnesota Press, 2002), 136–137, 143.

105. Jay, *Songs of Experience*, 373–375.

106. Walter Benjamin, "Theories of German Fascism: On the Collection of Essays *War and Warriors*, edited by Ernst Jünger," trans. Jerolf Wikoff, in *Selected Writings, Volume 2: 1927–1934*, 313–314.

107. Elisabeth Krimmer, *The Representation of War in German Literature: From 1800 to the Present* (Cambridge: Cambridge University Press, 2014), 72–73.

108. Giorgio Agamben, *Infancy and History: On the Destruction of Experience*, trans. Liz Heron (London: Verso Books, 2007), 41–42.

109. Kaes, "Cold Gaze," 108.

110. Ernst Jünger, *On Pain*, trans. David C. Durst (New York: Telos Press Publishing, 2008), 38.

111. Jünger, "On Danger," 372.

112. Jünger, *On Pain*, 39.

113. Werneburg, "Ernst Jünger and the Transformed World," 53.

114. Ernst Jünger, "War and Photography," trans. Anthony Nassar, *New German Critique* 59 (Spring–Summer 1993), 24. Originally published in Ernst Jünger, ed., *Das Antlitz des Weltkrieges. Fronterlebnisse deutscher Soldaten* (Berlin: Neufeld & Henius, 1930), an anthology.

115. Durst, *Weimar Modernism*, 159.

116. Magilow, *Photography of Crisis*, 122–124.

117. Werneburg, "Ernst Jünger and the Transformed World," 46.

118. Magilow, *Photography of Crisis*, 5.

119. Bohrer, *Die Ästhetik des Schreckens*, 328; Hervier, *Ernst Jünger*, 202.

120. Magilow, *Photography of Crisis*, 125.

121. Jünger, "On Danger," 372.

122. Walter Benjamin, "Little History of Photography," trans. Edmund Jephcott and Kingsley Shorter, in *Selected Writings, Volume 2: 1927–1934*, 510; Ernst Bloch, *The Spirit of Utopia*, trans. Anthony A. Nassar (Stanford, CA: Stanford University Press, 2000), 192.

123. Max Weber, "Science as a Vocation," in *The Vocation Lectures*, trans. Rodney Livingstone (Indianapolis, IN: Hackett Publishing Company, 2004), 13.

124. Weber, 12–13.

Chapter 4

1. I do not consider here *The Principle of Hope*, which is arguably Bloch's most important work. Although it includes some of Bloch's most penetrating ideas on the temporality of the instant, *The Principle of Hope*—written between 1938 and 1948 in exile in the United States and published throughout the decade of the 1950s in the German Democratic Republic—belongs to a decidedly different phase in the philosopher's intellectual life.

2. All quotes are taken from the English translation of the 1923 edition: Ernst Bloch, *The Spirit of Utopia*, trans. Anthony A. Nassar (Stanford, CA: Stanford University Press, 2000), 279.

3. Anson Rabinbach, *In the Shadow of Catastrophe: German Intellectuals between Apocalypse and Enlightenment* (Berkeley: University of California Press, 1997), 47, 57.

4. Michael Löwy, "El joven Lukács y el joven Bloch," in *György Lukács y su época*, ed. Graciela Borja (Mexico City: UAM-Xochimilco, 1988), 45.

5. Rabinbach, *In the Shadow of Catastrophe*, 27–28.

6. In 1911, Bloch and Lukács would also meet in Heidelberg, most notably in the Sonntags Gesellschaft, the intellectual salon organized by Max and Marianne Weber. His participation in this circle proved influential in Bloch's development as an intellectual. Although Max Weber had reservations about Bloch's messianic tone and attitude, he recognized the originality of the young man's thought. A few years later, it was Weber who recommended *Geist der Utopie* (originally titled *Philosophie der Musik*) for publication. See Peter Zudeick, *Der Hintern des Teufels: Ernst Bloch—Leben und Werk* (Moos: Elster Verlag, 1985), 44–45; Éva Karádi, "Ernst Bloch and Georg Lukács in Max Weber's Circle," in *Max Weber and His Contemporaries*, ed. Wolfgang M. Mommsen and Jürgen Osterhammel (London: Allen and Unwin/The German Historical Institute, 1987), 502.

7. David Kaufmann, "Thanks for the Memory: Bloch, Benjamin, and the Philosophy of History," in *Not Yet: Reconsidering Ernst Bloch*, ed. Jamie Owen Daniel and Tom Moylan (London: Verso, 1997), 36.

8. Rabinbach, *In the Shadow of Catastrophe*, 53.

9. Rabinbach, 32, 33.

10. Gershom Scholem, *The Messianic Idea in Judaism and Other Essays on Jewish Spirituality*, trans. Michael A. Meyer and Hillel Halkin (New York: Schocken, 1995), 33.

11. Jack Zipes, "Introduction: Toward a Realization of Anticipatory Illumination," in Ernst Bloch, *The Utopian Function of Art and Literature: Selected Essays*, trans. Jack Zipes and Frank Mecklenburg (Cambridge, MA: MIT Press, 1989), xiv.

12. Bloch, *Spirit of Utopia*, 3.

13. Bloch, 187–188.

14. Several decades later, Bloch would briefly devote his attention to a version of instantaneous temporality almost identical to Jünger's notion of terror in "Der unerträgliche Augenblick" ("The Unbearable Moment"), a piece originally published in *Verfremdungen I* (Berlin: Suhrkamp Verlag, 1962) and later included in the collection *Literarische Aufsätze*; Ernst Bloch, *Literarische Aufsätze* (Frankfurt: Suhrkamp, 1965); Ernst, Bloch, *Literary Essays*, trans. Andrew Joron (Stanford, CA: Stanford University Press, 1998).

15. Bloch, *Spirit of Utopia*, 199.

16. Edmund Husserl, *The Phenomenology of Internal Time-Consciousness*, trans. James S. Churchill (Bloomington: University of Indiana Press, 1964).

17. Georg Simmel, *Rembrandt: An Essay in the Philosophy of Art*, trans. Alan Scott and Helmut Staubmann (New York: Routledge, 1964), 57.

18. Arno Münster, *Ernst Bloch: messianisme et utopie* (Paris: Presses Universitaires de France, 1989), 99.

19. Georg Lukács, *Soul and Form*, trans. Anna Bostock (Cambridge, MA: MIT Press, 1971), 152–153.

20. Wayne Hudson, "Bloch and the Philosophy of the Proterior," in *The Privatization of Hope: Ernst Bloch and the Future of Utopia*, ed. Peter Thompson and Slavoj Žižek (Durham, NC: Duke University Press, 2013), 26.

21. Arno Münster, *Espérance, rêve, utopie dans la pensée d'Ernst Bloch* (Paris: L'Harmattan, 2015), 24.

22. Arno Münster, *Figures de l'utopie dans la pensée d'Ernst Bloch* (Paris: Aubier, 1984), 94, 108.

23. Friedrich Hölderlin, *Poems and Fragments*, trans. Michael Hamburger (London: Anvil Press Poetry, 1994), 483.

24. Münster, *Ernst Bloch: messianisme et utopie*, 6–9.

25. Bloch, *Spirit of Utopia*, 192.

26. Fredric Jameson, *Marxism and Form: Twentieth-Century Dialectical Theories of Literature* (Princeton, NJ: Princeton University Press, 1971), 126.

27. Bloch, *Spirit of Utopia*, 196, 201.

28. Peter Thompson, "Religion, Utopia, and the Metaphysics of Contingency," in *The Privatization of Hope: Ernst Bloch and the Future of Utopia*, ed. Peter Thompson and Slavoj Žižek (Durham, NC: Duke University Press, 2013), 82–105.

29. Bloch, *Spirit of Utopia*, 41, 158.

30. Bloch, 205, 248.

31. Bloch, 236–237.

32. Arno Münster, *L'utopie concrète d'Ernst Bloch: une biographie* (Paris: Édition Kimé, 2001), 112–113.

33. Münster, *Figures de l'utopie*, 95, 98. The mystical notion of restoration also plays a fundamental role in Walter Benjamin's late historical thinking.

34. Münster, *L'utopie concrète d'Ernst Bloch*, 80.

35. Ernst Bloch, *Thomas Münzer als Theologe der Revolution* (Frankfurt: Suhrkamp, 1969). On Bloch's Marxism, see Wayne Hudson, *The Marxist Philosophy of Ernst Bloch* (New York: St. Martin's Press, 1982), 21; Münster, *Ernst Bloch: messianisme et utopie*, 157.

36. Michael Löwy, "Utopie et romantisme révolutionnaire chez Ernst Bloch," *De(s)générations* 11 (May 2010): 82. This revolutionary enthusiasm led to Bloch being perceived as the "German philosopher of the October Revolution," meaning that he was a thinker on whom

the events of 1917 in Russia left such a powerful imprint that his philosophical will onwards would have been to promote the revolutionary powers latent in history and nature. See Oskar Negt, "Ernst Bloch, the German Philosopher of the October Revolution," *New German Critique* 4 (Winter 1975): 9–10.

37. Münster, *L'utopie concrète d'Ernst Bloch*, 124.

38. Münster, 80.

39. Bloch, *Thomas Münzer als Theologe der Revolution*, 19.

40. Neville Plaice, Stephen Plaice, and Paul Knight, translators' introduction to *The Principle of Hope*, by Ernst Bloch (Cambridge, MA: MIT Press, 1996), xxii.

41. Münster, *Figures de l'utopie*, 23, 93–94. Perhaps this explosive mixture of religious and materialist motifs can account for the difficulties in the reception of Bloch's Marxism in both the East and West during the Cold War. In 1949, after the end of his exile in the United States, Bloch chose to return to the German Democratic Republic (GDR), where he took on the chair of philosophy at Leipzig University. The apparatus of the Socialist Unity Party of Germany (SED) had kept him under surveillance during the early 1950s, and, after 1956, a period of great disquiet began for Bloch and his wife, Karola, which would end in their abandoning the GDR in 1961. The official attacks began in 1957, when the SED accused Bloch of representing "non-Marxist principles." In April, a conference at Bloch's own Leipzig University denounced his "idealistic-mystical" tendency and the conflicts between his philosophy and dialectical materialism; "Ernst Bloch—Die Vorlesung fällt aus," *Der Spiegel*, May 1, 1957, 57. That same year, Walter Ulbricht fulfilled his promise, reported by Hans Mayer, that *The Principle of Hope* should become a "book without readers." The printing of the work's third volume was stopped and the copies of volumes one and two were withdrawn from bookshops; Hans Mayer, *Ein Deutscher auf Widerruf. Erinnerungen* (Frankfurt: Suhrkamp, 1982), 2:242; "Ernst Bloch—Exkommunisiert," *Der Spiegel*, August 17, 1960, 54. During this period, close associates of Bloch were imprisoned. Bloch was next in the detention list, but Ulbricht cancelled the plan and granted him an enforced emeritus status instead; Mayer, *Ein Deutscher auf Widerruf*, 289–290. Bloch's philosophy of utopia represented a threat to the GDR's establishment because socialist nations themselves were not exempt from the criticism implied in his insistence on the distance between the present social conditions and the completion of utopia. Bloch's students had begun to use this perspective to criticize, not the capitalist world, but their own socialist reality; "Bloch—Aus der Neuen Welt," *Der Spiegel*, September 27, 1961, 86–88. In the West, Bloch's political views would represent another obstacle for the reception of his work. Bloch's combination of Marxism and religion and his communist stance reappear, for example, in Leon Wieseltier's review of *The Principle of Hope*'s English translation, from 1986. Wieseltier considers the work a "monumental apology for the Soviet Union" and "the most extravagant argument for Marxism ever assembled," a result of Bloch's "idiosyncratic mingling" of Marxism and mysticism; Leon Wieseltier, "Under the Spell," review of *The Principle of Hope*, by Ernst Bloch, *New York Times*, November 23, 1986.

42. Ernst Bloch, "Aktualität und Utopie," in *Geschichte und Klassenbewusstsein Heute*, ed. F. Cerruti, D. Claussen et al. (Amsterdam: De Munter, 1971), 180, quoted in Anson Rabinbach, "Unclaimed Heritage: Ernst Bloch's Heritage of Our Times and the Theory of Fascism," *New German Critique* 11 (Spring 1977): 17–18.

43. Hudson, *The Marxist Philosophy of Ernst Bloch*, 26–27.

44. Klaus Vondung, *The Apocalypse in Germany*, trans. Stephen D. Ricks (Columbia: University of Missouri Press, 2001), 245.

45. Rabinbach, "Unclaimed Heritage," 18.

46. Münster, *Espérance, rêve, utopie*, 173. Translation mine.

47. Rüdiger Graf, "Anticipating the Future in the Present: 'New Women' and Other Beings of the Future in Weimar Germany," *Central European History* 42, no. 4 (2009): 650.

48. Rüdiger Graf, "Either-Or: The Narrative of 'Crisis' in Weimar Germany and in Historiography," *Central European History* 43, no. 4 (2010): 594–595.

49. Graf, 604.

50. Graf, 604.

51. The genesis of *Traces* can be traced back to the writing of *The Spirit of Utopia* and Bloch's volume of essays *Durch die Wüste: Kritische Essays* (Berlin: Paul Cassirer, 1923). Many paralipomena from these works ended up as passages of *Traces*. See Klaus L. Berghahn, "A View Through the Red Window: Ernst Bloch's *Spuren*," in *Modernity and the Text: Revisions of German Modernism*, ed. Andreas Huyssen and David Bathrick (New York: Columbia University Press, 1989), 201.

52. Theodor Adorno, "Bloch's 'Traces': The Philosophy of Kitsch," trans. Rodney Livingstone, *New Left Review* 121 (May–June 1980): 49.

53. Tony Phelan, "Ernst Bloch's 'Golden Twenties': *Erbschaft dieser Zeit* and the Problem of Cultural History," in *Culture and Society in the Weimar Republic*, ed. Keith Bullivant (Manchester, UK: Manchester University Press, 1977), 106.

54. Berghahn, "View Through the Red Window," 203.

55. Gerhard Richter, *Thought-Images: Frankfurt School Writers' Reflections from Damaged Life* (Stanford, CA: Stanford University Press, 2007), 2, 7.

56. Rabinbach, *In the Shadow of Catastrophe*, 31.

57. Plaice, Plaice, and Knight, translators' introduction to *Principle of Hope*, xxxii.

58. Adorno, "Bloch's 'Traces,'" 51.

59. Martin Jay, "Mass Culture and Aesthetic Redemption: The Debate Between Max Horkheimer and Siegfried Kracauer," in *Fin-de-siècle Socialism and Other Essays* (New York: Routledge, 1988), 82.

60. Berghahn, "View Through the Red Window," 202.

61. Ernst Bloch, *Traces*, trans. Anthony A. Nassar (Stanford, CA: Stanford University Press, 2006), 50, 51, 97.

62. Bloch, 60.

63. Bloch, 136.

64. Bloch, 173.

65. Bloch, 72, 73, 89, 91.

66. Sándor Radnóti, "Lukács and Bloch," in *Lukács Revalued*, ed. Agnes Heller (Oxford: Basil Blackwell, 1983), 71.

67. Bloch, *Spirit of Utopia*, 116.

68. Berghahn, "View Through the Red Window," 202.

69. Maud Lavin, *Cut with the Kitchen Knife: the Weimar Photomontages of Hannah Höch* (New Haven, CT: Yale University Press, 1993), 29–30.

70. An extended second edition published in 1961 included some of Bloch's interventions in the Expressionism Debate of the late 1930s.

71. Phelan, "Ernst Bloch's 'Golden Twenties,'" 96, 100.

72. Phelan, 100.

73. Ernst Bloch, *Heritage of Our Times*, trans. Neville and Stephen Plaice (London: Polity Press, 1991), 97.

74. Phelan, "Ernst Bloch's 'Golden Twenties,'" 115.

75. In this sense, both *The Spirit of Utopia*'s apocalyptic time and *Heritage of Our Times*'s theory of noncontemporaneity belong to the same project of introducing new layers of temporality into the Hegelian dialectic, either as projections coming from the future (as in utopian anticipation) or from the past (as in the forms of noncontemporaneous consciousness).

76. Bloch, *Heritage of Our Times*, 106.

77. Bloch, 142.

78. Bloch, 102.

79. Bloch, 184–185.

80. Bloch, 78–79.

81. Rabinbach, "Unclaimed Heritage," 14.

82. Bloch, *Heritage of Our Times*, 110.

83. Bloch, 115–116.

84. Bloch, 116–118.

85. Löwy, "Utopie et romantisme révolutionnaire," 85.

86. Bloch, *Heritage of Our Times*, 140.

87. Bloch, 62.

88. Some of the other authors who participated in the debate were: Klaus Mann, Franz Leschnitzer, Herwarth Walden, Klaus Berger, Kurt Kersten, Gustav Wangenheim, Béla Balázs, Peter Fischer, and Hanns Eisler. See Hans-Jürgen Schmitt, ed., *Die Expressionismusdebatte: Materialen zu einer marxistischen Realismuskonzeption* (Frankfurt: Suhrkamp Verlag, 1973).

89. See Adorno, "Bloch's 'Traces,'" 51.

90. Rodney Livingstone, Perry Anderson, and Francis Mulhern, "Presentation I," in *Aesthetics and Politics*, eds. Theodor Adorno, Walter Benjamin, Ernst Bloch, Bertolt Brecht, and Georg Lukács, (London: Verso, 2007), 5.

91. Rabinbach, "Unclaimed Heritage," 15.

92. Katerina Clark, *Moscow, the Fourth Rome: Stalinism, Cosmopolitanism, and the Evolution of Soviet Culture, 1931–1941* (Cambridge, MA: Harvard University Press, 2011), 72, 211.

93. Zudeick, *Der Hintern des Teufels*, 153. Bloch, however, was probably not convinced of the trials' veracity. His wife, Karola, mentioned Bloch's private consternation before the Communist Party's defense of the trials and his anxious attempts to find a meaning in them. Nevertheless, Bloch supported them in order to maintain hope in the Soviet Union as the "revolutionary fatherland"; Zudeick, *Der Hintern des Teufels*, 155.

94. Münster, *L'utopie concrète d'Ernst Bloch*, 200.

95. Collected in Ernst Bloch, *Vom Hasard zur Katastrophe: Politische Aufsätze 1934–1939* (Frankfurt: Suhrkamp Verlag, 1972).

96. Münster, *L'utopie concrète d'Ernst Bloch*, 200.

97. Zudeick, *Der Hintern des Teufels*, 153, 169.

98. See Ernst Bloch, "Originalgeschichte des Dritten Reichs," in *Vom Hasard zur Katastrophe*, 291–317.

99. See Ernst Bloch, "Kritik einer Prozesskritik," in *Vom Hasard zur Katastrophe*, 175–183.

100. Ernst Bloch, *Literary Essays*, trans. Andrew Joron (Stanford, CA: Stanford University Press, 1998), 105.

101. Georg Lukács, "Expressionism: Its Significance and Decline," in *Essays on Realism*, ed. Rodney Livingstone, trans. David Fernbach (London: Lawrence and Wishart, 1980), 89, 109.

102. It must be noted that expressionism was a politically ambivalent movement. There were expressionist writers with Nazi sympathies (such as Gottfried Benn) and even Nazis with

expressionist sympathies (such as Goebbels); at the same time, expressionist works of art were the main target of the Nazi *Degenerate Art* exhibition of 1937.

103. Bloch, *Utopian Function of Art and Literature*, 160.

104. Martin Jay, *Marxism and Totality: The Adventures of a Concept from Lukács to Habermas* (Berkeley: University of California Press, 1984).

105. Rabinbach, "Unclaimed Heritage," 15.

106. Bloch, *Heritage of Our Times*, 3.

107. Bloch, 205.

108. Bloch, 207.

109. This text would later be included in the 1962 edition of *Heritage of Our Times*.

110. Bloch, *Heritage of Our Times*, 240.

111. David C. Durst, *Weimar Modernism: Philosophy, Politics, and Culture in Germany 1918–1933* (Lanham, MD: Lexington Books, 2004), 20.

112. Bloch, *Heritage of Our Times*, 246–247.

113. Georg Lukács, "Realism in the Balance," in Adorno et al., *Aesthetics and Politics*, 41.

114. This text would later be included in the 1962 edition of *Heritage of Our Times*.

115. Bloch, *Heritage of Our Times*, 250–252.

116. Bloch, *Traces*, 129.

117. Bloch, 130.

118. Bloch, 130.

119. Douglas Kellner and Harry O'Hara, "Utopia and Marxism in Ernst Bloch," *New German Critique* 9 (Autumn 1976): 15.

120. Mark Lilla, "What Is Counter-Enlightenment?," in *Isaiah Berlin's Counter-Enlightenment*, ed. Joseph Mali and Robert Wokler (Philadelphia: American Philosophical Society, 2004), 9.

Chapter 5

1. Georg Simmel, "The Metropolis and Mental Life," in *On Individuality and Social Forms: Selected Writings*, ed. Donald N. Levine (Chicago: University of Chicago Press, 1971), 325.

2. Dorothée Brill, *Shock and the Senseless in Dada and Fluxus* (Lebanon, NH: Dartmouth College Press, 2010), 45.

3. Howard Eiland and Michael W. Jennings, *Walter Benjamin: A Critical Life* (Cambridge, MA: Belknap Press of Harvard University Press, 2014), 125.

4. Walter Benjamin, "Experience and Poverty," trans. Rodney Livingston, in *Selected Writings, Volume 2: 1927–1934*, ed. Michael W. Jennings, Howard Eiland, and Gary Smith (Cambridge, MA: Belknap Press of Harvard University Press, 1999), 731.

5. Walter Benjamin, "The Storyteller: Observations on the Works of Nikolai Leskov," trans. Harry Zohn, in *Selected Writings, Volume 3: 1935–1938*, ed. Michael W. Jennings and Howard Eiland (Cambridge, MA: Belknap Press of Harvard University Press, 2002), 143–144.

6. Benjamin, 143–144.

7. See Walter Benjamin, *The Origin of German Tragic Drama*, trans. John Osborne (London: New Left Books, 1977), 55; Eiland and Jennings, *Walter Benjamin: A Critical Life*, 552.

8. Examples include the work of John Heartfield and Hannah Höch. See Matthew Teitelbaum, ed., *Montage and Modern Life: 1919–1942* (Cambridge, MA: Institute of Contemporary Art/MIT Press, 1992).

9. Some of these artists later gathered around the journal *G: Zeitschrift für Elementare Gestaltung*, founded by Hans Richter, and to which Benjamin was a contributor. See Eiland and Jennings, *Walter Benjamin: A Critical Life*, 422.

10. Walter Benjamin, *One-Way Street*, trans. Edmund Jephcott, in *Selected Writings, Volume 1: 1913–1926*, ed. Marcus Bullock and Michael W. Jennings (Cambridge, MA: Belknap Press of Harvard University Press, 1996), 444–488.

11. Ernst Bloch, *Heritage of Our Times*, trans. Neville Plaice and Stephen Plaice (London: Polity Press, 1991), 335, 337.

12. László Moholy-Nagy, "Production-Reproduction," trans. Mátyás Esterházy, in *Moholy-Nagy*, ed. Krisztina Passuth (New York: Thames and Hudson, 1985), 289.

13. Benjamin, *One-Way Street*, 486.

14. Benjamin, 486, 487.

15. Howard Caygill, "Non-Messianic Political Theology in Benjamin's 'On the Concept of History,'" in *Walter Benjamin and History*, ed. Andrew Benjamin (London: Continuum, 2005), 224.

16. Walter Benjamin, "Surrealism: The Last Snapshot of the European Intelligentsia," trans. Edmund Jephcott, in *Selected Writings, Volume 2: 1927–1934*, 207–221.

17. Benjamin, 209.

18. Benjamin, 210. Benjamin's reference to "the revolutionary energies that appear in 'the outmoded'" can also be interpreted as a version of the Blochian not-yet—that noncontemporaneity of history and being that opens up the present to utopian possibility.

19. Benjamin, 217–218.

20. Eiland and Jennings, *Walter Benjamin: A Critical Life*, 763.

21. Walter Benjamin, "Little History of Photography," trans. Edmund Jephcott and Kingsley Shorter, in *Selected Writings, Volume 2: 1927–1934*, 510.

22. Walter Benjamin, "The Work of Art in the Age of Its Technological Reproducibility: Second Version," trans. Edmund Jephcott and Harry Zohn, in *Selected Writings, Volume 3: 1935–1938*, 118. All quotes from the "The Work of Art" come from the text's second and most comprehensive version, written between December 1935 and February 1936, and usually referred to as the "Urtext."

23. Benjamin, "Little History of Photography," 510.

24. Benjamin, "Work of Art," 117.

25. Benjamin, 132n22.

26. Benjamin, 108.

27. Eiland and Jennings, *Walter Benjamin: A Critical Life*, 422.

28. Uwe Steiner, *Walter Benjamin: An Introduction to His Work and Thought*, trans. Michael Winkler (Chicago: University of Chicago Press, 2010), 131.

29. Benjamin, "Work of Art," 104–105.

30. Jürgen Habermas, "Walter Benjamin: Consciousness-Raising or Rescuing Critique," in *On Walter Benjamin: Critical Essays and Recollections*, ed. Gary Smith (Cambridge, MA: MIT Press, 1988), 119.

31. Benjamin, "Work of Art," 124n10.

32. Henri Bergson, *Time and Free Will: An Essay on the Immediate Data of Consciousness*, trans. F. L. Pogson (Mineola, NY: Dover Publications, 2001); Edmund Husserl, *The Phenomenology of Internal Time-Consciousness*, trans. by James S. Churchill (Bloomington: University of Indiana Press, 1964); Martin Heidegger, *Being and Time*, trans. John Macquarrie and Edward Robinson (New York: Harper and Row, 1962).

33. Prompted by Adorno's criticisms, "On Some Motifs in Baudelaire" is a reelaboration of the section on the figure of the flaneur from "The Paris of the Second Empire in Baudelaire," an essay that Benjamin projected to become the middle section of his unfinished book on

Baudelaire, *Charles Baudelaire: A Lyric Poet in the Age of High Capitalism*. Benjamin conceived of the Baudelaire book as a "miniature model" of the *Arcades Project*. See Eiland and Jennings, *Walter Benjamin: A Critical Life*, 422.

34. Walter Benjamin, "On Some Motifs in Baudelaire," trans. Harry Zohn, in *Selected Writings, Volume 4: 1938–1940*, ed. Michael W. Jennings and Howard Eiland (Cambridge, MA: Belknap Press of Harvard University Press, 2003), 313–355.

35. Benjamin, 318.

36. Giorgio Agamben, *Infancy and History: On the Destruction of Experience*, trans. Liz Heron (London: Verso, 2007), 41.

37. Benjamin, "On Some Motifs," 318.

38. Sigmund Freud, *Beyond the Pleasure Principle*, trans. James Strachey (New York: W. W. Norton and Company, 1961), 26–28. For a discussion of Freud's theory of trauma, see Thomas Trezise, "Trauma and Theory," chap. 2 in *Witnessing Witnessing: On the Reception of Holocaust Survivor Testimony* (New York: Fordham University Press, 2013).

39. Steiner, *Walter Benjamin*, 163.

40. Benjamin, "On Some Motifs," 314, 320.

41. Benjamin, 327.

42. Benjamin, 328.

43. Benjamin, 343.

44. Benjamin, 337.

45. Agamben, *Infancy and History*, 41, 42.

46. Benjamin, "On Some Motifs," 336.

47. Benjamin, 335–336.

48. Benjamin conceived of the project in 1928–1929, abandoned it for a few years, and then resumed his research in 1934, which continued until his death in 1940.

49. My reading of this stage of Benjamin's thought takes into account the reconstruction of another of his (unfinished) writing projects, derived from the *Arcades* and made available in *Charles Baudelaire: A Lyric Poet in the Age of High Capitalism*. This reconstruction is based on the manuscripts discovered by Giorgio Agamben at the Bibliothèque Nationale de France in 1981. I had access to the English version of the reconstruction prepared by Michael W. Jennings when I was a student in Prof. Jennings' graduate seminar Benjamin's Baudelaire: Towards a Theory of Modernity, held at Princeton University in 2010. An Italian translation of the reconstruction is available in print: Walter Benjamin, *Charles Baudelaire: Un poeta lirico nell'età del capitalismo avanzato*, ed. Giorgio Agamben, Barbara Chitussi e Clemens-Carl Härle (Vicenza: Neri Pozza Editore, 2015).

50. Walter Benjamin, "The Study Begins with Some Reflections on the Influence of *Les Fleurs du mal*," trans. Edmund Jephcott, in *Selected Writings, Volume 4: 1938–1940*, 96.

51. Walter Benjamin, *The Arcades Project*, trans. Howard Eiland and Kevin McLaughlin (Cambridge, MA: Belknap Press of Harvard University Press, 1999), 351 [J69, 5]. In notes citing the *Arcades*, the page number will be followed by the number (in square brackets) of the note according to the alphabetized grouping of the *Arcades* manuscript.

52. Benjamin, "Study Begins," 96–97.

53. Benjamin, 97.

54. Letter by Benjamin in Walter Benjamin, "Exchange with Theodor W. Adorno on the Essay 'Paris, the Capital of the Nineteenth Century,'" trans. Edmund Jephcott and Howard Eiland, in *Selected Writings, Volume 3: 1935–1938*, 51.

55. Benjamin, *Arcades Project*, 458 [N1,9].

56. Walter Benjamin, "Paris, the Capital of the Nineteenth Century," trans. Howard Eiland, in *Selected Writings, Volume 3: 1935–1938*, 33–34.

57. Benjamin, 44.

58. Eiland and Jennings, *Walter Benjamin: A Critical Life*, 314.

59. Richard Wolin, *Walter Benjamin: An Aesthetics of Redemption* (Berkeley: University of California Press, 1994), 113.

60. Michael Löwy, *Redemption and Utopia: Jewish Libertarian Thought in Central Europe, A Study in Elective Affinity*, trans. Hope Heaney (London: Verso, 2017), 108.

61. Löwy, *Redemption and Utopia*, 98.

62. Wolin, *Walter Benjamin*, 14–15.

63. Sandor Radnoti, "Benjamin's Politics," *Telos* 37 (1978): 66.

64. Steiner, *Walter Benjamin*, 148–149.

65. Walter Benjamin, "The Metaphysics of Youth," trans. Rodney Livingstone, in *Selected Writings, Volume 1: 1913–1926*, ed. Michael W. Jennings and Marcus Bullock (Cambridge, MA: Belknap Press of Harvard University Press, 1996), 6–17.

66. Walter Benjamin, "The Life of Students," trans. Rodney Livinsgtone, in *Selected Writings, Volume 1: 1913–1926*, 37.

67. Letter of August 9, 1935, in Gershom Scholem, ed., *The Correspondence of Walter Benjamin and Gershom Scholem, 1932–1940*, trans. Gary Smith and Andre Lefevere, with an introduction by Anson Rabinbach (New York: Schocken Books, 1989), 165.

68. Eiland and Jennings, *Walter Benjamin: A Critical Life*, 27.

69. Friedrich Nietzsche, "On the Utility and Liability of History for Life," in *The Complete Works of Friedrich Nietzsche 2: Unfashionable Observations*, trans. Richard Gray (Stanford, CA: Stanford University Press, 1995), 129.

70. Benjamin, *Arcades Project*, 392.

71. There is a coincidence between this aspect of Benjamin's historiographical method and his own ideas on the "optical unconscious." In the *Arcades'* epistemology of history, certain historical objects or configurations, if seen retrospectively, are perceived as being anticipated in previous objects or configurations, just as photographs looked at in the present feature an "inconspicuous spot where in the immediacy of that long-forgotten moment the future nests so eloquently that we, looking back, may rediscover it"; Benjamin, "Little History of Photography," 510. Photography, Benjamin affirms, is to the optical unconscious what psychoanalysis is to the instinctual unconscious. A comparable observation could be made about Benjamin's historical method: that the historical materialist standpoint would be the "psychoanalysis" of the "dream images" of the collective.

72. Rolf Tiedemann, "Dialectics at a Standstill: Approaches to the *Passagen-Werk*," trans. Gary Smith and André Lefevere, in Benjamin, *Arcades Project*, 935.

73. Benjamin, *Arcades Project*, 486 [N18,4].

74. Steiner, *Walter Benjamin*, 113.

75. Walter Benjamin, "Eduard Fuchs, Collector and Historian," trans. Howard Eiland and Michael Jennings, in *Selected Writings, Volume 3: 1935–1938*, 262.

76. Benjamin, *Arcades Project*, 460 [N2,2].

77. Benjamin, "Eduard Fuchs," 262.

78. Benjamin, *Arcades Project*, 463 [N3,1].

79. Theodor W. Adorno, "Introduction to Benjamin's *Schriften*," trans. R. Hullot-Kentor, in Smith, *On Walter Benjamin*, 12.

80. Benjamin, *Arcades Project*, 461 [N2,6].

81. Dimitris Vardoulakis, "The Subject of History: The Temporality of Parataxis in Benjamin's Historiography," in A. Benjamin, *Walter Benjamin and History*, 123.

82. Philippe Simay, "Tradition as Injunction: Benjamin and the Critique of Historicisms," in A. Benjamin, *Walter Benjamin and History*, 147.

83. See Søren Kierkegaard, *Philosophical Fragments and Johannes Climacus*, trans. Howard V. Hong and Edna H. Hong (Princeton, NJ: Princeton University Press, 1985); Søren Kierkegaard, *The Concept of Anxiety*, trans. by Reidar Thomte in collaboration with Albert B. Anderson (Princeton, NJ: Princeton University Press, 1980); Bergson, *Time and Free Will*; Heidegger, *Being and Time*.

84. See Benjamin's letter to Ernst Schoen of September 19, 1919, in Gershom Scholem and Theodor W. Adorno, eds., *The Correspondence of Walter Benjamin, 1910–1940*, trans. Manfred R. Jacobson and Evelyn M. Jacobson (Chicago: University of Chicago Press, 1994), 148; Eiland and Jennings, *Walter Benjamin: A Critical Life*, 264–265.

85. See Ernst Bloch, "Recollections of Walter Benjamin," trans. Michael W. Jennings, in Smith, *On Walter Benjamin*, 339–340.

86. See Benjamin's letter to Gershom Scholem of October 17, 1934, in Scholem, *Correspondence of Walter Benjamin and Gershom Scholem*, 154.

87. Adorno, "Introduction to Benjamin's *Schriften*," 7.

88. Tiedemann, "Dialectics at a Standstill," 936.

89. Tiedemann, 936.

90. Eduardo Cadava, *Words of Light: Theses on the Photography of History* (Princeton, NJ: Princeton University Press, 1997), 79.

91. Benjamin, "Paris, the Capital," 33–34.

92. See Walter Benjamin, "First Sketches," in Benjamin, *Arcades Project*, 845 [H°,17], 861 [O°,50].

93. Benjamin, *Arcades Project*, 388–389 [K1,2].

94. Steiner, *Walter Benjamin*, 148–149.

95. Anson Rabinbach, introduction to Scholem, *Correspondence of Walter Benjamin and Gershom Scholem*, xvi.

96. Anson Rabinbach, *In the Shadow of Catastrophe: German Intellectuals between Apocalypse and Enlightenment* (Berkeley: University of California Press, 1997), 57, 59.

97. Löwy, *Redemption and Utopia*, 101.

98. Löwy, 106.

99. Walter Benjamin, "Critique of Violence," trans. Edmund Jephcott, in *Selected Writings, Volume 1: 1913–1926*, 240–241.

100. Georges Sorel, *Reflections on Violence*, trans. T. E. Hulme (New York: Collier Books, 1950), 246.

101. See Rabinbach, *In the Shadow of Catastrophe*, 60; Eiland and Jennings, *Walter Benjamin: A Critical Life*, 320.

102. Sorel, *Reflections on Violence*, 123, 128.

103. Stephen Kern, *The Culture of Time and Space: 1880–1918* (Cambridge, MA: Harvard University Press, 1983), 103.

104. Sorel, *Reflections on Violence*, 135.

105. Habermas, "Walter Benjamin: Consciousness-Raising," 119.

106. Eiland and Jennings, *Walter Benjamin: A Critical Life*, 325. It is as if in Benjamin's thought the revolution were a political "category of the unreal," comparable to Karl Heinz

Bohrer's identification of the surrealist instantaneous experience as a "perceptual category of the unreal," given surrealism's tendency to relativize the event's "realizability" and "dispense with reference"; Karl Heinz Bohrer, "Instants of Diminishing Representation: The Problem of Temporal Modalities," trans. James McFarland, in *The Moment: Time and Rupture in Modern Thought*, ed. Heidrun Friese (Liverpool: Liverpool University Press, 2001), 121.

107. Walter Benjamin, "Theological-Political Fragment," trans. Edmund Jephcott, in *Selected Writings, Volume 4: 1938–1940*, 305–306.

108. Löwy, *Redemption and Utopia*, 102.

109. Löwy, 103.

110. Leopold von Ranke's dictum for historiographical research. See Simay, "Tradition as Injunction," 148.

111. Stéphane Mosès, *L'Ange de l'histoire: Rosenzweig, Benjamin, Scholem* (Paris: Éditions du Seuil, 1992), 23.

112. David S. Ferris, "The Shortness of History, or Photography *in Nuce*," in A. Benjamin, *Walter Benjamin and History*, 63.

113. Michael Löwy, *Fire Alarm: Reading Walter Benjamin's 'On the Concept of History'*, trans. Chris Turner (London: Verso, 2005), 62–63.

114. Löwy, *Redemption and Utopia*, 111.

115. Löwy, 111.

116. Andrew Benjamin, introduction to A. Benjamin, *Walter Benjamin and History*, 1.

117. Gershom Scholem, "Walter Benjamin and His Angel," trans. Werner Dannhauser, in Smith, *On Walter Benjamin*, 52.

118. Tiedemann, "Dialectics at a Standstill," 944.

119. Rabinbach, *In the Shadow of Catastrophe*, 32.

120. Benjamin, "Theological-Political Fragment," 305.

121. Wolin, *Walter Benjamin*, 117.

122. Reinhart Koselleck, *The Practice of Conceptual History: Timing History, Spacing Concepts* (Stanford, CA: Stanford University Press, 2002), 240, 243.

123. Walter Benjamin, "On the Concept of History," trans. Harry Zohn, in *Selected Writings, Volume 4: 1938–1940*, 397.

124. Jürgen Habermas, *The Philosophical Discourse of Modernity: Twelve Lectures*, trans. Frederick Lawrence (Cambridge, MA: MIT Press, 2000), 11.

125. Benjamin, "On the Concept of History," 395.

126. Benjamin, 396.

127. See Peter Osborne, *The Politics of Time: Modernity and Avant-Garde* (London: Verso, 1995), 156, 159.

128. Werner Hamacher, "'Now': Walter Benjamin on Historical Time," in A. Benjamin, *Walter Benjamin and History*, 52.

129. From this fact, Eduardo Cadava has derived an interpretation of photography as Benjamin's "model for the understanding of history." Cadava, *Words of Light*, xx.

130. Benjamin, "On the Concept of History," 396. Giorgio Agamben has put forward a different interpretation that associates Benjamin's messianic ideas, not with Jewish mysticism, but with the Christian messianic stance articulated in Saint Paul. According to Agamben, there are textual correspondences, not merely conceptual, between Benjamin's theses and Paul's epistles, so that "the entire vocabulary of the theses appears to be truly stamped Pauline." For Agamben, Benjamin's now-time, for example, exhibits a direct correlation with the Greek phrase *ho nyn*

kairos—that is, the "technical designation of messianic time in Paul." Giorgio Agamben, *The Time That Remains: A Commentary on the Letter to the Romans*, trans. Patricia Dailey (Stanford, CA: Stanford University Press, 2005), 143, 144.

131. Gottfried Wilhelm Leibniz, *The Monadology and Other Philosophical Writings*, trans. Robert Latta (Ithaca, NY: Cornell University Library, 2009), §22, §61, and §62.

132. Löwy, *Fire Alarm*, 100.

133. Benjamin, "On the Concept of History," 392.

134. Peter D. Fenves, *The Messianic Reduction: Walter Benjamin and the Shape of Time* (Stanford, CA: Stanford University Press, 2011), 243–244.

135. Löwy, *Fire Alarm*, 94.

136. Benjamin, "On the Concept of History," 395.

137. Walter Benjamin, "Paralipomena to 'On the Concept of History,'" trans. Edmund Jephcott and Howard Eiland, in *Selected Writings, Volume 4: 1938–1940*, 402.

138. Benjamin, 402.

139. Benjamin, 402.

140. Hent de Vries, "'The Miracle of the Dancing Ball: Walter Benjamin, Mechanical Mysticism, and the Apocalyptic Epistemology of Changing Everything, All at Once" (talk, Program for European Cultural Studies, Princeton University, Princeton, NJ, April 17, 2013).

141. Slavoj Žižek, *Event: Philosophy in Transit* (London: Penguin Books, 2014), 116.

142. Benjamin, "On the Concept of History," 390.

143. Hamacher, "'Now': Walter Benjamin on Historical Time," 42.

144. Benjamin, "On the Concept of History," 391.

145. Benjamin, 397.

146. Hamacher, "'Now': Walter Benjamin on Historical Time," 45.

147. Benjamin, "On the Concept of History," 395.

148. Andrew Benjamin, *Style and Time: Essays on the Politics of Appearance* (Evanston, IL: Northwestern University Press, 2006), 33.

149. Benjamin, "On the Concept of History," 395.

150. Benjamin, *Arcades Project*, 392 [K2,3].

151. Benjamin, "On the Concept of History," 392.

152. Giorgio Agamben, "The Messiah and the Sovereign: The Problem of Law in Walter Benjamin," in *Potentialities*, trans. Daniel Heller-Roazen (Stanford, CA: Stanford University Press, 1999), 163.

153. Carl Schmitt, *Political Theology* (Chicago: University of Chicago Press, 2005), 5.

154. Horst Bredekamp, "From Walter Benjamin to Carl Schmitt, via Thomas Hobbes," trans. Melissa Thorson Haule and Jackson Bond, *Critical Inquiry* 25, no. 2 (1999): 251–252.

155. Benjamin, *Arcades Project*, 474 [N9a,7].

156. Benjamin, 474 [N10,2].

157. Gershom Scholem, *The Messianic Idea in Judaism and Other Essays on Jewish Spirituality*, trans. Michael A. Meyer and Hillel Halki (New York: Schocken, 1995), 7.

158. Mosès, *L'Ange de l'histoire*, 20.

159. Mosès, 150.

160. Benjamin, "Paralipomena," 403.

161. A. Benjamin, *Style and Time*, 5.

162. Osborne, *Politics of Time*, 115.

163. Benjamin, "Paralipomena," 403.

164. Karl Heinz Bohrer, *Suddenness: On the Moment of Aesthetic Appearance*, trans. Ruth Crowley (New York: Columbia University Press, 1994), x.

165. Mosès, *L'Ange de l'histoire*, 24, 155.

166. Scholem, *Messianic Idea in Judaism*, 3.

167. Bohrer, *Suddenness*, 65.

168. Nietzsche, "On the Utility and Liability of History for Life," 94.

169. Friedrich Nietzsche, *Thus Spoke Zarathustra*, trans. Adrian del Caro (Cambridge: Cambridge University Press, 2006), 175.

170. Rabinbach, *In the Shadow of Catastrophe*, 61.

171. Benjamin, "On the Concept of History," 397.

Conclusion

1. Darrin M. McMahon, "The Return of the History of Ideas?," in *Rethinking Modern Intellectual History*, ed. Darrin M. McMahon and Samuel Moyn (Oxford: Oxford University Press, 2014), 23.

2. Reinhart Koselleck, *Futures Past: On the Semantics of Historical Time*, trans. Keith Tribe (New York: Columbia University Press, 2004), 22, 263.

3. Koselleck, 265.

4. Koselleck, 266.

5. Reinhart Koselleck, "Crisis," trans. Michaela Richter, *Journal of the History of Ideas* 67, no. 2 (2006): 372.

6. François Hartog, *Regimes of Historicity: Presentism and Experiences of Time*, trans. Saskia Brown (New York: Columbia University Press, 2015), xviii, 193; Hans Ulrich Gumbrecht, *Our Broad Present: Time and Contemporary Culture* (New York: Columbia University Press, 2014), xiii, 30, 32.

7. Koselleck, "Crisis," 393.

8. Ernst Bloch, *The Spirit of Utopia*, trans. Anthony A. Nassar (Stanford, CA: Stanford University Press, 2000), 187–188.

9. Ernst Jünger, *The Adventurous Heart: Figures and Capriccios*, trans. Thomas Friese (Candor, NY: Telos Press, 2012), 7.

10. David Bathrick and Andreas Huyssen, "Modernism and the Experience of Modernity," in *Modernity and the Text: Revisions of German Modernism*, ed. Andreas Huyssen and David Bathrick (New York: Columbia University Press, 1989), 6.

11. The instant would play, from this perspective, an important role in the *dialectical* formulations of the disenchantment thesis: the conviction, articulated by intellectuals such as Lukács, Bloch, Benjamin, and Adorno, that "modern disenchantment is renewed enchantment"; Daniel Weidner, "The Rhetoric of Secularization," *New German Critique* 42, no. 1 (2014): 8. Therefore, although the history of the concept of instantaneous temporality in modernity can be interpreted as exemplifying the narrative of secularization, this history can, at the same time, also question this narrative's historical and conceptual applicability. The instant would represent a concept of mediation between religion and secularism, the sacred and the profane, just as it performs the role of a mediating notion between the subjective and the collective, the aesthetic and the political. As mentioned previously, one of the instant's characteristics is its capacity to migrate to different conceptual spaces, bringing with it characteristics and assumptions from one realm into the other.

12. On the migration of ideas through "provinces of conceptual 'space,'" see McMahon, "Return of the History of Ideas?," 25.

13. Jan-Werner Müller, "European Intellectual History as Contemporary History," *Journal of Contemporary History* 46, no. 3 (2011): 589.

14. For a discussion of postmodernist aesthetics and its relations with the states of capitalist development, see Fredric Jameson, *Postmodernism, or, The Cultural Logic of Late Capitalism* (Durham, NC: Duke University Press, 1991).

15. Giorgio Agamben, *The Time That Remains: A Commentary on the Letter to the Romans*, trans. Patricia Dailey (Stanford, CA: Stanford University Press, 2005); Alain Badiou, *Metapolitics*, trans. Jason Barker (London: Verso, 2005); Alain Badiou, *Being and Event*, trans. Oliver Feltham (London: Bloomsbury Academics, 2013); Slavoj Žižek, *The Ticklish Subject: The Absent Centre of Political Ontology* (London: Verso, 1999).

16. François Dosse, *Renaissance de l'événement: Un défi pour l'historien, entre sphinx et phénix* (Paris: Presses Universitaires de France, 2010), 81.

17. Slavoj Žižek and Glyn Daly, *Conversations with Žižek* (Cambridge: Polity, 2004), 136.

INDEX

ACKNOWLEDGMENTS

Many people have helped me in the development of this book. Writing it would have been impossible without the substantial advice from Philip G. Nord, Thomas Trezise, Hent de Vries, and, above all, Anson Rabinbach. Andy's generosity, lucidity, and erudition accompanied me throughout its conception and progress and still represent an enduring source of inspiration.

I also want to show my gratitude to Ilan Bizberg, Francisco Gil Villegas, and Guillermo Zermeño, my professors at El Colegio de México who first oriented me in my initial incursions on the history of instantaneous temporality more than a decade ago.

Very special thanks to Samuel Moyn for his encouragement, and to my editors at University of Pennsylvania Press, especially to Damon Linker, for his invaluable guidance. I also need to thank Mary Murrell, whose suggestions improved the final product in significant ways.

Marcel Lepper, the former director of the Deutsches Literaturarchiv Marbach, and Paul Michael Lützeler, president of the American Friends of Marbach, provided advice and support in the realization of archival research in Germany in the summer of 2013.

Charles Dellheim, Jonathan Zatlin, Muhammad Zaman, and Carrie Preston provided crucial support during my stay as a postdoctoral fellow at Boston University's Kilachand Honors College in 2015–2018.

I am grateful to CONACYT (Consejo Nacional de Ciencia y Tecnología) for the research funding provided during the academic year 2014–2015.

At different points of the elaboration of this book, a number of friends and colleagues provided valued insights, comments, and criticisms: Samar Farage, Cristina Florea, Carlos Fonseca, Sergio Galaz García, Rubén Gallo, Laura Gandolfi, Marcela García, Juliana Jiménez, Rafael Lemus, Lorena Marrón, Natalia Mendoza Rockwell, B. Richard Page, Daniel Purdy, Jean

Robert, Carolina Sá Carvalho, Ana Sabau, Sajay Samuel, Melissa Teixeira, Mauricio Tenorio, Marc Volovici, Nathaniel Wolfson, and Enea Zaramella.

Finally, I want to thank Gladys and Leonel for a life of encouragement. This book is dedicated to them.